THE OPTION METHOD

The Myth *of* Unhappiness

The Collected Works of Bruce Di Marsico on The Option Method and Attitude

Behavior

Myths

Happiness without Reason

Enjoying Your Happiness

Option Mysticism

Practicing The Option Method

Stories and Meditations

A Comprehensive Overview

The OPTION METHOD
The Myth *of* Unhappiness

The Collected Works of Bruce Di Marsico on The Option Method and Attitude

Edited and with commentary by Aryeh Nielsen

Foreword by Frank Mosca

Introduction by Deborah Mendel

With contributions by Wendy Dolber

DIALOGUES IN SELF DISCOVERY LLC ❖ MONTCLAIR, NEW JERSEY

The Option Method: The Myth of Unhappiness
The Collected Works of Bruce Di Marsico on The Option Method and Attitude
Volume 3

Dialogues in Self Discovery LLC
P.O. Box 43161, Montclair, NJ 07043
www.DialoguesInSelfDiscovery.com

Disclaimer
The information provided within is not a substitute for professional medical advice and care. If you have specific needs, please see a professional health care provider.

Design by Williams Writing, Editing & Design
www.williamswriting.com

Volume 1
Paperback, ISBN 978-1-934450-01-7

Volume 2
Paperback, ISBN 978-1-934450-02-4

Volume 3
Paperback, ISBN 978-1-934450-03-1

Printed in the United States of America

Listen to your heart, for that is where knowledge acts.
Do only what attracts you.
Do what you feel like.
Cor Super Ratio. *The Heart above logic.*

Bruce Di Marsico

Contents

Foreword by Frank Mosca | xiii
Guide to the Collected Works | xv
Introduction by Deborah Mendel | xix
Notes to the Reader | xxi

PART I: BEHAVIOR

Changing Behavior | 3
"I Did It Again" | 4
From Now On | 6
Considering Work | 9

PART II: EVERYDAY MYTHS

Common Myths | 13
Myths and Habits | 14
Mistakes | 16
Importance | 17
You Have No Rights | 19

PART III: THE GREAT MYTHS

Section I: Self | 23

There Are No Secrets About the Meaning of *Your* Life | 25
The Will | 27
Free Will | 28
The Mind | 29
There Is Nothing Hidden within Us | 31
The Kernel and the Husk | 34
Option Ontology | 36

Section II: The World | 37
The Purpose of the World Is Your Happiness | 39
Section III: Time | 41
The Two Nows | 43
The Experiential Now and the Intentional Now | 44
Hesitating to Say Yes | 46
Section IV: Sex | 51
Sex Is a Mystery | 53
Section V: Life, Health, and Death | 57
Happiness and Health | 59
The Option View of Death | 60
The "Problem" of Death | 62
Life and Death | 63
Commentaries by Aryeh Nielsen on "The Great Myths" | 65
The Meaning of Life | 67
The Will | 68
You Are Your Happiness | 70
The Self Is a Location | 74
The World Is You | 76
PART IV: HAPPINESS WITHOUT REASON
Section I: About Happiness without Reason | 81
There Is Nothing to Believe | 83
Section II: Nothing Prevents Happiness | 87
There Are No Obstacles to Perfect Happiness | 89
There Is No Reason to Be Unhappy | 90
There Is No Need to Understand Yourself | 91
If You Seem Unhappy, You Can Know You Are Not | 96
Section III: There Are No Reasons for Happiness | 99
Happiness Is Not the Result of Having Good Things | 101
No Beliefs Are Necessary | 102
What Happiness Does | 107
Justifying Your Wants | 110

Section IV: Perfect Happiness | 113
You Can Be Happy Now and At All Times | 115
Realizing Perfect Happiness | 116
We Can Be Happy Because We Want To | 117

PART V: ENJOYING YOUR HAPPINESS

Section I: About Enjoying Your Happiness | 121
The Enjoyment of Happiness | 123
Being Happy Now | 125
Enjoying Your Freedom | 127
Miracles and Happiness | 130
Everything Is Good | 133
Are You Good? Are All Things Good? | 135
Section II: Practical Enjoyment | 137
I Am Not the Cause of Your Happiness | 139
Being in Society | 144
On Fervor | 145
Acting Unhappy | 148
There Are No Emotional Problems | 149
On Being Private | 151
Trusting Your Learning | 152
Section III: You Are Your Happiness | 153
The Two Principles | 154
Perfect Happiness Moves You | 156
There's Nothing Wrong with You | 160
What Is Happening? | 162
Section IV: A New World | 165
The Future | 167
Wait, Watch, and Enjoy What Happens in You and Around You | 168
Happiness Opens Up a New World | 176
Section V: Perfect Freedom | 181
The Freedom Not to Change | 183
Doing Nothing | 184

Section VI: The Experience of Happiness | 185
On Quiet | 187
Peace and Joy | 191
Gladness | 193
Being Grateful without Reasons | 194
Commentaries by Aryeh Nielsen on "Enjoying Your Happiness" | 199
The Worst of Humanity | 201
Option and the Play of Existence | 203
Emotions Are Happiness | 205
PART VI: OPTION MYSTICISM
On God | 209
Option Theology | 216
Ancient Wisdom | 220
Option Mysticism | 221
God's Prayer to Man | 223
I Am Your God | 226
Contemplation Is Joy | 228
Commentaries by Aryeh Nielsen on "Option Mysticism" | 229
Option, Mysticism, and Pragmatism | 231
PART VII: PRACTICING THE OPTION METHOD
Section I: About Practicing The Option Method | 237
Learning the Practice of The Option Method | 239
How to Do The Option Method | 241
The Practice of Option | 246
Section II: The Option Method Questions | 257
Introduction to the Questions | 259
Dialogue Model | 264
Variants of the Option Questions | 266
The Goal of the Guide | 268
Exploring "I Don't Know" | 270
There Are No Option Statements | 272

Section III: Applying The Option Method | 273

I Am Not the Cause | 275

The Best Way to Help | 276

The Client Is the Expert | 278

Everyone Does Not, in Practice, Want Happiness | 283

Option as Therapy | 285

The Four Attitudes | 292

Guidance in Questioning | 300

Using The Option Method with Others | 306

Applying The Option Method Personally | 311

Using The Option Method with Yourself | 315

Commentaries by Aryeh Nielsen on "The Practice of The Option Method" | 317

The Attitude Behind the Questions | 319

Necessity Is the Only Belief That Matters | 320

Option Restores the Awareness of Choice | 321

PART VIII: STORIES AND MEDITATIONS

Section I: Stories | 327

Going Off to College | 329

Holding Your Breath | 332

Genesis | 333

The Troubadour | 335

The Man Who Found Diamonds | 338

Section II: Meditations | 343

Choice | 345

The Absolute Truth Is Simple | 347

Cor Super Ratio | 349

PART IX: A COMPREHENSIVE OVERVIEW

A Brief Compendium of The Option Method for The Option Method Professional | 353

Section I: The Option | 355

The Natural Laws of Happiness | 357

Section II: Further Axioms of Option | 363

Axiomatic Corollaries of Option | 365

Section III: What Is Option About? | 373

Option Ontology and Epistemology | 375

What is the Purpose or Meaning of Life? | 376

Section IV: Summary | 377

The Option Message | 379

The Right to Be Happy | 380

Commentaries by Aryeh Nielsen on "A Comprehensive Overview" | 381

A Summary of Option Teachings | 383

Acknowledgments | 409

The Editing Process | 411

About Bruce Di Marsico | 413

Index | 415

Foreword by Frank Mosca

THE READER OF THESE WORKS IS GOING TO FIND A ROADMAP TO THE vast and varied workings of Bruce Di Marsico's mind. But despite the sometime appearances of complexity, there will be a road sign pointing always, always in one direction: to your happiness. That is the key to remember as you set out on your journey. I know that this is what has sustained and enriched my own journey, one that began decades ago when I was fortunate to come upon Bruce's ideas and then had the great fortune to meet and learn personally from him. This brief introduction is really simply one person's experience of Bruce, of The Option Method and what that has meant in my life.

First at the core, it has meant everything. It has meant ongoing happiness to the degree that I learned to remember my happiness should I forget it. It has meant the disentangling of what seemed to be impossible knots of contradictions, complexities and conundrums that seemed never to yield to whatever I would bring to bear to try and help myself. The image of Bruce like Alexander cutting the Gordian knot of human misery comes to mind. But it was not an act of hubris, but one of immense insight that allowed him to see through the apparent insurmountability of the problem of human happiness. He could then dissolve what stood in the way and open to view that most profound but simple truth: your happiness is always yours; it is in fact what and who you are. Beliefs are the artificial blockages to that direct and incredible knowledge. Questions are the key to removing them.

Like Socrates, from whom he drew some inspiration, Bruce relished the dialogue and the coming to the key "I don't know" moment. The moment when we stand on the edge of two worlds. The one we could now leave behind. The one we have constructed with the aid of culture in all its forms and configurations. Once the veil of our dedication to the pseudo-certainty of what we think we know is rent, we are naked to the possibility of taking that giant step to acknowledging the unshakeable truth of our own happiness now and in every moment we are privileged to allow ourselves to know it.

As you read these volumes it will at times seem that Bruce may be going off in endless tangents of discussions. But these are not tangents at all. Remember, that one blinding truth about happiness is resisted by us in almost endless ways. His students and clients raised doubts and difficulties at every turn as they wrestled with the import of surrendering their beliefs in some apparently necessary miseries, some absolutely irreducible requirements to be unhappy. Remember, our whole world rests upon these assumptions. It is no wonder then that Bruce brought his particular eloquence to elaborate and draw out incredible subtleties of argument, wit, and pure intellectual power to counter these objections and to continue thereby to hold out hope to those who continued to bury themselves in needless labyrinths of their own making. But he was patient; it was his signature strength. He knew what seemed to us to be at stake, and he wanted for all who would to hear, that joy that he himself was living.

So, don't hold back in your engagement with Bruce; he will not disappoint you. In all these decades, he has been my constant companion in life and even in death. His words, his vision, his immense verve in being willing to take on your fears and doubts with extraordinary intellectual skill will get you to that place you yearn for. So it has been with me, through so many unexpected turns and twists my life has taken.

Now in my seventies, I am filled with joy at the prospect of his work being made widely available. He has shone a bright, inextinguishable light into the shadows and darkness of the human condition. Do not fear it. It will not consume but will enlighten and elevate. I am so glad you are taking this opportunity to discover this for yourself. Written with deep gratitude,

Frank Mosca
May 5th, 2010
Hampton Bays, New York

Guide to the Collected Works

The Collected Works of Bruce Di Marsico span three volumes, which together constitute his explanation of the truth about happiness: that we are already perfectly happy, and unhappiness is merely the belief that we could somehow not be.

These writings are created from lectures and writings created over a period of a quarter century. Bruce taught a number of extended courses on Option, and this book attempts to follow the general order of presentation in his teaching work, and to serve as a course in The Option Method and Attitude for those who were not able to experience Bruce firsthand.

The course progresses in this manner: first, an introductory overview is presented (*Overview of The Option Method*). This is followed by core Option concepts (*Happiness, Unhappiness, Feelings, Beliefs, Desires, Emotions, Motivation, Wanting, Doing, Knowing*).

Next are the most immediate, everyday implications of these teachings (*Relationships, Believing Yourself, Forms of Unhappiness*), more advanced implications (*Arguments against Happiness, Behavior, Myths*), and then the most esoteric implications of Option (*Happiness without Reason, Enjoying Your Happiness, Option Mysticism*).

Only at this point is *Practicing The Option Method* considered. The Option Attitude is the foundation of The Option Method. Just as "technically correct" music empty of emotion is an empty exercise, so is The Option Method practiced without the Option Attitude. Bruce did not cover the practice of The Option Method until well into his courses, so that the fundamental Option Attitude was well-established in those who used the Method. He demonstrated and taught that once the Option attitude is well-understood, the practice of the Method flows organically.

Finally, *Stories and Meditations* and *A Comprehensive Overview* provide a summing up and review of Option teachings.

The material, while presenting an overall arc of argument, has many loopbacks and repetitions. Bruce often said the same thing in many different ways so that everyone would have a chance to understand the implications of knowing that unhappiness cannot happen to us.

The truth of happiness is simple. Why does it take three volumes to explain? Because the belief in unhappiness takes many forms, and is incredibly complex. But to be happy, there is nothing to know. All the medicine contained within these volumes is to help release unhappy beliefs, and as they fall away, they become of no importance. After studying the Collected Works, you will know far less than you did when you started. What you will no longer "know" and believe is that you have to be unhappy. And you will find that, without these beliefs, you will know your own happiness.

The three volumes of *The Collected Works of Bruce Di Marsico*

Volume I

An Overview of The Option Method
Happiness
Unhappiness

The first part of Volume I provides an overview of The Option Method, and touches on all aspects of Option, to provide a framework for understanding the details. The remainder of this volume explains happiness and unhappiness: happiness is what you are. Unhappiness is believing that what you are is somehow wrong.

Volume II

Feelings, Beliefs, and Desires
Emotions
Motivation
Wanting, Doing, and Knowing

Relationships
Believing Yourself
Forms of Unhappiness
Arguments against Happiness

Volume II starts by explaining how unhappiness happens. Believing, or predicting the consequences of an event for how you feel is how emotions happen. Why does unhappiness happen? It is the (unnecessary) use of emotions to motivate your wanting. It also discusses happiness in the context of relationships, how happiness is synonymous with perfect self-trust, and the forms that unhappiness takes. It concludes by dismantling arguments commonly made against happiness.

Volume III

Behavior
Myths
Happiness without Reason
Enjoying Your Happiness
Option Mysticism
Practicing The Option Method
Stories and Meditations
A Comprehensive Overview

Volume III addresses myths: the myths that behavior has anything to do with happiness, and myths such as "the meaning of life." It continues with discussing how we need no reasons to be happy, and then discusses enjoying your happiness, as you get more and more in touch with it (perhaps ultimately manifested as a form of mysticism). It explains how to practice The Option Method to help you or others get more in touch with their happiness. It concludes contemplations on happiness in the form of stories and meditations, and two summaries of Option teachings, one comprehensive and one reductive.

Introduction by Deborah Mendel

The Option Method takes unhappiness from that vague cloud of confusion and that which just happens to you and brings it down to the real dynamics that cause your emotions . . . your beliefs and your judgments.

Bruce Di Marsico

Fundamental to Bruce's Option Method is the nonjudgmental approach to exploring unhappiness. This attitude, combined with The Option Method questions, unravels the mystery and "cloud of confusion" that usually surrounds our emotional upsets. The Option Method helps you let go of those beliefs that are fueling your unhappiness.

Bruce understood that we are our own best experts. We each have our own individual, specific reasons for becoming unhappy when we do. The Option Method questions are designed to help us identify those reasons. Unlike other modalities, The Option Method does not require you to rethink, memorize, or adopt a new belief or thought pattern. The Option Method questions present a painless process that allows us to simply let go of self-defeating beliefs. The Option Method reveals the beliefs behind our bad feelings and unhappiness. Through this process we discover it is painless and easy to let go of the beliefs that cause our unhappiness.

Did you ever notice that when you anticipate getting upset about something you begin immediately to feel upset? The moment we begin to fear or predict that we are going to feel any way that we don't want to feel in the future, we have already begun to feel that way in the present. It is likewise true of our good feelings. When we are looking forward to feeling good about something, we immediately feel good and are in a good mood.

I believe that one of the most profound discoveries that Bruce made in his creation of Option is that our current unhappiness is derived from our predictions and imaginings of ourselves as unhappy in some way in the future—more specifically, our *beliefs* about what we will feel in the future. The answer is not to convince ourselves that our future will always be bright. We know from experience that life does not always work out the way we want it to. The Option Method gives us a tool to question our beliefs and realize that, whatever our future holds, we don't have to feel unhappy about it. When we are free from these "future fears," we will naturally be happier.

Deborah Mendel

Notes to the Reader

1. Whenever an entire passage appears in this sans serif font, it is editorial commentary.
2. Bruce developed Option Method in the early years of his psychotherapeutic practice, initially calling it Existential Analysis, Option Psychotherapy, and other similar names. At that time, he was teaching mostly to mental health care professionals. He quickly saw that his teachings—concerned specifically with unhappiness and beliefs about unhappiness—really did not fit into the paradigm of the medical or psychotherapeutic model. They had a much wider application to all those interested in personal growth and development. From 1970 on, he used only the name Option Method. It was his intention to make the Method available to as wide a group as possible so those who were trained could carry on the teachings. Early lectures often included the words "therapist" and "patient," which soon gave way to terms like "practitioner" and "client." These terms should be considered to be used interchangeably.
3. The purpose of editorial commentary in this book is twofold: sometimes to clarify areas that Bruce spoke about during many talks, but did not create any central document or lecture on. Other commentary is meant to provide a roadmap to essays or talks that some have found particularly difficult to understand. By reviewing a roadmap of the teaching first, it is hoped the reader will be able to absorb the works more easily.
4. More resources can be found online. In the archives sections of the ChooseHappiness.net website there are many study guides for topics featured in this book, and audio recordings of Bruce's original lectures. **http://www.choosehappiness.net**

PART I
Behavior

Changing Behavior

Do we care about patterns of behavior? As a practitioner, no; but if a person feels bad about their repetitive behavior, I care about their feeling bad. What I help them with is not their pattern of behavior but their feeling bad. Now, if their pattern of behavior, which is a long phrase for "being unhappy a lot," is based on an unhappy belief, then if they were not unhappy their pattern of behavior might change.

Some people are very defensive. And they're always asking, "What do you mean?" They're always worrying that somebody's going to judge them as not worth loving. When and if they stop being afraid of not being loved, I doubt if they're going to be defensive. So some behavior will automatically change, since it's connected to what people believe will change.

But the behavior only changes insofar as it's connected to the emotion, since it's an expression of a kind of an emotion or a belief or an attitude. And what I like to teach my students is that attitudes are bodily stances. They're the way we hold ourselves in the world. Anyone who's ever learned to pilot a plane learns about attitude. That's the way you maneuver through the sky, by the plane's attitude. Attitude is your approach, your attack, the way you're coming at things in life. An attitude is a well-established set or pattern of behavior that reflects a well-established set or pattern of beliefs, because they've long been believed in and never had any reason to be challenged or questioned.

"I Did It Again"

November 11, 1995

WHAT about people who do change their beliefs and yet get unhappy again and again and again? What about recalcitrants? What about those kinds of so-called stubborn, crazy people?

Let me tell you something. There's no such thing. I don't care how long you have been believing that your water supply is safe where you live. You may get up in the middle of the night, every night, and get yourself a drink of water. But if you found out today that that water was poisoned, you would not accidentally drink the water, and then say, "Oh, boy. I did it again." I don't think so.

You're only doing it because you think you can get away with it. It's as simple as that. If you know it's not something to be unhappy about, then you were fooling around, and you thought you could get away with it. Really what it means is you still believe that this indeed is something to be unhappy about for the same but different reasons. In other words, when you stopped being unhappy about it, for the reasons that were looked at when you stopped being unhappy, you *did* stop being unhappy about it for that reason. But you have since realized *another* reason to be unhappy about the same thing. And that's why, and that's all, and you're still unhappy about it for *your* reason. Perhaps a different reason than you used to have. But a different reason why you still believe you have to be unhappy about that.

I'll tell you an experience of my own. After learning quite a number of times that I didn't have to be unhappy about all kinds of things, I pretty much counted myself very lucky and extraordinarily happy. And indeed, I was. And I felt that way. And it all was true. And then I would see myself acting this weird way I didn't like. I mean, similar to a pain in the stomach or somebody coming into a room and my looking away and not wanting to look at them. "Why am I doing that? I'm not usually shy. Do I *look* shy?" So, all those kinds of behaviors.

And I would look at each behavior and I would realize that it was an expression that I thought I wasn't allowed. What if, really, what I wanted to do when this person walked into the room was to look away, for reasons I don't understand and don't need to understand, because I agree with myself? And I just thought that I would have been doing that for years, if I felt allowed—this is just the first time I was feeling allowed.

What's it got to do with happiness or unhappiness? It has everything to do with happiness and nothing to do with unhappiness. And yes, it's weird. So as long as you're not worried about being weird, just honest about being weird, you may find that you're admitting some truth that you never did before. And you're allowing yourself some freedoms you never allowed yourself before.

From Now On

November 11, 1995

I'VE never been one for hitting myself over the head if I found that I was feeling bad, or for anything that I would find out later that one could label as bad. All that matters is that I could be done with it if I wanted to be. That was the greatest of all freedoms that I ever discovered. Hey, you tell me that I did it. I'll tell you, well, as far as I'm concerned it's done. I just have to realize I did it. So I questioned myself this way; why would I want to feel that way about that? And I knew immediately that I didn't have to be unhappy. I don't know whether that counts as unhappiness or not. It doesn't matter, you see, because I'm done with it anyway. It's gone.

Another example: after I learned that I didn't need to be unhappy about things, I was talking to somebody in apparently a very excited, intense way.

And he said, "Hey, Bruce, don't be angry."

"What?" I said. "Oh, I'm not angry at you at all."

He said, "Well, you sure looked it."

"Well, I'm sorry if you thought I was angry. I really wasn't. And if I was, I'm not. Honestly. And I don't know *what* I was. I was just being really intense. And if you call it anger, I don't care. I'm not now. I promise you I am not angry. I know I'm not angry now. I have nothing to be angry at you for. I was just making a point. I didn't know you were so delicate!"

And then I realized that people are very sensitive to what they think they see and hear. And they're very much concerned if you're angry. I didn't know if I was angry or not, but I also didn't care because I wasn't any longer. It doesn't matter to me whatever I have been as long as I'm happy now.

I don't want yesterday's happiness. Do you? I don't know anybody who does. I want it fresh. I'm happy now. And that's all I know. And if I was unhappy a minute ago; thanks for reminding me. Because

I'm fine now. I can't imagine I was really angry about anything. So anyway, I'm willing to cop to it, as long as you believe me now when I say I'm not angry. I'm really not.

The whole point of knowing The Option Method is to know that you don't have to be unhappy *now.* Not to find out that you were an idiot for being unhappy in your past or an idiot for being unhappy yesterday or that you didn't have to be unhappy. No, that's not what you're here for. In The Option Method, we've discovered that there are two "nows." Among people who come with unhappiness there is "up 'til now"—and every time they're talking about now, they're talking about themselves up 'til now. They *always* get unhappy about this. They're *always* tired about that. They're *always* worried about the other thing. And they're *always* talking about their past. Everything they know themselves to be up 'til now. Albeit that they may have been happy 90 percent of the last week since I saw them, they describe themselves in terms of only the unhappiness they've had in the last week. And that's who they are. They're the one who failed at this. They're the one who's unhappy about that. And that's who they are now.

But there's another now. There's who we are "from now on." Both "nows" are psychological nows. And all we're looking to do is change the "up 'til now" to what we are "from now on." We don't want to change who our clients have been up 'til now. No need. No reason. They don't either. They just want to feel better from now on. And that's all we're concerned with.

So, very frequently, people describe themselves in an ever-running, continuous past. You know, the past is always present. This is who I am. This is what I do. I do this. I do that. And they're talking about their past more often than not, and bemoaning the fact that in the future they won't be doing that, implying in some way, "I wish I was going to not be doing that from now on."

So that's another thing that The Option Method does. It helps people change their perspective on time. When people stop being unhappy, they are no longer concerned with *up 'til now*; they are really only concerned with *from now on.*

You probably recognize that in your own life, easily. When you're happy, you're always looking forward, never looking back. You're always looking forward to the next good thing, the next feeling, the next whatever. And when you're unhappy, it's like you've always been unhappy, and you're never going to stop being unhappy. But those are just illusions and that's why it's nice to have somebody ask real questions, somebody who will help you while you are living in that nightmare of unhappiness, that illusion that you're stuck with always getting unhappy over and over again.

Considering Work

September 23, 1974

At work, consider . . .

The right to, and rightness of, showing off.

The right to be paid for playing rather than working.

The right to play at making play look like work.

Consider . . .

The fear of being burnt out.

The fear that work is hard.

The fear that past failures take away the right to desire success.

You have . . .

Permission to feel "raring to go," regardless of past lack of progress.

Permission to be free of previous success.

Permission to be creative.

Permission to be free of traditions.

Permission to be free of others' expectations.

Permission to acknowledge to yourself your unique motivations.

You are . . .

Free to broaden your interests.

Free to follow your hunches.

Free to like something for personal reasons as well as for "objective" reasons.

Choices . . .

Spreading the wealth vs. creating new wealth.

Need to justify vs. no need to justify.

Should share vs. *want* to share.

Respecting one's own skills and talents is the same as respecting the products of one's skills and talents (material things). Loving what is, the world, matter, self, etc., is the result of happiness.

PART II

Everyday Myths

Common Myths

UNLESS I'm happy (feel good), I won't get what I want.

Unless I do what I want, I won't be happy.

Unless I get what I want, I won't want to (feel like) doing what I want.

Unless I'm happy, I won't do what I want.

Unless I get what I want, I can't be what I want to be (feel good, etc.).

Unless I get what I want (from you), I won't feel like (enjoy) doing what I (you) want (for you).

If I don't feel like doing what I (you) want (for you), I become unsure of my desires to be with you.

You won't feel like doing what I want (from you) if you see I'm unsure about what I want to do (for you).

I want to be with you, but if I or you don't feel good, I'm afraid I won't want to be with you, and I want to be with you.

If I or you don't feel good, I'm afraid you won't want to be with me.

Myths and Habits

1975

SOME of our beliefs (predictions) have no current rationale.

Unhappiness is *not* a habit but a new response each time to a new situation (although the mind may perceive it as similar experience or situation, it is still new in *this* time frame).

Many beliefs and behaviors are mythical in the sense that they may have once served a purpose or had a reason (for believing or behaving in a particular way) and that reason is no longer relevant, but the belief is still operative because it has not been questioned and is still believed to be existing for some good reason—which, in fact, may no longer be convincing, relevant, or in any way attractive and believable. For example:

* finishing everything on your plate;
* thinking it's bad to undress in front of someone (being embarrassed, still, with doctors and nurses, say);
* feeling bad if someone disapproves of your behavior; and
* requiring parents' permission to go out at night.

There are also general mythical fears in every culture. For example: the fear of growing older because I will not have the energy to do the things I want to do. (Older people do not want to go to the playground and run around the climbing bars, and need not be sad about leaving those desires behind. If an older person is unhappy about being old, that is a mask of blame to cover some other feelings and fears of not being able to be happy.)

My past has as little to do with me (i.e., my freedom to choose my beliefs) as *your* past has to do with me. Past attitudes cannot continue, they must be recreated (remembered and reaffirmed anew each time it is relevant).

Habits (beliefs that are believed, because they were re-believed or once believed, and we don't believe anymore) still exist *only* because we believe they do or have to. "I will have trouble or difficulty stopping (believing, doing, etc.) because I have not stopped for a long time. So it must be hard. I have tried in the past." Yes, you have tried while believing it was difficult. And your beliefs always win.

Mistakes

November 11, 1995

A MISTAKE is doing something expecting one result, and winding up with another.

You try to put the watchband on the watch and everything flies apart—instead of putting on the watchband, you broke the watch. That's a mistake—you got an unintended result that's also an undesirable result. An unintended result that's a pleasant result is usually called a lucky accident.

Often, we judge that other people made a mistake when they're merely expecting a different result than we are. The minimum to decide that someone else made a mistake would be that they stated a certain goal, and they achieved another. They said that they were trying to bake a pie and instead they roasted a turkey. But you could also be misunderstanding what they said they were doing: "baking a pie" could be a family in-joke when they were growing up that they used to describe roasting a turkey. So you can't really know if anyone else made a mistake or not unless they tell you. And even then, they may have *actually* gotten the results they wanted and be telling you that they did *not*, for their own reasons: "If I had known that was the last piece of pie, I wouldn't have eaten it—my mistake."

If you believe that what someone is doing will lead to a result that they don't intend and that you don't want—for example, they are setting the furniture on fire to keep the house warm—then, in that case, maybe you just give your advice, and run!

Importance

May 4, 1979

THE whole discussion of values, attention, happiness, patience, hope, safety, etc. hinges on the basis for the notion of importance.

"Dramatically important" means obviously important or undoubtedly important. No one is ever interested in whatever they consider unimportant. There is no such thing as Important. There are only things that are important to a person. Nothing is Important to Life, People, God, etc. These are non-existent generalizations that may or may not relate to individual experiences and notions of importance. Unhappiness is believing in Important Events and the Importance of their happening.

The determination of the importance of a thing is therefore the crucial mental activity and the common pivotal factor in the question of peace and joy. There can only be unhappiness when a person believes they are judging Important that which is "Truly" Unimportant and/or disregarding the Importance of something else they should consider Important.

The clarity with which I express this concept is a question which some consider important. "Clarity is Important" is a church to which many belong. If you are happy, you already know what I mean. If this bothers you, it is because you worry about the clarity of meaning. If you are bored, you are afraid of misjudging the Importance of this writing; if you knew it was important to you, you would be interested; if you knew it was unimportant to you, you would put this paper down.

There is even no such thing as a fool. A fool would be someone who gets Importance all mixed up and values the Wrong things.

To believe that 2 + 2 = 5 is to be mistaken or wrong, but to be a fool one would also have to believe that the correct answer was Important and Wrong answers were anti-Important answers.

To be against what is Right is "Foolish."

To know what is Right is to know nothing.

Things are Important because they are seen as Right for something. Other things are Important because they are believed to be Right, period. There is no Right or Correct. There is only that which is correct for something.

That 2 + 2 = 5 is incorrect is applicable to and wrong for balancing a checkbook, but relevant and not incorrect for the demonstration of the meaning of the concept of synergy. With regard to other areas, 2 + 2 = 5 may be irrelevant and neither right nor wrong for those fields or the people involved.

Importance for, or relevance to, or correctness to, imply a fundamental relevance to the person's goals and desires, which also seem to be formed around the concepts of Right and Wrong.

Could it be that 2 + 2 = 5 is an important issue in math or chemistry (wrong in some mathematics and correct as a chemical analogy) and is unimportant emotionally to a person—even a mathematician or a chemist or a banker?

For example, for a banker to find an error in someone else's bank account could mean nothing to him; but if his account was incorrect, it could be important to him.

Could it be that the person (banker or layman) who finds an "error" in their account would not have to believe it was important to them—for example, an error of $10 in a $10,000 account, or a $1,000 error in a million-dollar account?

Could it be that no matter the size of the error, say a complete "loss" of the account, the person would not have to consider it important to them?

"Important for something" and "important to me" are totally separate concepts unless I connect them.

What is important to a person is just that: that which is important to *that* person. Not to people on paper, discussions like this.

What seems to be important to unhappy people is the fear of getting their importances wrong. The fear of embarrassment and feelings of shame are direct consequences of mixing up importances. Only "fools" and "bad people" don't do what is "right" or don't want to.

What is important to happy people is nothing. That would be a way of saying that their happiness becomes the important thing, or is a result of not making things important *to their happiness.*

You Have No Rights

December 12, 1992

If you want to start playing around with rights, we'll just say, all right, you have a right to a pen and they have a right to steal it from you. If you want to keep on using the word "right," then you have to use it everywhere. And I always believe in the phrase, "You underline everything, you underline nothing." So if you have rights, then they've got rights to take your rights away from you. So if you've got rights, and they've got the right to take your rights away from you, what are you talking about, anyway?

There really are no such things. There's either your ability to get something and keep it, or not. I hear "rights" as people crying all the time, and feeling they're "supposed" to, and they're not having what "should" be, and there's always the feeling there's something wrong: "I'm not having what I'm 'supposed' to have," and "this 'shouldn't' happen."

These "rights" ideas go into every question. How did you get the unhappiness you have? Because your parents didn't treat you "right," or society didn't treat you "right," or they "shouldn't" have done this to you, they didn't have a "right" to talk to you that way, on and on and on. It's all based on this false concept that you have any rights whatsoever. You have no rights, whatsoever. Once you get that in your mind, everything you get is because you got it. Either somebody gave it to you, or you got it, in which case that's how you got it. That's it. That's just simple facts. You can only sit on a chair if there's a chair to sit on. You don't have a "right" to sit on a chair in a field unless you bring that chair with you.

And lots of rights just seem to me as ludicrous as that, like somebody drowning in the ocean and saying they have a right to fly. What are you talking about? It's all got to do with unhappiness. People talk about rights and debts and oughts and shoulds. It's just unhappiness. And it's very freeing to understand that nothing can make you unhappy.

You don't need these things that you lose in order to be happy. But you have every right to try to get them back. You can have them if you can have them, but you don't need to be unhappy. What makes you unhappy is believing you have lost something that you had a right to, something you're supposed to have. That's what makes you unhappy—believing you should have had this and you've lost it, or it was stolen from you, or you destroyed it through your own ignorance or stupidity and believing it should be there, and you have a right to this.

Understand this: in every unhappy way, "right" means an obligation. Everything you have a right to, you have an obligation to get. I don't know if you've ever noticed that. So, it's a two-edged sword—it's a real pain in the ass. You have to be unhappy until you get it and you have to be unhappy if you lose it, because then you have to win it back; because if you have a right to something, you have an obligation to have it. You have an obligation to fight for it, even if you don't want to. If you don't take your rights, you're allowing people to walk on you, step all over you; you have no self respect. See, it's that double-edged sword of rights.

There are no such things as rights. Let's just get that truth for today, December 12, 1992: learn once and for all that you have no rights. There are no such things as rights. There is only ability or ableness or power. If it's not those things, there's no magic, there are no rights.

There are no such things as duties. There is only your choice to do or give as you wish, or as you are able. To believe that you have a duty is a meaningless phrase. You have an "obligation"—what does that mean? If that convinces you to want something, fine; some bullshit convinced you to want something. The truth is, you can only now do it because you want to.

Group Member: *It's the attempt to constrain others by fear to do what you want them to do.*

Absolutely! Unhappiness is apparently a very useful tool. But it's self-engendering, because those people are unhappy in the first place; that's why they want to constrain you by fear—because they operate by fear, too.

PART III
The Great Myths

SECTION I

Self

There Are No Secrets About the Meaning of *Your* Life

October 7, 1981

THERE are no secrets about the meaning of *your* life. There are nothing but "secrets" about the meaning of "Life" (in the abstract). *You* are the meaning of your life. *You* give it meaning.

"Meaning" usually means "equals," " implies," "purpose," "is defined as," "has connotations of," "translation," etc.

Meaning also means "the use of" or "the usable information." Meaning points out, in order to point toward a lesson, a learning. "What does it mean?" means "What can I learn from it? How can I use it? What are its secrets?"

Any thing or concept can have any meaning or no meaning. No thing can be usable apart from a learner desiring to use, and a learner can desire to use anything in any way he or she chooses.

Fire means heat if heat is how it is used. Fire means light if that is how it is used. Fire used as light may not mean heat. Fire used as heat may not mean light.

The ultimate determiner of meaning is the learner's beliefs or desires. Learners learn meanings that they believe they ought to learn or that they want to learn. Conversely they *cannot* learn meanings that they believe they ought *not* to learn (even if they wish they could).

What does learning meaning mean? It means anything or nothing. If it means anything, it means either interpreting data into "shoulds," "oughts," or "supposed to's," or it means using meaning as a means to another end.

Another use of meaning other than "what should it mean?" is: "What could it mean?" Or "What does it mean to *me*?"

Why do things?

Since no thing needs to or must have a given meaning, then meaning can be anything or nothing. There is no such thing as meaning (in itself) if something does not *have* to mean something. Or there really is incontrovertible meaning, for *you*.

The Will

THE will is the name of relationships between beliefs and behavior. The will would not even seem to exist were it not for an apparent disparity between the desire of the heart and the behavior of the body. The will seems to exist because it seems necessary to acknowledge that "I did do what I don't like." It seems necessary for integrity's sake to admit that "my will is ineffective."

But, since, in every real sense, the will is the servant of the heart and mind and soul, it cannot fail. We cannot blame the tool for its misuse. The will simply manifests what is desired. Behavior only reflects belief.

What happens when it no longer seems necessary to acknowledge that "I did do what I don't like?" When the idea of "the will" is no longer necessary?

Desires become manifest. What becomes manifest is now judged. This judgment is the basis for another desire. And this *new* desire now becomes manifest. The process continues. This is Joy (active involvement in unfolding). When the process is completed, there will be a change. This is Peace (restful satisfaction in completion), or Quiet (being done for now).

Each moment of desire-manifestation-judgment is a re-creation of your whole existence. There is no before and after that can be known, hence no before and after at all, hence no emotional experience of time at all.

All emotional feelings of time are a sense of waiting and disparity, of unfulfillment, and in the continuous re-creation of desire-manifestation-judgment, time would not be emotionally related to or reflected upon, as there is no sense of deprivation in the continuous motion of desire.

Free Will

FREE Will is an explanatory principle and concept meant to explain the hypothesis that one who has "it" is totally free in regard to activities of the will. The confusions surrounding the concept are based on how will is understood. Just what are the activities of the will and what does free will affect and effect, if anything?

The concept, in my understanding, can be used to explain choice and the questions regarding the ability to choose.

The most profound implications of will and its freedom concern what truly "belongs" to us and what does not. The question of ownership is merely one of effectiveness of control. Degree of ownership and degree of effectiveness of control are so exactly proportionate as to be interchangeable terms. Effectiveness of control involves both the resultant effects as well as the primary activity; e.g., it can be said that I own or have total control of a business if I control all aspects of its conduct *and* full control of the profits. This, of course, does not exist in a country that taxes or otherwise controls business or assets. Therefore such questions arise:

Does man control his body or his world? If he has free will, does it have pure effectiveness? Or are its activities modified by phenomena not under his control? Is his will subject to laws and limitations such as gravity, disease, aging and the like? Or is the subject matter and the proper sphere of activity of the will in another realm altogether?

The object of free will must be happiness. Even if it is proposed that the object of free will is control of matter, what is the object or purpose for such control? The will to create or control matter may be the same as the happiness to be effected by the creation or control of such matter.

If the question "How does control contribute to my being?" is answered in terms other than happiness, then we may consider the term "Free Will" to be ill-defined.

The Mind

1992

Self-Teaching

The human (probably the human brain and its relevant mechanisms) invents the mind as a means of teaching itself things that would not otherwise be learned by simple, biologic, sensible experience.

Self-Experimenting

The ability to induce, deduce, discern, and refine what is learned into concepts and meanings such as pertinence and relevance, and to extend those ideas into possibilities, is what we call the mental faculties of a person. This ability to experiment in fantasy, and imagine various consequences by mental trial and error is, in itself, the greatest aid to invention, and perhaps the only evolutionary difference from other animals. It may be what caused the evolution of the mind and the body.

The Mind Is a Mental Fiction

Although there is no need to speak of a bicameral mind as if it were un-integrated, there is the functional experience of thinking: the person (mind) speaking to itself, or reflecting on itself. This, of course, is a mental fiction. The one mind can be three, or four, or more contestants in the experiment for development if it so imagines or determines itself. Argument is the name for mind. Or vice versa. Resolution is not a necessary requirement for mental exploration. That is a value to be determined by the mind. The mind is neither satisfied nor unsatisfied, save by its own determinations. The person's mind creates itself as a function of the person.

An Expression, Not a Component

The so-called split between mind and body is a proposition of the mind itself to reflect its own arguments within itself. The mind is a mental fiction; it can no more exist without a whole person than can a state without people, or the ring of a bell without the bell. The mind is an activity or expression of a person, not a component of a person.

Self-Changing

What is believed by the person to be that person/self can now causally change what it can feel and seem to be like as that person. A person may very well believe that his/her mind is a component, a partner, or even a rival. The various attributes of mental states *are* reflections of the beliefs of the person, and, as such, are an idiopathic condition.

Creates Self-Beliefs

Learning is response to stimulus, even if that stimulus is the belief about self which is autogenously independent of external experience. External experience is, after all, subject matter for belief, and as such is subject to responses based on judgments. Judgments (beliefs) that an experience is bad, or the experiencer is a bad person, certainly cause responses different than contrary judgments.

Creates Unhappiness

Unhappiness, or the "disturbed" emotional state, is the illusion that there is a non-integrated mentality to be suffered. In short, an unhappy person believes that his/her mind is in danger of being unable to experience the person as he/she chooses/wishes to experience the self/mind. It is the mind-created belief (fear) that the person will be forced or convinced (influenced) to believe it is against itself.

There Is Nothing Hidden within Us

March 20, 1976

THERE is nothing awful hidden within us. No evil, no problems, no secret thoughts, no hidden beliefs, no fears, no reluctance, no unhappiness, etc.

These are ways of behaving when and only when we behave that way.

There are also no great things hidden within us.

No love, no secret urges, no beauty, no greatness, no unborn children, no goodness that we hide, no holiness, no happiness, no secret magnificence, no creative ideas, no unwritten songs, books, no unpainted paintings, no hidden sexuality, no secret masculinity or femininity waiting to be disclosed. Nothing.

We are whatever we are when we are being that way. We are not unfolding or blossoming flowers.

There is no future self hidden within us waiting to emerge.

Although we can talk of ourselves this way and there can even be a real truth about what we are potentially, we have to understand potentiality in a more real and present sense.

We are what we are now. What is that, though?

It is the sum total of all that I am now. My thoughts, my desires, my feelings, my awareness of myself, and all that I am doing that I am not aware of in addition to what I am aware of.

It is in the reality of what I am doing unawares that the question of capability arises.

If I wish to speak of what I am capable of, I can only be referring in some way to who I already presently am and what I am presently doing that I don't seem to be aware of. We must realize that when we refer to that activity of ours that we are not seemingly aware of, we are not talking about a hidden, not yet manifested, self.

It is like saying "I am hiding the true showing of my liver, which someday could be disclosed to the world, or to me, in its full glory." As if someday our livers will be enshrined outside our bodies.

Hidden, in the sense of unseen, unaware, does not mean "shall be seen, should be seen or even desired to be seen."

Simply, that which is hidden, unseen, or unaware is not desired to be manifested unless, or until, it is actually manifested.

It is not desired while it is hidden or unaware because desire means to be aware of desiring something. If we find ourselves desiring to be beautiful, loving, wise, etc., it must be because we are already becoming aware of the reality that we are already beginning to do that.

To want to be loving is the awareness of becoming loving, etc. This "being loving" does not come from some hidden vault within our something-or-others (mind, heart, soul, etc.). It is not "coming" from anywhere. We are doing it, now!

We know how to do it and we know ourselves, so we know when to do it. It "comes from" our knowing when to do what we do. What we call desires is really our knowing when to begin doing that which we now say we desire.

"Knowing" ourselves does not mean we are aware, but it certainly means that since we do indeed do whatever it is that we do—for example, heartbeat—without awareness, we must know that we do it. We do not do it without our own "permission." We do it by ourselves, by using ourselves, by being ourselves. We do whatever we do for ourselves. Simply—our unaware activity is to serve our awareness. Our awareness is our happiness and joy, and feeling and doing what we are aware of wanting and beginning to feel and do.

Nothing is hidden other than what we know must be done without awareness (such as the function of our liver), so that our awareness can be served best.

We only believe in secret selves because we are aware of becoming (that is, desiring to be) what we are naturally beginning to be.

If we are aware (or have a fear) of that secret self as undesirable sometimes—if we believe we may have hidden fears, unhappiness, self-destructiveness, etc.—it is because we are beginning to become aware that we do not want to be that way. "Do not want" means "beginning to want something else." "Wanting" means becoming aware of being what we want to become aware of being, etc.

The belief in a secret self is the desire, or becoming aware, that I serve myself and am doing what I am doing (both aware and unaware) in just the way that I am beginning to approve of, in just the way I am beginning to enjoy. I am beginning to be happy about the way I do things, which is the way I become happy.

All desires are the beginning of actually doing that.

We know when to manifest our desires.

Our desire to be aware of doing only what we want to do, which is our enjoyment, is the cause of our doing all that we do.

Our beginning to become aware of doing only what we begin to do is the cause of our doing all that we do.

The Kernel and the Husk

March 10, 1975

THE only "law" of human nature is: You are free. You are good. You are happy. Your life does not exist to balance things. It is not for the species. It is not for a food chain. It is not to serve Nature or some momentary station along the continuum of evolution. Your life is not for another's happiness; it is for yours. Your life *is* for happiness. Your so-called biologic entity, your body, is yours, for you to do with as you wish. Your body is not limited, though, to what you see. There is a way of understanding the body as visible and invisible rather than as a body/soul duality.

Imagine, if you will, a seed: a kernel or germ within, and a shell or husk without. The future plant comes from the growth of the kernel and the shedding of the small, limited, somewhat inflexible shell. Consider the body as a seed husk, and the kernel of the body as invisible; but not because it is hidden within, but for another reason. In fact, consider the kernel as much, much larger than the husk—in fact, infinitely large.

The body, besides a physical description of its visible and tangible parts, is also discussed in terms of its non-visible but tangible parts such as internal organs. Another aspect by which we know and designate a body is by its effectiveness on our senses. Basically, another person's body or ours is called that because we perceive it with our senses. The term "body" can be parsimoniously described as the "person that I perceive."

In other words, I will affirm that you have a body if I can see it or feel it or smell it or hear it. All my perceptions of you are products or movements or sensations of my body. I say *you* have a body if *I* vibrate; I say *you* have a body if *my* body knows it. You *may* have a body, but I can't know that if you are out of my perceptual range; I can only know your body if you are within the limits of my body's vibration range. If something of you vibrates something of me, then I perceive your body and its effectiveness.

The kernel of your body may be much larger than the husk I call your body because it has effectiveness, perceptual effectiveness, like any aspect of your visible body. The kernel of your body is the pure effectiveness of you, your being.

Because you may have imagined yourselves *inside* your bodies, I want to counter with the concept that perhaps your so-called body is your visible material manifestation, and that *you* are everywhere. Perhaps your body is the center from which you radiate, or the center toward which you concentrate your being. Perhaps it is not the center of anything, not a geographical or cosmic location, but merely one aspect of the reality of your body.

Any two persons, as beings and as effectiveness, can occupy everywhere at any time. If I love you, all you have is mine and vice versa, and it doesn't matter if you agree.

Option Ontology

WHAT Is "You" and "Being Self"?

A person can believe that how they look is them.

One could believe that what they want is them.

One could think that the way they behave is them.

One could think that the real them (real self) is essentially unknowable, but is revealed and expressed by behaviors and attributes, and physiology.

You are the one who thinks and believes. What you think is what you do, not merely who you are.

How you feel about you is something you do. This is the same as what you believe about you.

Since *all* things you do are your doings, who are you behind those doings? Are you the chooser of what you do, or think or believe? Are you the expression of your choices? Are you the initial "yes" or "no" which activates and motivates your behaviors?

Since you are not who you were, are you who you are now only? Are you the sum total of anything you were? Are you the sum total of all you now choose to be?

Although there may be many ways to understand you, there is the question of what is the most relevant and meaningful way. What is the you that has the most meaning to you?

No description of you is who you are. Your essential experience of yourself is your emotional state. You are happy, or you believe you are not. Every other experience of life is known through that emotional state. Everything is "colored" or not by your emotions.

SECTION II

The World

The Purpose of the World Is Your Happiness

December 12, 1992

It's good to realize that you're egocentric. It's just a way of describing self. You can only know yourself from yourself. You can only be motivated from yourself. It's only yourself that you can ever experience as yourself. And you move from there. Everything you perceive you perceive from there. Everything you bring in, you bring in to there. And it doesn't matter if there was ever such a thing as selfish or not selfish. It's as good a word as any; it just comes from what your self is. And it really is all you know.

Let me put it this way . . . there are some obvious kinds of truths that you know that you may not have related to or called upon just yet. There is no past universe. There is no past world. Simply put, all that ever was (the past), is gone, or is part of now, as now (it's not the past). All that ever was, was part of creating now, so all that ever was, is gone. All that preceded now was part of creating now. Given that, I want to ask you, why does the world exist now? Why is there a now? For what purpose?

Since there is no "why" apart from what happens, or I make happen, the question is really a form of "What will I do with the world and the universe?" See, when I am asking you "Why does the world exist?" it really means, "What will you do with this world? What will you do with the universe? What's the world supposed to be for?" or "What's the purpose of life?" or "What am I supposed to do?" or "Why should I want to live?" These are all related questions. What's the answer? Whatever *you* say.

But . . .that isn't the answer. Whatever you say is not *the* answer because I have *my* answer. So you can say that whatever I say is not the answer, it's what *you're* saying. *If* you say that—if you are still one of the people who say, "What's the world for?"—then I'll tell you: for *me* to be happy.

The whole world that ever existed, all the world that ever existed, the universe that ever was and has been, has conspired to bring me to this moment, so that I can be here to be happy. Everything had to be what it was in order for me to be here now to be happy. That's what I say. And if you say that, then that's what you say. If you say the world is for some other purpose better than yours, what kind of schmuck are you? Why should you be the one to volunteer to back off and say "The world is for some other purpose than mine?" You don't have to do that.

You know what you want. You want to be happy. You want happiness. And you want to exist to be happy. Or you know something, and you know then what I know, that it IS your happiness, doing what's going on. Your happiness is what's going on.

Too mystical? Fine. Let's deal with the facts. What's the world for as far as you are concerned? What is the purpose for your life, if it isn't for you to know that you want to be happy? You want to be fertilizer? Somewhere down the line that's what *we'll* say. The purpose of your life is to add a little more fertilizer. Because that's what we saw happening.

The point is, you're not going to leave it for *us* to say what your life is for. You can; you can join a religion and have them define what your life is for. You can act like you don't know what your life is for.

You want to be part of humanity as you know it. You want to be normal. And you spent your whole life trying to be that. That's exactly why you get unhappy and not happy, and why you could get unhappy. You created yourself through this effort of constantly wanting to be something you call "good" or "normal."

SECTION III

Time

The Two Nows

THERE are two unhappinesses as there are two "nows":

Any unhappiness that you've had up until now has only been a question which says: "Do you believe from now on that you will have to be unhappy?"

The question of future unhappiness is a question that says, "Will you keep asking yourself this question?" The question of future or "from now on" unhappiness is, "Will you believe or do you now believe that you will do, feel, think, what you now know you no longer want?"

The question is whether you will believe, or are now believing, that you have to ask this question now, because you've asked it up till now.

Do you have to be unhappy now because you have been up till now?

Two Nows:

I am feeling unhappy now.

Now I do not believe I am unhappy.

The Experiential Now and the Intentional Now

September 26, 1975

I DON'T have to be unhappy. I simply do not have to believe that I will ever be unhappy again. I simply do not have to *believe* that I will ever again believe that I am unhappy. I do not have to believe that there is anything that is happening in me or around me or to me that can cause me to be unhappy. I do not have to believe that there ever could be.

I do not have to believe that anything that is, or could be, could cause me to believe that I have to be unhappy. I do not have to interpret, or understand, or discover, or consider, or be open intellectually, or allow the possibility for my own sake, or for the sake of truth, or any value, that I have to be unhappy or that I may be unhappy. I do not have to, for my sake, allow the possibility that anything that I experience could mean that I may be unhappy.

I do not have to consider that anything I find myself doing or feeling or thinking means that I may be unhappy.

No matter what I feel or think or experience within me or outside me, I do not have to consider that it is happening because I believe that I have to be unhappy.

I don't have to believe that I may be believing that I have to be unhappy.

Even if it were possible that what was happening was caused because of what I may have believed before then that I may have to be unhappy, it would not be for my sake to consider that it proves that now I am believing that anymore.

I do not have to believe that I now believe I have to be unhappy. I do not have to believe that I could make myself believe that I am unhappy.

I do not have to believe that I could "accidentally," or because of my past beliefs and attitudes, cause myself now, or ever again, to believe that I am or may, or will be, unhappy.

If I find that what I am doing or feeling or thinking may have come from past unhappiness, then I do not have to believe that it was accidental. I must have chosen to believe it and forgot I did. I must have believed that something that was happening meant I was believing that I had to be unhappy. I do not have to ask why I did that, since I have intended to not believe that I don't have to be unhappy. I did it because I believed I had to. I do not have to believe it now, no matter what.

To know or discern that what I am feeling may be from unhappiness is of no use, unless I know that I do not have to believe I am unhappy anymore.

If I ever was unhappy, I do not have to believe that anything means that I now believe that I have to be unhappy now or in the future.

No matter what I may have been feeling or experiencing because of what I was believing, I do not ever have to believe that it is happening because I *now* believe that I have to be unhappy.

I do not have to believe that anything, even feelings that have been unhappy up till now, can make me be unhappy from now on.

Even if I experienced what may be unhappiness, I do not have to believe that from now on I am unhappy. It does not have to mean I am now unhappy.

You could experience unhappy feelings (from believing up till now) and at the same time (from now on) believe you don't have to be unhappy.

You do not have to believe that anything can cause you to be unhappy now or again.

You could experience unhappy feelings (from believing up till now) and at the same time (from now on) you don't have to believe you are now believing, and are any longer, unhappy.

There are two experiences of now. "Up till now" is a feeling. "From now on" is thoughts and beliefs. "Up till now"—effects. "From now on"—intention. I could be unhappy, right now, up till now (the experiential now) and not be unhappy, right now, from now on (the intentional now).

Hesitating to Say Yes

January 30, 1975

THERE are many questions that if we ever chose to answer them, we would only choose one answer. The one that seemed best to us—the one that we knew would be the happy answer.

When we refuse to actually answer the question the only way we really want to, we may feel that we are answering it another way. But we are not. We cannot say "no" when we know we want to say "yes." But since we did not actually hear or feel ourselves saying "yes," we think or feel we said "no." We experience it as if we were forced into saying no or feeling as if the "no" is happening to us and we are seeing ourselves as perverse. The truth is that we are in that hell, that abyss, which is really no more than a prolonged hesitation—a hiatus, a gap—in which it could seem that we don't believe anything we actually do believe, and are ourselves enemies to all our best instincts.

There are many situations wherein we know that if we decided, *really* decided,

whether we were enjoying ourselves or not,
whether we really consented or not,
whether we really approved or not,
whether we really were glad or not,
whether we really were free or not,
whether we really were happy or not,
we would only choose one choice—the happy one.

We know that if we were to make any decision about how we really felt, we would only make it one way: the happy way. Sometimes (if not always), we do not really decide. We hold the decision in abeyance (internally) and instead mouth the words to ourselves or others. There is a kind of "but" in the back of our minds. A slight holding back from a full energetic confession and/or decision which would flow freely.

Instead we will then "act as if" we consented, approved, were glad, were free, were happy, etc. It will not be fully convincing. We will wonder if we are lying to ourselves or our friends.

"Are you glad to be with me now?" Translate to self: "Am I glad to be here now?"

Immediately the words come: "Sure! Of course. Yes. Uh huh." All lacking real joy, real believability, and we hear it. Our friend hears it. We both wonder, but don't say anything. Yet we wonder, we think "Why isn't he, she (why aren't I) more glad to be here?"

Here is what happens: we all know (on some level in our hearts) that being glad to be with someone is just simply a decision which is totally independent of where the other person is at and even independent of where we have been at ourselves up till that moment of decision. We know that we are indeed glad, that we have no real reason not to be glad, to be with our friend. Yet before we make the decision, at the time of the question of gladness, we realize we are not feeling deeply the gladness we know is or could be there. We make our mistake then. We believe that since we are not feeling it, we may not be really all that glad for some reason (God knows what reason—just some vague reason, some feeling that we always have, that we lack energetic joy or deep happiness).

Remember, this is what happens at the time of the question before we decide the answer to the question. In a sense, we translated the question from "Are you glad?" to "Have you *been* feeling glad?"

We are in a small dilemma. We know there is no reason to not be glad; we know we are glad (somehow) but we have not been especially feeling it.

We are also very much aware that there is only one answer which we really want to give to the question, to ourselves, to our friend. "Yes, Yes, I am glad."

If we go no further at this point in the emotional dynamics and introspection process, we can say something to ourselves and/or our friend. We will say "Yes"—but that is all. We only *say* it. We don't really feel it.

What we said was kind of true but only *like* the truth. Not really true, yet not untrue. True but not honest.

The reason for this is that we simply never got to the point of deciding the answer to the question but were only reporting what our answer would be, could only be (knowing our heart) *if* we decided. But we didn't decide. There was nothing new in our statement. No new moment, nothing fresh, alive, no renewed self—just reporting, and not even exactly true reporting.

We say where we would like to be as if we were there, yet tempered modified, spoiled by the tone, the feeling of where we *were*.

The old feelings, the past feeling, which was there at the time of the question, remained, even though our words leapt forward to our dreams, our hopes, to the only answer we really wanted to give.

My words express my desire and my hope, but the sound of my words (my tone and feelings) reflects my past and my despair.

There may even be the feeling that we wish we weren't asked because of this dilemma. We feel lacking, uncommitted, unenthusiastic, and we don't like it. We wish we were really the way we would like to be: alive, joyous, convincing, convinced.

How can we be? Only one way. Go ahead and be that way. Don't just answer the question, decide on the answer. Don't look back for the answer. Decide the answer for this *new* now. Decide for this moment of the question. The other answer we gave was based on how we felt before the question, combined with how we'd like to decide.

Instead of reflecting on how we have not been feeling before the question, let us decide how we are going to feel, now that we think of it.

Perhaps it is good to understand that there was no reason to "feel" especially glad until it occurred to us as something desirable. Before the question, it just wasn't a question. How we were feeling may have simply been okay, peaceful, waiting, floating, etc. Only when a question becomes an actual question is it relevant. It simply was not relevant to be feeling deeply until it was relevant.

To *feel* really glad, we have to believe we *are* truly glad. What we choose to believe about ourselves can be derived one of two ways: 1) consistent with our past or 2) in spite of our past.

Another way of saying this is, we believe about ourselves according to which self we believe is the true and determining self, the most powerful self. Of course only one of these views of self can be the true one, but we can believe in either one.

The two "selves" in this context are:

1. I can believe that the way I have been feeling, behaving, etc., is

my true self and this self must be allowed to continue to live and operate, and in fact is so powerful that it will anyway.
or

2. I can believe that which is in my heart. What I'd love to feel, love to show, etc. is my true self and will come to life at this moment and emerge from within. I can believe that this is my most powerful self.

There will never be two "selves" when we are behaving and feeling what we really want to. It is only when we wish to change and are no longer desiring our old behavior that we might feel there are two choices.

If, when we wish to change, we look only at our heart as our true emerging self, and our past (our "up till now" feelings and behavior, etc.) as our passing self, which once came from our heart, but is now being renewed, redirected, refreshed, and re-enlivened, we will be able to allow the past to recede and allow the new moment of the now self to be alive and operant.

Since to be truly glad (or any good feeling) we must *believe* we are truly glad, we have to see this quality as one of our own, as coming from our real self. We have to know that we wouldn't be wanting to be that way unless it was about to emerge from us. We have to know that the whole question of wishing we were more glad, more happy, etc., in a given situation couldn't even be a question unless it was prompted by an urge in our heart.

In seeing this desire as our true new self (instead of our past lack of feeling, etc.), we will believe it about us. It is by seeing this that we can then go to the next step, deciding without hesitation. We can simply decide that that is the true me.

I am not putting down the old feeling. It had its meaning in its own time. The point is that the old feeling just isn't relevant anymore when I wish I felt differently, more, deeply.

We must remember that feelings come from beliefs and decisions. Full feelings come after decisions. We do not have to base our decisions on our past feelings but can know that future feelings will only reflect our decisions or lack of them.

When we are in a situation where we suddenly realize or question our feelings and want to make them deeper or different, let us not be misled into believing that they reflect where we are now. Where we are now is up for grabs. Where we are now and are going to be is up to us now, again, and again. Our feelings never reflect where we are right now at the moment we are questioning them. They only reflect where we were before.

"Am I glad?" Pause, heartbeat, smile, now, "Yes, I'm so glad!"

When we want to feel a certain way, let us just look closely. We will find that we have actually begun to feel that way. To decide is really to discover that what we want to feel we are beginning to feel. To decide means "Don't decide for the past; the future is beginning."

SECTION IV

Sex

Sex Is a Mystery

Monday Night Study Group, 1973

Sexual feelings, as physical sensations, may be judged as either a sign of attraction to having good feelings or as a sign of deprivation from good feelings.

Emotional feelings about sex are judgments on the repercussions of sexual activity.

There is no form of having good feelings with others that is inherently included or excluded from the idea of sex. "Sex," in itself, is a mystery; it is a way that some people set aside some ways of having good feelings with others as "special."

Sex Is a Mystery

The body is homeostatic: you start to get hungry so that you can get back to homeostasis. You get thirsty so your body can return to homeostasis. That's not an emotional feeling; it is the physical sensation of well-being. It's the knowledge that nothing is going wrong.

Sexual feelings can come from a sense of deprivation, of lacking something that you believe you require for happiness. You *can* do anything just because you want to, without any sense of deprivation, but there are some things that essentially you *wouldn't* do if you did not have a sense of deprivation, for example, having sex with someone without their consent.

If you experience the sensation of well-being, are you just going to stand and stop moving, or might you just move? Happy people might still move, but they wouldn't make judgments in order to move. They would go places not in order to do anything, but just to do it. It just may happen that to go to sexual activity would not be the same as going to sexual feelings. A person might very well go through intercourse just as they go through going outside and inside.

If you were happy, would you go through anger? If you were happy, would you go through depression? Would that be part of your movement? So if you are talking about feelings, when you are happy, there are going to be certain feelings that you are just not going to have. If sex is like any other feeling, there might be a chance that you wouldn't have sexual feelings, because there are a lot of other feelings that you just wouldn't have if you were happy. The question is, is sex a movement back to homeostasis in the sense of well-being and being happy? In the absence of homeostatic movement, would there be such a thing as a sexual feeling?

Would you have to feel hungry in order to know to eat? Hunger is another thing that is apparently homeostatic. Some people are hungry and other people are not hungry, but they still eat, because that's what keeps them alive. Your body doesn't necessarily get miserable in order to tell you to eat.

What you call "hungry you might never feel if you actually went along with your body. That may be something that only comes from ignoring all the sensations, or the awareness. For your convenience, you limit eating to three times a day. You will eat before you go to work, once you while you are working, and then after work. People will notice hunger like anything else having to do with happiness or unhappiness; some notice hunger as an attraction towards food, and some will feel that same sensation as a deprivation from food, and it is the whole difference in hunger between being happy and unhappy.

Unhappy people notice hunger as a deprivation; happy people may notice an attraction to food. And they are two humans with the same physical sensations.

Sex could be something you're attracted toward or feeling deprived of. Good feelings from other people seem to be part of sex. So one could be attracted to having good feelings with other people, or feel deprived of them. If one was attracted to having good feelings with other people, there might not be any such thing as sex, but simply an attraction to having good feelings with other people. That would be the homeostatic position. Some of what is the so-called "sex drive" or "sex feelings" is when you are feeling deprived of having good feelings with other people, or deprived of having good feelings with yourself.

For example, take masturbation; there is a whole question of how much of it occurs from a sense of deprivation. For many of the teenagers that I have talked to, it was something they did to make themselves feel good when they felt bad. After having a rotten day, that was the way they made themselves feel good. Just because something is not bad, that doesn't motivate people to do something; very few people sit and tie and untie shoes all day.

The only reason we have emotional feelings about something is because we have questions about the repercussions. The feelings of good and bad are always connected to the future. With an open judgment, there are no good or bad feelings, there are just feelings. When you judge the repercussions, then you create emotional feelings.

Perhaps the only reason that a human being would have any thought or belief or anything about sex would be because they might have thoughts or beliefs about the desirability of the repercussions.

SECTION V

Life, Health, and Death

Happiness and Health

February 3, 1975

ALL emotional states are produced by beliefs. (If a feeling is not caused by a belief, it is not what we mean by an emotion.) All other feelings are caused by knowing. If the body is not directed by beliefs, it will behave in a natural way—in other words, as it knows to, in response to stimuli other than those stimuli of beliefs. Beliefs are very powerful stimuli.

Given certain beliefs, the body knows to respond in ways we call happy (healthy).

Given other beliefs, the body knows to respond in ways we call unhappy (unhealthy).

It does not follow that in seeking more happiness one will have to become healthier. The body works with the best at its disposal. It is conceivable that certain health-restoring mechanisms have been irrevocably destroyed in the past—our own past or during the course of history.

It is certain that if it is possible to become healthier, being happier will actualize that possibility. A happier person could be healthier than *they* were when unhappier, but not necessarily healthier than an unhappy other person. What is "healthier"? The body doing whatever it wants, unimpeded by internal or invading counter-forces or obstacles.

The Option View of Death

October 21, 1990

THE truth about death for man, from the attitude engendered by The Option Method, would be derived the same way as any other phenomenon. "What do you mean by death? What does that mean to your happiness?"

The death of another human being, especially a loved one, usually means the loss of that person, with no hope of regaining them, their presence, their company, their loving and happy ways. The death of an unwanted person, especially an enemy, means quite a different thing. The meaning makes the difference in the emotional response, and in the very human meaning of death itself. To deny the difference would be to ignore that all events are relevant or not, according to their impact on and pertinence to our values and desires.

Death simply does not have one scientific, factual meaning, although it may seem to allow for an objective scientific, biologic description. But even that word "objective" actually is an emotional reference, a description of death for an organism that has no affective meaning to the describer—in other words, the death of an organism that is either unreal (theoretical or generic), or for which the describer has no emotional opinion.

A definition such as "cessation of all movement and irreversible decay, without animation or life" is paltry at best, not thorough or exclusive; and as with all definitions, it risks being irrelevant and needing further explanations of the other terms in the definition. Besides, that is not what most people mean to ask when they ask about death and its meaning.

Definitions as meanings are deficient when they lack the relevant information, and are presumptively judgmental when they assert subjective value. Semantics can only render utility when the questioners can truly learn to ask what they really want to know, and why they want to know. Then semanticists can refer to the appropriate authorities for material information.

The most meaningful and therefore useful answer would have to take into account what is really being asked. I dare to say that whenever I have heard that question about the "meaning of death" or something like it, the questioner was really asking, "How can I not be unhappy about the loss of a loved one?"

As to the question of one's own death, the meaning is usually, "How can I not be unhappy about losing all that 1 love?" Succinctly, in both cases the idea of being unhappy about loss (and the "death" of hope) is the relevant fear, and the real meaning of "death."

This fear, of course, is the fear that The Option Method deals with, and the very fear that it allows a person to question. The person's actual answers that follow from The Option Method of questioning that person's beliefs about loss as a cause of sadness or anger, etc. are what are going to be THE answer to the person's meaning of the question of "How can I not be unhappy?"

The "Problem" of Death

THE philosophical problem of disease and death as being or non-being is irrelevant or absurd.

If they are being, they cannot end happiness. If they are non-being, they do not exist and are only believed to exist at best.

A perfectly happy person cannot believe in the death of his perfect happiness, since perfect happiness is a "knowing that one is perfectly happy."

If death is non-being, then I will never "know" the end of my happiness since there will be no "I" to experience such a knowing or ending. I will never be aware of knowing that I am no longer being or knowing.

If physical death is not what it seems, if it is not the end of my knowing my being, then I will always know I am perfectly happy.

The two approaches to death could be summed up this way:

1. I will never know non-being or non-happiness, or
2. I will always know being and happiness.

Life and Death

ARE there any truths we can discover about living and dying that have not been seen to be because of fear? Is it necessary to die? Is it necessary for the ones I love to die? Is it necessary for me to die?

It may not be necessary or inevitable for people to die. It depends on what we mean by death. If there is no question of unhappiness about loss, then we have the issue of desire. The truth could be approached as a question of wanting; perhaps of wanting to remain healthy, or or regaining health.

Is health (feeling well and able) what we mean by living? Is getting health and all the other things that we want while alive what we mean? It is still all a matter of wanting what we want, and getting what we want. If it is possible for a loved one not to die, and if we could have anything to do with their living, then it would begin with our desiring them to live, and acting according to that desire.

Since healing miracles have happened, and we have experienced them, it would seem that there is a truth to be enjoyed in that. Healing is surely a sign of the happiness and the knowledge of the healer being given to the ill person. Being healed is newly having the ability to feel well, and have the desired ableness of the body and mind; to be a whole, well, happy person. Healings have happened to people who never explicitly wanted one, or thought it was possible. That shows it is truly by the choice of that which heals.

Life, health and other things are all matters of knowing how to get what we want, or gladly receiving gifts. We can be grateful and still want what we want to come to us however it will.

Many things are possible which are believed to be impossible, even miracles. Miracles show the truth that there is more to life than ever we imagined. Every time I experience a miracle, I am newly reminded of that.

COMMENTARIES

by Aryeh Nielsen on

"The Great Myths"

The Meaning of Life

This commentary is a synopsis of ideas that Bruce Di Marsico expressed in many writings or talks, but did not express summarily in a single writing or talk.

WHAT is the meaning of life? To answer that, first we must answer, "What is meaning?" Meaning is the implication or the purpose of something. "My illness means that I can't go to the party tonight" is equivalent to "The implication of my illness (for me) is that I can't go to the party tonight." "My illness means that I need to eat healthier" is equivalent to "The purpose of my illness (for me) is to let me know that I want to change my diet."

So, what is the meaning of life? It is the implications of life, for *you*, or the purpose of life, for *you*. "The implication of *my* life is that, as someone who can play piano, I am able to entertain by playing piano. The implication of *your* life is that, as someone who can paint, you are able to entertain by painting." "The purpose of *my* life is to see my children flourish. The purpose of *your* life is to commune with nature."

But need life *have* implications or purpose? Not at all. You are doing what you are doing. What you are doing doesn't need to imply anything except that you are doing it. What is the meaning of what is in your peripheral vision now? That is part of your life. Perhaps it has no implications for you. What is the purpose of what is in your peripheral vision now? Perhaps it has no purpose; it just is what it is. Things have meaning for you if they have meaning for *you*, and they do not if they do *not*.

There are no secrets about the meaning of your life, because you already know perfectly what implications events have for you, and what purposes you have for yourself. That is because implications and purposes are a form of knowing, and you can no more not know these than not know your own experience.

The Will

This commentary is a synopsis of ideas that Bruce Di Marsico expressed in many writings or talks, but did not express summarily in a single writing or talk.

WHAT do people mean when they say they are lacking in willpower?

What do people mean when they say (in a distressed manner) that they have been waiting for something?

How are willpower and unhappy waiting related?

"The will" is the feeling of trying to "make" behavior match desires. Behavior could only not match desires if it was felt necessary to behave other than you desired.* This feeling of necessity is unhappiness. For those who are perfectly in touch with their desires (in particular, their happy desires, which are those desires arising in the context of knowing they are perfectly free to feel as they would like), there is a perfect unity between desire and behavior.

For example, if I "lack the will" to stick to a diet, I believe I *should* stick to the diet. If I truly want to diet, then I will diet—unless I want *more* to not feel *obligated* to stick to the diet!

In the example above, I did indeed desire to diet, and "lack of will" explains why I did not do so, despite my desire. In truth, though, I

---

* More precisely (but a mouthful): "Behavior could only be experienced as not matching *what you would most desire if you knew you could always feel the way you wanted to feel* (sometimes called colloquially "your deepest desires") if it was mistakenly felt necessary to behave other than in the way you would find most attractive *in the absence of any presumption that it was necessary to get what you want in order to feel the way you want to feel.*" Bruce Di Marsico often used the phrase "being in touch with your desires" to refer to *these* desires, as opposed to desires based on the mistaken presumption of needing to get what you want in order to be happy.

didn't "lack will"; rather, more than to lose weight, I desired to not be "trapped" or obligated by a diet.

Therefore, "the will" is as illusory as unhappiness. In realizing that you can feel however you would like to feel, the feeling of "having" to use willpower to "make" behavior match desires disappears. Desires and behavior become a perfect unity. As a corollary, since "the will" (like evil) doesn't actually exist, the question of "free will" is as meaningless as a question about a "square circle."

Behavior manifests changes in the world, which yields a new judgment on the state of the world, and new desires. Ultimately, without any beliefs about how things "should" be to impede the natural cycle:

* desires arise from judging the state of the world,
* manifestation (the state of the world) arises from behavior (which changes the state of the world),
* behavior arises from desires . . .

Bruce Di Marsico sometimes refers to this desire-behavior-manifestation-judging-desire cycle as Doing.

The feeling of waiting, unhappily, is the feeling that "I am not doing what I could be doing, or should be doing, to manifest the changes I desire." Therefore, there is no unhappy waiting (or unhappy feeling of time passing) when desires and behavior are a unity. This is often called, in psychological literature, "Flow." But those who advocate "flow" seek out the conditions in which they believe they can experience their desires and behavior as a perfect unity, such as sports, sex, or meditation, not realizing that desires and behavior are inherently in perfect unity in every circumstance when unhappiness does not "interfere."

A most prosaic example: we desire to eat, and so we manifest behavior to partake of food. With each bite we eat, we newly judge the result of our action, and find ourselves with a different desire, being less hungry than in the last moment. The joy of eating continues until our hunger is satisfied, which commences the peace of having eaten.

Especially when picnicking on vacation, we may experience this "joy of eating/satisfaction of having eaten" cycle without any sense of time or deprivation. And this is our experience of living, whenever we have no belief of how things should be: merely a continuous motion of desire, enacted.

You Are Your Happiness

This commentary is a synopsis of ideas that Bruce Di Marsico expressed in many writings or talks, but did not express summarily in a single writing or talk.

A WORD that Bruce Di Marsico used even more than the word "happiness" was the word . . . "you"! He occasionally talked about what he meant by this word. Most summarily, he said "You *are* your happiness," also "You *are* what you value."

To set the context, try this thought experiment:

If you changed your hair color, would you still be *you*?

If you lost the use of your body, would you still be *you*?

If you suddenly found yourself, seemingly against your will, liking what you don't like (attracted to foods, people, and behaviors you don't like), would you still be *you*?

What is "you"?

As you read these words, there is a tacit experience of valuing things, now.

"You" is a reference to this experience.

In Bruce Di Marsico's example, if you value the taste of olive oil, then "you" *is* the experience of valuing the taste of olive oil (among other things also valued).

Valuing things is synonymous with emotional beliefs. Emotional beliefs always take place in the context of practical beliefs, each individual's model of the world (in the above case, such beliefs as: "olive oil exists," "olive oil is edible"). It is worth noting that practical beliefs have nothing to do with unhappiness. For example, if someone believes that a spaceship of aliens is docking in the back of their skull, to quote Bruce Di Marsico, "Maybe somebody you are helping knows better than you what is really going on. If a belief someone has doesn't matter for their *happiness*, what does it matter to *you* if their understanding of 'reality' doesn't match yours?"

"You" Is a Reference to an Experience

Consider the declaration, "I am here."

Throughout the day, in each moment, this declaration would have a slightly different meaning, because in each moment, "here" is a different place. "Here" is a reference, a way of pointing to a relative location, not a thing-in-itself.

Similarly, in each moment, "I" is different, because the experience of valuing changes moment by moment. When hungry, food is valued more highly. When not hungry, food is valued less highly. An individual's beliefs can change radically, at any time. "I" is a reference, a way of pointing to an experience of valuing, not a thing-in-itself.

"I" also has practical use: "I" can be a reference to an individual body. In this sense, "I" means "this body right now." This practical use of "I" has no consequences for happiness in any way. In this case, "I" is used as an object of experience, not the subject of experience. "I like the hair I have" can be elaborated as "I (as an experiencing subject) value the hair this body (as an object of my experience) has."

The "I" that is relevant to happiness is the subjective "I," which is the experience of valuing; not the objective "I," which is an object (the body) that is valued.

"Happiness" Is the Taste in Your Own Mouth

One definition Bruce Di Marsico used for "Happiness" is: the ultimate explanatory principle, the goal of everything you do. The goal of everything you do is simply what you value most. "You" is a reference to the experience of valuing. So, we see that "you" and "happiness" actually refer to the same thing! Your taste is what you value. The goal of everything you do is what is most to *your* taste. It is *your* happiness.

As Bruce Di Marsico put it poetically:

Happiness is admitting that you like that you want what you want.

Happiness is admitting liking that you don't like what you don't like.

Happiness is admitting liking that you change your mind whenever you think that's best.

Happiness is admitting liking that you don't change your mind until you really change your mind.

Happiness is admitting liking that you feel just the way you like to feel about everything you do.

What Happens to "You" after You Die?

After the death of the body, if there is still an experience of valuing, then that "you" is no more limited in happiness than before the death of the body, because there would still be the experience of doing and being whatever is valued most, in the context of after-bodily death.

If there is no experience of valuing, then there is no "you" to talk about, and the question becomes the equivalent of "What happens to a ripple on a pond when it has completed?" A ripple is a process, not a thing, and once the process has completed, the process does not exist.

In sum, after bodily death, either there is no "you," or happiness is perfectly available. Either way, then, death presents no obstacle to *your* happiness.

Did Something Make You Who You Are? Parents, Past Lives . . .?

If someone says "I am who I am because of my childhood," or "I am who I am because of my past lives," what are they saying?

In Bruce Di Marsico's example, if you value the taste of olive oil, then you *are* the experience of valuing the taste of olive oil. What does it mean to say "I value the taste of olive oil because my parents fed it to me every day," or "I value the taste of olive oil because I was an olive farmer in my past life?" These "explanations" don't add any information about who you are, because you are simply the experience of valuing olive oil. Whether these "causes" are true, false, impossible to verify, or meaningless has no bearing on your present-time valuing of things, and so is irrelevant to the question of who you are.

Not Believing Yourself

Bruce Di Marsico has described unhappiness as not believing yourself. He elaborates by saying that unhappiness is the impossible belief that you don't value what you value. Feeling you "should" have values other than you do in order to be happy is an example of this impossible belief.

The experience of valuing things right now is exactly what is meant by "you." If these values change, then that is the "you" of right now. Happiness is valuing things as you do. To fully elaborate out the statement, "You should be different (in order to be happy)" means "You 'should' have values other than you do, in order to fully value things as you do." This is clearly an impossible statement! This is what is meant by "being against oneself." And this is what unhappiness is.

Consenting to Happiness: "Watch and Enjoy What Happens"

Since you *are* your happiness, you can never truly be unhappy; you can only mistakenly believe you are unhappy. Bruce Di Marsico called being free of this mistaken belief "consenting to happiness." It is the perfect knowledge that you value what you value, and never do not.

What is there to do when you know that you value what you value and never do not? "Watch, and enjoy what happens," as what is happening is the process of *your* happiness. This process alternates between what Bruce Di Marsico called Joy, or moving toward what you value, and Peace, or the satisfaction of having arrived at what you value (for now), which Bruce Di Marsico sometimes summed up as "Happy, and not done for now" and "Happy, and done for now."

The Self Is a Location

This commentary represents the editor's synthesis of ideas Bruce Di Marsico expressed only in fragments.

THE "self" refers to a location in experience that is used to measure the experienced world. The "self" is the center of experience, in the same sense that "here" is the center of space. It is an arbitrary origin of measurement. It is not an entity that persists through space and time. For example, it would seem absurd for someone to say on Tuesday, while standing in Tokyo, "Here I am," and then on Wednesday, in London, to say "How on earth did 'here' change so much between Tuesday and Wednesday?" The obvious retort is, "because it is a different 'here'." Yet the natural limitations of space and time mean that there is some consistency in where "here" is over time—for most of us, "here" has always been on the earth, and never located outside the solar system.

Similarly to "here" as the origin of measurement in space, the "self" is the origin of measurement of experience. The "self" can be described in detail by describing the values experienced at a given moment. Before dinner, we say "I (my self) am hungry." After dinner, we say "I (my self) am not hungry." The "self" is no more an entity that persists through space and time than "here" is, and it might seem absurd to ask "How on earth did who I am change so much during dinner?"

Some values shift rapidly, some slowly, and some seem to stay the same the whole of a bodily lifetime. In accordance with how values shift, at any two moments in time the earlier "self" may be more or less like the later "self," just as we often find the "here" where we are sometimes similar to a previous "here," and sometimes not.

Who we are has patterns of consistency and change, just as *where we are* does.

Some religious texts discuss the "separate self-sense," the feeling of differentiation between self and universe. Similarly to how lines of demarcation separate nation-states, yet are fundamentally arbitrary divisions of geography, lines of demarcation are naturally drawn in experience: does the "self" include emotional feelings? The body? The universe? Fundamentally, the lines are arbitrary and can shift. Some may feel "I am the universe"; others may feel, "I am not my body, not my thoughts, not my emotions"; and most others will demarcate the self from the world in a complex way that neither makes the self equivalent to the world, nor makes the self completely vacuous. There is no "better" or "best" way to demarcate the self from the world, there is only the ever-shifting way each of us lives this demarcation.

The World Is You

This commentary represents the editor's synthesis of ideas Bruce Di Marsico expressed only in fragments.

WHAT does Bruce Di Marsico mean when he says "The world *is* you?"

There Is Only Your World

He is not proposing that what arises is purely a figment of the imagination, and is also not claiming that there is no reality "out there." Insofar as there is, and it represents limitations on your actions, you find out. Bruce Di Marsico: "If you thought there was a door there, and there is only a wall, you'll find out when you bump into it."

But everything you know about the world is *your* knowing, and is not an aspect of the world-in-itself. For example, take sugar: only a being who found classifying some patterns as sugar as relevant to their life would conceive (whether verbally or non-verbally) a substance as sugar. For deep-ocean bacteria that feed on methane, recognition of "sugar" is completely irrelevant to their existence. Even when a scientist classifies two molecules as similar in some way, and therefore both sugar, he or she is making a practical judgment about what it means to classify things as similar. Similarly, a particle physicist has their own criteria for classifying things as "particles."

No one knows the world-in-itself; they only know the world as they understand it.

An example that many have strong feelings about, in the abortion debate, is the question of when life begins. There is no "right" answer out there in the universe. There is each of our understandings. If you want others to see the world as you see it, then that is *your* wanting, and the universe allows you to want others' point of view to change (though if they do change their point of view, it will be *their* choice, perhaps in response to your communication). This does not imply anything about what you do: with your understanding, you may choose to practically co-operate with, work at cross-purposes to, or be indifferent relative to those who disagree with your point of view.

You Create the Distinction Between Yourself, Others, and the World

Consider two adjacent countries. In this case, it is obvious that the borders between them are humanly created, and there is no division inherent in the universe that separates the two lands. Nonetheless, the distinction can be very practical, as when we talk of the weather in one country. The distinction is fuzzy, useful, and can shift over time as political regimes rise and fall.

Now consider the border between "you" and the "world." There are clinical cases in institutions of people, often classified as "extreme paranoid-schizophrenic," who believe that all thoughts in mind and actions in body are not their own. There are also cases of those who stare out the window at traffic all day, experiencing everything they see as their own action. If you are reading this, you are probably between the two extremes of "I-am-everything" and "I-am-nothing."

But if someone touches your clothes, are they touching you? There is no universal answer, only your answer of this moment. The boundary between you and the world fluctuates from moment to moment. When using a familiar tool, such as a hammer, the sense of "you" may expand to the tool, only to exclude the tool the moment you are no longer engaged in its use. There is no "right" border between "you" and the "world," only the one you experience. But remember—everyone else will have a different border, which may be very similar to your experience, or wildly different!

Consider the border between "you" and "others." Meditating yogis have confessed that they make no such distinction. Those with what is labeled as "Multiple Personality Syndrome" confess that they are other to themselves. Infants only gradually begin to make distinctions between self and other. People in love confess a merging of self-and-other. Those falling out of love confess the opposite. There is no "right" border between "you" and "others," only the one you experience. But remember—everyone else will have a different border, which may be very similar to your experience, or wildly different!

PART IV
Happiness without Reason

SECTION I

About Happiness without Reason

There Is Nothing to Believe

December 1987

THE student's approach is that what you have to do is *learn* something and remember something. The Option Method is learning how to *forget* something. It's a question of what you've been believing, not what we're going replace that belief with. When a person stops believing in demons, do you replace that with a belief in something else? When you believed the devil existed, you believed it. But when you no longer believed it existed, you no longer believed it existed. So if you don't believe that what's going to happen to you on Monday, for instance, could make you unhappy, could make you not free, then you're just going to see things happening without judging them as reasons for unhappiness. Believe it or not, there is a point at which you can see somebody yelling and screaming and ranting and raving right at your face, and you just see it. It is just what's happening.

When you can start hearing unhappiness as meaning the same thing as "possessed by a demon," you can start seeing how ludicrous the whole thing is. When people say, "You shouldn't do that," you'll go, "Huh? Means nothing to me. I really don't know what it means." You can realize how wise you are. You can appreciate it. "You ought to feel bad about that." "Aren't you ashamed?" These have no meaning. You wouldn't even know how to go about doing that thing that they're telling you to do. How could I go about feeling bad? How could I go about feeling ashamed? I don't have what it takes. I'd have to be believing something, wouldn't I? "You shouldn't have done that. You should have done this. That's not supposed to be. That's wrong." You'll hear that as the same meaningless thing as if you hear someone saying to you, "That's a sin" or "That's evil." All of the expressions of unhappiness and the statements of unhappiness and the beliefs about unhappiness can become meaningless.

May I suggest to you that all the expressions of unhappiness are *already* meaningless to you, but you've been struggling with thinking that somehow you have got to have them have some kind of a meaning before you can dismiss them? When you were a kid, somebody told you that you were bad. You didn't know what that meant. "Huh? What?" You knew that somehow it meant something about them, that they're doing something to themselves, that they're thinking and saying and feeling something.

When someone didn't like you, you didn't know what that meant about you. You heard about evil and bad and right and wrong, and you tried to give it meaning, and you wound up in this world of illusion. Your attempts to give it meaning is what we will call unhappiness. "Should" and "shouldn't," you've tried to give that meaning. They never did have meaning, if you think about it. You thought all your life you knew what "should" and shouldn't" meant. In fact, all your life, up until not too long ago, all you were concerned with was "What am I supposed to do? How am I supposed to be? What should I be? Should I go to this school? Should I go to that school? Should I take this job? Should I take that job? Who should be my friends? Should I be friends with her? Should I let them say this? Should I do that? Am I supposed to do this? Am I supposed to do that?" You tried to give those things meaning. You lived your life with them as if they had meaning.

They never had meaning. You were trying to give them meaning all the time, and that attempt to constantly give them meaning and live up to the meaning would be called "stress," "anxiety," and "unhappiness." So we're going back to them having no meaning, where we came from. You'll then see the world for what it really is.

Some live their lives in order to go to heaven and avoid hell and things like that, but it all starts with the presumption that they're not in heaven now. My joke is, why isn't it entirely possible that you've died and gone to heaven or—depending on your theology—you've been reincarnated into this perfect state now? The only thing is, you just don't believe it, that's all. You were born, you appeared on this heaven, this earth, and you're in heaven. There's nothing wrong. Everything's perfect. Have fun. And that's the way it is. And then you start saying, "But I can't do this, I can't do that, I can't say this, I can't do that. This can't be heaven."

Who said this wasn't heaven and paradise, and why did you believe them? Isn't it a fact that the only problem *is* that you believed them? If they're right, believe them. If they're not right, and you're not believing them, why are you here? You don't believe them. So what are you doing, asking me for permission to believe yourself? Well, you have an absolute right to do that—but you might want to know that is what you're doing, if that *is* what you're doing: needing some authoritarian, bright guy to support your belief so that you can believe in yourself.

I see that with every client. They're always playing devil's advocate with themselves and with me. I'm there to try to help them to be happy and they're showing me how that isn't really possible because even if they do, they'll mess it up somehow. Whose side have you come to believe you're on?

SECTION II

Nothing Prevents Happiness

There Are No Obstacles to Perfect Happiness

September 29, 1990

THERE are no obstacles to perfect happiness.

Nothing prevents happiness. Nothing causes unhappiness.

Nothing (outside one's own beliefs) makes a person believe in unhappiness.

All beliefs are choices to accept *as* true what "seems" evident.

What seems evident may only seem evident because of previous beliefs of what is true. Assumed facts or false premises can lead to the mistakes that appear to be "evidence," but are merely logical deductions or interpretations based on those false assumptions.

One universal false assumption is that our unhappiness happens against our will or desire, and not by our choice. The choice involved here is the choice to believe that false assumption. Once believed, it will seem that unhappiness happens to us.

The belief that *not getting what you want* (to whatever degree of relative personal importance) *makes you unhappy* (according to those same degrees of value) *is* the belief that is the actual cause of the unhappiness. For example, the greater the subjective loss, the greater the sadness. The greater the supposed insult, the greater the anger. Can a person be unhappy about something they do not believe is something to be unhappy about?

The universal belief underlying all the errors and assumptions of unhappiness is this one simple belief: happiness is wrong at certain times or under certain circumstances and conditions. And so, unhappiness is felt.

There Is No Reason to Be Unhappy

THERE is no reason to be unhappy. You have made yourselves unhappy, believing there were reasons (or causes) to be. You believed you ought to. You don't have to believe that anymore. It isn't true. There is no reason at all to be unhappy. You are fine. You are perfect and happy.

You will do whatever you want, whatever you feel like. You will feel however you wish. Nothing can make you unhappy. You have only believed you could be made unhappy. You now know the truth.

Don't worry anymore. Do whatever you do without question. The last judgment was yesterday. You're okay now.

You don't ever have to lie by believing you can gain by being unhappy. To tell such a now-obvious untruth doesn't mean that you realized it or intended to lie to yourself. You passed on a myth you sincerely and terribly believed. The lie was long ago. Don't repeat the trap.

There Is No Need to Understand Yourself

March 17, 1975

Is wanting to be happier any different than who you are? Is being happy any different than being who you are? If you are going to be happier, if you are going to be free from fear, if you are going to change from what you no longer want to something else which you more want, where did that wanting come from if not from you? Why is it not a promise, rather than a cause for more of what you don't want? Why is not the awareness that you would prefer to feel differently than you feel now the beginning of feeling differently than you feel now? What can you do except want to be happier?

You begin with that, and then whatever follows is part of that. It is either that or it is part of some innate tendency to be self-destructive. Which is it? If you want to be happier, what would follow? Since you want to be happier, only being happier could follow. If not, then not. You are only unhappy because of what you believe. But it is only one belief that we are talking about—because you believe that you will not naturally be happier. That takes many forms, of course. Once you believe that, you can believe that things around you are causing you to be unhappy; you can believe that seeing yourself not change is making you unhappy, you could believe anything. What those things depend on is the moment, it depends on something we may more sometimes call your "style," which may be more biologically determined than anything. You will grab on to something that has to do with who you really are and be against it.

But it is not the being against it that causes you unhappiness. It is *why* you are against it. It doesn't even matter if you could hypothetically, theoretically, be against yourself—that doesn't even matter as long as you didn't believe you were. And it isn't even being against yourself or even seeing yourself being against yourself in that sense that is unhappiness—it is how you account for it. It is why. If you believe that even if you were against yourself, it was because of pollution or something, that then you couldn't do what you wanted to do, or it was because you had some vitamin deficiency or something that you couldn't cure—that it was constitutional—that it really was imposed upon you—that you were really crippled and that you couldn't help yourself—you wouldn't be unhappy. It is *why* you believe you're against yourself that makes you unhappy. If you really believed you weren't able to do the things you wanted to do, to be the way you wanted to be, would you be unhappy? Perhaps even if you believed that you weren't able to be perfectly happy—you physically were not able to experience perfect happiness, or physically weren't able to be it—it is *why* you would believe that that is the point, even though some of these beliefs are impossible. But why you would believe that it is possible is what would matter.

Questioner: *But what about somebody who has no legs and is unhappy because he can't walk?*

Well, didn't you at least start by knowing that he is certainly believing on the surface that he needs legs in order to be happy? Isn't that his first statement, though? "I am unhappy because I don't have legs" is the same as saying "I need legs in order to be happy." Why does he believe he needs legs to be happy? Why does he believe he needs anything in order to be happy? Because he believes that he doesn't naturally have what it takes in order to be happy. He isn't saying he wants legs, he is saying that he should, ought to, must, is supposed to, is the law of nature that he have them, and why doesn't he have them?

Questioner: *Even if a person believed he was physically incapable of knowing perfect happiness, if he believed that was because of some physical incapacity, what then?*

He could be perfectly happy. If by "perfect happiness" he means perfectly himself, he would have to believe he is against himself to be unhappy. He would have to not believe he would naturally be himself. It isn't possible that a person could know that they physically weren't able to be perfectly happy. It would depend on what they meant by "perfect happiness"; and if you actually looked at it, they wouldn't be talking about perfect happiness, probably, but about being perfectly capable of doing what is necessary in order to be perfectly happy, because they are believing that there is something to be done in order to be perfectly happy.

What if you "know" that the way you are presently constituted physically, you might not be able to experience perfect happiness? That still would not be a cause of unhappiness, because you would immediately start wanting to be constituted physically different in order to be able to experience perfect happiness. The question is, why don't you believe that you could change physically if you needed to change physically, if you needed another arm or another leg or two more? And it is *why* you don't think you would, that would make the difference.

If you want to call it a primordial belief, a basic belief, you can. The hunch, the doubt that you are naturally not going to be happy—that you might not naturally be happy—is there. It is behind everything else. And if you ask "Why do I believe it?" you are still believing it. Do you believe it or not, is the only question. It is the belief about which it only matters that you are believing it or you are not believing it. Do you feel somehow that you are naturally not going to be happy? Yes or no, that is what you are feeling. If you said "yes," you said "yes"; if you said "no," you said "no." That is who you are.

The reason you would ask why is because you didn't believe that everything that comes from you is perfectly happy, is motivated by your happiness, including your beliefs, including that belief. It is not *what* you ask that will make you unhappy, it is *why* you ask it. It is not *what* you don't ask that will make you unhappy, it is *why* you don't ask it. It is not *what* you do or don't do that will make you unhappy, it is *why* you don't do it or do it. It really doesn't matter whether I want to sit in this chair or I want to stand up. It is why I sit in this chair. If I am wanting to sit in this chair or not wanting to sit in it—it is why I am doing that. Let's say I am wanting to sit in this chair. If I believe I should do what I want—if that is the reason I sit in the chair, if that is the reason I go with my wanting, if I do what I want because I believe I should—then I will be unhappy.

It doesn't matter that I did what I wanted. It is *why* I did it that I will be happy or not. If I believe that I didn't want to sit in this chair and I believe that I shouldn't want to or should want to, then I will be unhappy. It doesn't matter. If I do what I want or I don't do what

I want, it is why I do or don't do it. If I don't get into the "whys," then I will always just do what I want. If I were to say to you now, right now this moment—"Do something you don't want to do," I don't care what thought, what action, what behavior you choose—it doesn't matter, does it? You can't really feel that you did what you didn't want to do. You can only feel you did what you didn't want to do if you first feel you should or shouldn't want to or be able to do that. It isn't the thing itself, it never is. It is *why.* It isn't whether you believe you want to or not, even. It is not even "Do I really want to do this or do I not want to do this?" Even if it were possible that you could do something that you didn't want to do, as soon as you did it, you just realized you wanted to do it—as long as you didn't say "should" or "shouldn't have"; as long as you didn't say your unhappiness was against it, that it was against your happiness, that it came from your unhappiness.

In one way, which I suppose often will seem theoretical, you are only unhappy because you believe you are. You just believe that there is something called "unhappiness" in you right now and something causing it or something not causing it, or something has to rout it out or something has to not rout it out, and that there is a war—and that you can be believing in unhappiness is the only problem. Whenever you are unhappy, it is only because you believe you are. It sounds glib sometimes, and yet I think it is the most profound understanding of it.

It can get to a point where you no longer want to understand that or anything else. That understanding yourself and what you do and why you do it can be totally undesirable to you. Then there can be a point where you do want to understand some things. It is *why* you want to understand and *why* you don't want to understand that would make the difference. If you find that you just don't want to look at yourself anymore and you just don't want to analyze and you are fed up with it and you are sick and tired of it, what matters is *why* you are feeling that way. It is because you are afraid, because you are believing that somehow you are going to be unhappy. If you find that "Lo and behold! Wow, I am really not wanting to look at why I did what I did and I am really not wanting to explore or understand myself, isn't that marvelous!" then that is something else altogether different. If you find yourself not being very ecstatic, now, hearing the greatest truths in the universe—if you find yourself not jumping for joy, if you find yourself not doing this or that—it doesn't matter. It is *why* you are not. If you are not because you are not and you are wanting to be happier, you are not unhappy. You are unhappy, if you are, because you are not believing you are wanting things and changes; you are believing you should have had them.

If You Seem Unhappy, You Can Know You Are Not

December 12, 1992

So is it true that people don't have to be unhappy, but just believe in it? Since that's true, what follows from that in your life? Every time you experience that you might be unhappy (if you are wondering if you really are or were unhappy), ask yourself, "What do I know to be the truth?" That, at worst, if you *had* been unhappy, it was because you believed you had to be. And what's pertinent and relevant for you to know now? That you don't have to be.

But that has all kinds of ramifications. If you seem to get unhappy, you can just know that, if that really was unhappiness, it was because you thought you had to be unhappy—but what's the truth, now?

And so anytime you may seem to get unhappy, you just experience this, and realize, "I've been unhappy," or "maybe I've been unhappy," or "maybe this was unhappy"—or, "I don't want to be unhappy," and it's over.

Because unhappiness doesn't have a substance, it's not reality, so it can't have its own life. It doesn't even exist with or without your permission; it's just an illusion. It's believing you have to feel a certain way. So once you realize, "I've been unhappy," what does that really mean? You really mean you don't want it.

So, I want you to know that it's over. And at that moment, your unhappiness is over. Now, although you could worry and feel bad that you didn't realize it sooner, then you could realize THAT is just being unhappy, and that could be over. Because as soon as you realize you're unhappy, it's over. There's no way to be unhappy about something you don't want to be unhappy about. And there's really no way to want to be unhappy about something, when you know about yourself that you don't want to be unhappy.

So even what we've called "wanting to be unhappy" is still people who believed it was necessary.

Here's a medicine that does you no good but it doesn't have a bad taste. Here's a medicine that does you no good, but it tastes bad. Which will you want? If you take the one that tastes bad, it can be for no other possible cause than you believing it was necessary. Even though people have experiences like, "I'm pretty sure I want to be unhappy," that's actually an experience in the unhappiness itself. How they got to that was because they felt, in the first place, that they had to be unhappy.

If you understand this, if you have this attitude, everything comes from this without me really teaching you much.

SECTION III

There Are No Reasons for Happiness

Happiness Is Not the Result of Having Good Things

June 1982

HAPPINESS is not, nor ever has been, the result of having good things in themselves. What we always meant by "good" merely granted us the right to be happy. Happiness is the right to be happy and is the result of not doubting that you have that right to be, no matter what.

All that people want is to be happy. Happiness is the ultimate desire. Happiness is the prime mover. Happiness is the goal of all desires.

The desire for happiness is the sole motivation of all people. The desire for more happiness is the sole motivation for all people.

No Beliefs Are Necessary

January 28, 1974

When will we stop forgetting; when will we start remembering? This is only another way of saying, when will we really be happy, or when will we believe what we know? When will we stop forgetting that we don't have to be unhappy?

The attitude of the method really makes that model unnecessary; but without the model, one part of the attitude might always have been missing. So in a sense, you have the attitude, and you have the model, and sometimes there is something a little missing in the attitude that the model helps you to restore. Sometimes there is a little something missing in the model that your attitude can help to restore.

I think that it is an important thing to remember: that any work with anyone, including yourself, is based on your attitude. Sometimes you may feel that there is something missing in your attitude, and if you go back to the model of the method, "Why are you unhappy, etc.?" that may help you restore to your attitude what would be missing, and the attitude may restore the method. If you can't remember the method, you might just go back to your attitude and rediscover the method.

There are two fundamental belief states of motivation: needing to be happy and wanting to be happy. Motivation means tending towards. We can motivate ourselves by wanting: happy if I get it or happy if I avoid it. So if we are using happiness as the *goal* of our motivation and we believe that we are happy if we get happiness, if I want to become happy, I am happy if I get happiness. "Unhappy if I don't get it" would be the belief of needing to be happy and unhappy if I don't get it as a way of motivating myself to get the happiness. So basically, those two beliefs in the kinds of being are really two kinds of motivation towards happiness.

In many ways they are the same thing, and they are the two ways people use to become happy. They either need to become happy or they want to become happy.

There is a third kind of motivation, which, because it is ignored, the other two come into play. You could call it God, or peace with a capital P or happiness with a capital H or destiny with a capital D; it hardly matters because it is all inadequate. What does that have to do with motivation? Simply that if one needs any motivation, either wanting or needing, one is denying knowing. Simply, even if one is wanting to become happy, that wanting to become happy would be in some way a denial. It would be a way of saying "I need to try," that the trying is necessary in some way.

This is progressing from trying, from using need—unhappiness—to motivate ourselves to be happy, to understanding that a happier state, a more pleasant way to try to be happy is by using *happiness* to become happy, and by wanting to be happy, and by not being unhappy if we are not. The third state, which we can call "no belief," shows us that in that state, there couldn't be any question of trying, and shows that wanting and needing are both in a way a kind of lie.

What we get down to is that beliefs and motivations are the same thing, and the very fact that we believe we need motivation of any sort is to say that it is not yet so. If I am tending towards going over to that side of the room, that in itself is an admission that I am not yet there. If I were to know myself to be over there, it would be inadequate somehow to say that I *wanted* to be there. I was there a few moments ago and here I am now. To say that I tend towards being here right now becomes totally irrelevant because I *am* here. I know myself to be here.

Some things, like our own nature, things that are essential to our own being, have to be surer than just tending towards. We can all tend towards going to the kitchen later, which we would all kind-of-notice in ourselves as a wanting. We would become aware of our tendency towards going to the kitchen and discovering that we want to go there for coffee. But that still is a very uncertain thing, that still is not sure, and that kitchen may fall down before we get there or we may fall down before we get there. Tending toward something in itself does not give any surety or any certainty of achievement. So in wanting things, somehow, no matter how we motivate ourselves, that motivation itself never gives any surety of your goal.

But there are some goals that we just can't tolerate not being assured of accomplishing, and one of these (perhaps the only one) is happiness. We cannot allow for ourselves for happiness to be an uncertain thing. Insofar as it is to us uncertain, we resort to these two types of motivation (wanting and needing) in order to tend toward it, because we believe it is uncertain. And only if a thing is not certain do you have to tend toward it. Only if a thing is certain can you, in a sense, forget it and ignore it—which accounts for why we would forget our happiness, even though we are always there, and why we would be unhappy: simply because happiness must be certain.

How could something that is so important to us be forgotten all the time? Simple. It is not so important to remember. Why not? We don't forget that we wanted to go home tonight, and yet in so many ways it would be much less important to any of you than your own happiness. But there is no way that any of you would forget that you wanted to go home. But when you want to go home to happiness, go home to your real self, how can you forget that? And yet you seem to.

It could be because we are simply caught up in that whole thing of motivation, the whole thing of desire and the whole thing of needing, that insofar as we *want* to become happier we are much happier than when we *need* to be happy, and are believing we need something in order to be happy and that we will be unhappy without this or that. We are in that state of non-being which is a state of believing "I am lacking, I am non-existing, not fully existing, and I need something to complete my existence."

The state of becoming happier is still presuming that I am not yet fully existing, but that I am being born, I am coming into existing, I am coming into fullness, that I am still not yet complete but I am wanting to be. In itself, it is a kind of denial of fulfillment. The denial is warranted only by the evidence. We all have enough evidence to say that we are still becoming happier. So that the fact that we can deny that we are perfectly happy doesn't seem to be unwarranted. It seems to be a perfectly sane thing to do, logical, sensible. But by the very fact that it implies that denial, that that denial is part of it, we will have to vacillate between the wanting and needing, and stay in the beliefs all the time.

We will still use beliefs as a motivation. We will still motivate ourselves because we want to or need to because we have a reason. We don't just *do* because we *do*. Whereas when we are knowing being—which is the same as knowing doing—we *do* at that point because we *do*; we *be* because we *be*. We *are* whatever we *are*. We *want* what we *want*. And in that way, wanting at that point is not the wanting as in "wanting to be happy." In the state of knowing being, there can very well be a sense of wanting, but that sense of wanting is no different than knowing. My wanting to do something is just simply my knowing to do it—my knowing that it will be, my knowing that it is to be done. If we try to see that in terms of our happiness, it might make a little sense.

If you know that you are happy, there isn't any question of beliefs. When there is no longer any question about it and there is no longer any tending toward it, there is no reason for beliefs. Beliefs have no raison d'être. They have no justification. They have no value, in fact. And if you look from that point back, you see that the only value beliefs had were to deceive. That to believe anything was to confess your not knowing, was to deny knowing. I am not talking about the belief that Paris is in France. That is not necessarily what concerns us. But there is certainly no value in terms of our happiness, to believe that *this* will help us to be happy or *that* will help us to be happy or *this* is evidence that we are not, and *that* is evidence that we are. And there is no value in any of those beliefs about ourselves, especially beliefs about our potential for being, and beliefs about where we are at this very moment.

Believing means acting. Beliefs aren't just a mental set, an intellectual construct; and when we turn something into a belief, it doesn't just exist as some kind of a symbol in the brain but it exists throughout the whole body as an act, which the body can manifest.

A belief is not in the so-called brain; a belief is in the mind and the mind is between the top of the scalp and the bottom of the soles of the feet. If you feel what we call a psychosomatic pain, that is your mind, because your mind is at that point in your side or your leg or wherever the pain happens to be. The whole idea that your mind is in your head is archaic. So believing is believing with the whole body. What is knowing with, then?

I think if you look more closely, you will see that believing is with the body in a certain way. It is actually a destruction of the body. Believing always manifests itself in the body as some kind of a problem, as something uncomfortable.

So, the more we believe, the less of our body we will have. The stronger the beliefs, the stronger the pain. And so every belief is a hole in the body—if you want to see it that way, if you understand it. It is a void in the mind because it implies a not being yet.

If I believe something about myself, I am saying I am not being something yet that I want to be.

Because of our experience in this world, we have come to very much learn that we could want things to be true but just because we want them, that doesn't mean they are so. All of you think you have a lot of evidence that has proven to you that you have wanted many things but couldn't always get what you want. What if that is simply just not true? But because you have been believing that you could want something and not have it, you have also been believing this about your own state of mind. You have believing this about your own destiny. You have been believing this about your own happiness. But is it knowledge? Do you really know that wanting doesn't make it so? Or have you just been believing that way all of your life?

Because wanting and knowing are not different. And your wanting happiness is a revelation to yourself that you know what happiness is. Otherwise, how could you want it? You can't want something that you can't even conceive of. Your wanting happiness demonstrates that you already know what your happiness is. And consenting to that knowledge *is* happiness.

What Happiness Does

April 29, 1976

WHAT happiness is—it does.

Since happiness is feeling good in the best possible way, it relegates the whole realm of doing to that which is part of, and integral to, feeling good in the best possible way. The best possible way of feeling good is "simply" feeling good, in a way that is unencumbered, un-dependent, and unnecessary (for no reason).

Happiness is the experience of knowing that whatever is done (by others or by me) is unnecessary. It is also unnecessary to "know" that you are happy.

It is never necessary to be happy. Neither is it necessary to be unhappy, but unhappiness is the believing that something is necessary. The feeling and compulsively "natural" conviction that unhappiness is sometimes necessary is merely the attitude of reflecting upon ourselves as part of a necessary phenomenon or unfolding experience of existence.

Naught is necessary. Happiness proves it. Happiness is the feeling of being unnecessary, feeling what is never necessary to feel, choosing what is never necessary to choose, doing what can never be necessary to be done. Nothing needs to be begun. Nothing needs to be completed or left undone.

The feelings of happiness feel good precisely because they are free feelings of feeling freely, and choosing freely to think, feel, and do whatever, or not.

The specific physical sensations are never necessary and are the resultant feelings of whatever makes feelings, no matter how or why or when those feelings are set in motion.

The feelings of happiness are the feelings that we are feeling while not "knowing" necessity.

It is the true knowledge (so say the happy) of not believing, not perceiving, not choosing on the basis of necessity but *because, just because.*

When we are happy, the concepts of "because," "validity," and "justification" get cloudy and lose "meaning."

The meaning or cause of a thing is the understanding of why it is necessary. When things are not necessary, they lose meaning in reference to necessity; and happiness can be called the "cause"-with-"meaning"—in a sense, better than the previously understood causes. "It is because I am happy" means "I do not believe it needs to be, so it is because 'because' has lost meaning." To say "because, *because*" is the happy way of expressing that because is only a point without reference or meaning in terms of necessity.

"It is because I am happy" means "It *is*, I am happy," or "It *is* (it need not have been) and I am happy (I have no need)." When an unhappy world (a necessary world of necessary people necessarily searching for what is "really" necessary) asks "why" something happens, or "why" a person does or is a certain way, it means to find and judge the goodness of the reason or the believed cause in terms of necessity. The "asking" is the assumption of things being necessary, and an expectation of "necessary" acquiescence to that dogma.

All "just" courts acquit anyone who acts from a commonly accepted standard of necessity. Even a unique belief in the necessity of one's behavior exempts the most extreme behaviors from the charge of guilt (i.e., hypocrisy) and judges them at worst "crazy, deluded, sick," but necessary in context of such a demented state (devoid of reason or true knowledge of real necessities). The crazy person's best defense is to demonstrate a deep conviction of his or her "necessary" priorities, which they believe override normal social concepts of necessity.

When a happy person is asked *why* they choose as they do, they realize there can be two motives for the question. Is the question asked by someone who believes in necessity and judgment, or by someone who knows of freedom and wishes to share information (whatever information you choose of your own free choice to share) and the knowledge of happiness?

Questions are happy, or not happy, because people are. The difference between them is all the difference, in any meaning of differentness. No two things could be more different from each other. The difference goes beyond the concepts of opposites: it is the difference between a thing (happiness) compared to nothing (unhappiness). The unhappy question has less than no meaning. It is perceived as the preachment it really is and an invitation to play in hell.

Happiness does that which is unnecessary. Seen from the mind of necessity, it does what seems impossible.

Justifying Your Wants

November 11, 1995

Sometimes someone says that it looks to them like you're irrational, because you're skipping over a lot of things you're already convinced of. Some people are going to decide that you shouldn't have reached your conclusions because you haven't convinced them why you've reached the conclusions you have. But you have all the justifications you need, and once you know that it's okay for you to do something, you don't remember all the reasons why it's okay.

You've already settled your argument with yourself, and if you're talking about being convincing to somebody else, that's a whole other issue. Judgmental people require all kinds of things; they may never be satisfied, but sometimes they can be. They think they require some kind of better knowledge of you before they say that what you're doing is okay. Well, that's just too bad. That's what being judgmental is all about. People who think they need to know more to let it be that what you do is okay—that's what we'd call a very unhappy person. Why would they need to let what you do be okay? Why would they have to look upon what you do as okay? Can't they just know that they like it or don't like it or it's none of their business? When you're satisfied that what you want is really what you want, for the reasons that you want it, you're okay.

We don't always remember all the logic that went behind it. When you're trying to figure out what movie to go to, you go through each movie that's playing: "What about that one? What about this one?" And you turn down 30, and settle on one for whatever reasons, and now that you've settled on it, all you need to know is that you've got to get to the theater by 9:00. Someone says, "But why are you going to see *that* movie?" "I forget, we just gotta get there." And that's the way our real lives work. We don't remember the justifications for what we want. If we had any doubts, we solved them. And that's all anybody needs to know about what I'm doing. If I had any doubts, I've solved them or I wouldn't be doing this, whatever it is I'm doing.

But maybe it's somebody you promised to tell the rationale of what you do to, and so they're confused. In other words, you said one thing, but you look like you're doing another thing. They ask, "Could you fill me in on that?" And you could simply say, "I'm sorry. I have no time now. But I understand what you're talking about. But I have no time." Or take the time to show them what you skipped over. You told them you were going to do one thing and now you're doing another. So maybe you want to share with them what changed your mind. But you know that what you want is what you want. And that's okay with you.

SECTION IV

Perfect Happiness

You Can Be Happy Now and At All Times

November 1, 1977

The Option Message is: You can be happy now and at all times because you are able to and want to enjoy yourself now and always.

The reason is: Nothing can make you be unhappy (and you don't want to be).

The reason for this is: Nothing ever *made* you feel bad.

The reason for this is:

You felt bad whenever you thought you were supposed to,

or

You believed you would naturally have to be.

The reason for this is: You believed it was the way things were. You thought that unhappiness was natural. You believed you had a problem being okay.

The reason was: You believed others. You never knew better.

You believed that thinking otherwise was really another worse version of thinking that would make you more unhappy.

You can enjoy yourself now, be happy now and always.

You want to; you are able to; and nothing can stop you, since it is only you who does it.

Whatever reasons you think you have, they have not made you unable to be happy nor have they made you not want to be happy. If you believe you are unable or not wanting to be happy, that is what feels bad to you.

Realizing Perfect Happiness

August 8, 1975

WHEN did we become perfectly happy? When did it happen that nothing was wrong with me? That evil disappeared from the earth? That unhappiness no longer needed to be feared or avoided or borne?

Perhaps we always were, and it took time for us to *realize* it.

It seemed that perfect happiness, once experienced, could leave me, and leaving me wanting, striving for what I believed was in the future.

I now know that I was always all that I ever wanted, without realizing it before.

Since I was *already* perfectly happy, I can have only been seeking happiness *from* my happiness.

All that I called unhappiness, since I realized perfect happiness, has seemed unreal, phony, mysterious, unaccountable, unbelievable, confusing, and deeply awesome—and yet has seemed at times to be for some purpose.

It has all been the wanting to believe that I am perfectly happy, but not believing that such a desire does not come from *wanting to avoid* unhappiness, but does indeed come from *having* happiness.

All "unhappiness" has been believing that I have not yet become perfectly, permanently, unchangeably, happy. Because I did not feel the joy I had when I *knew* I was perfectly happy, I was *seeking* the joy, because I was believing I was lacking the knowledge of happiness.

Now that I know my happiness, I know: Joy is for when I have it.

We Can Be Happy Because We Want To

May 16, 1975

If I am unhappy, I want to be happy, and want the way I want to use as the way to become happy. I am not dependent on help to become happy, I do not need help to be happy, but if I am helped I will be glad.

We can be happy merely because we want to.

It is wanting to be happy that will work, not one method or another. The message of The Option Method is not that it is the best method, but that we never have to be unhappy and can be happy by wanting to be.

Know that you don't want to be unhappy, and that you want real happiness, and do whatever you want. Be happy and do what you want.

You may know that you don't have to be unhappy, but unless you know why, you will not be happy.

Why don't you have to be unhappy?

Because you don't want to be.

You are unhappy because you believe you have to be, not because you really want to be.

You are unhappy because you now or once believed you had to be as a way of being happy, staying happy, getting happy, or getting happier.

Sometimes you are not unhappy but experience a strange feeling or see or become aware in some way that things are not as you want them.

This is a test. You are asking yourself, "Does this or that mean that I am unhappy?"

The only answer is: "I want to be happy. I do not believe I have to be afraid or unhappy about what is happening."

Another name for this experience is "Are you afraid of being unhappy now?"

The only answer is "No. I want happiness."

If the tests continue, realize that you are not wanting to test yourself. Your awareness is from your happiness. Do what you want. Do not think that being aware of what you don't want means you are unhappy. Just affirm that you ARE happy.

PART V

Enjoying Your Happiness

SECTION I

About Enjoying Your Happiness

The Enjoyment of Happiness

September 7, 1991

To Enjoy Means to Employ

To the degree to which we are employing something, it can be said that we are enjoying it. For example, to enjoy a bike is to use it to ride it, not leave it in the garage. To enjoy art is to use it for rest, or associative memories, or cultural education, etc., not leave it in a box. To enjoy an experience is to use it for feeling good or whatever other value we use it for. To enjoy a friend is to use their companionship for its value, whatever it is. To enjoy an idea is to learn it and use it in your life. To enjoy what you learn is to employ what you learn. Whether it be a musical skill like playing an instrument, or an abstract skill like problem solving, you enjoy the skill by employing it. Using The Option Method is enjoying it, and vice versa.

Conversely, we don't usually say we enjoy things we don't use. If we enjoy things at the moment we get them and then not later, it is usually because we anticipated using them later, even though we didn't. Some things are enjoyed because we believe we will use them. That enjoyment is momentary. Lasting enjoyment comes with actual employment. It is all proportional. The more we use something, the more we enjoy it. The less we use it, the less we can enjoy it.

Many, upon realizing the truth and relevance of The Option Method, really enjoy that realization. They expect it to be useful and see that it could change their lives toward being happier. Then they do not use it. They wait instead for new moments of insight, or a new twist, or a new relevance to be shown to them. They are not enjoying *or* employing what they already know. They seem jaded, saturated, or somewhat indifferent or resigned to their unhappiness. The next step is depression about repeated problems they thought they had dealt with. The problem they didn't deal with is the lack of enjoyment of the real possibility of happiness. They stopped enjoying that they really did deal with that problem. Happiness is easily accessible yet, but they are not used to enjoying that knowledge.

The most common unhappiness of people who have benefited by The Option Method is that they regret "having to" remind themselves. They often deny that, because of the way it sounds to them. The usual way that belief is experienced is that "I should not need to remind myself not to be unhappy. I already learned that." Why would it be a resentful task to use the most wonderful procedural tool man ever had for being happy, The Option Method? If it is not seen as a privilege to be enjoyed (employed), but if instead is seen as a shameful remedy to a shameful condition, like a medicine or therapy to be endured (or ignored), it would be no wonder that they would experience a reverting to some of the old ways. Enjoy what you learn by employing it at every opportunity.

Being Happy Now

December 1987

QUESTIONER: *How can I be instantly happy at all times?*

You don't have to now start believing new things; you have to stop believing certain things. If you don't believe you're going to be unhappy, then what you are is happy.

But here is my answer: what makes you think you're not perfectly happy right now and for all times? If you believe it's not for all times, you have condemned yourself already. These are questions, not a statement. What makes you think there's a problem? Maybe, even, you were believing in unhappiness until I asked you, up till now. What makes you think there is still a question?

Who asks the question, "How can I start being instantly happy and never unhappy again?" Only somebody who believes that he's going to be unhappy in the future, which is why you're even asking the question.

Believing means "what you think is true." A belief is not something like you pick and choose from a smorgasbord. Believing something is true is what you think is true. Will you be getting unhappy in the future? Do you believe that is true?

Once you learn, though, that it's by believing it that you're burning yourself, I'm not so sure you're going to keep sticking your hand in the fire. But you have to see that that is what you are doing. You thought he was asking a question; I heard a person screaming, "I'm going to get unhappy in the future."

The question "How do I stop being unhappy?" comes from somebody who already believes in unhappiness. If somebody asked "How can I keep the devil away from me, now and the rest of my life?" you might say "The *what* away from you?"

You're free and you know it. Nothing is making you do anything, so the question is, what makes you think you're not free? To start with, are you sure that what you're feeling is a bad feeling? What if I told you that what you were feeling was excitement for the future?

You're either free or not free. It is as if you are saying, "My knowing that I'm free isn't good enough," when it *is* perfectly good enough, and your freedom is doing its job perfectly well right now, but you just don't believe it and think there's a problem.

Enjoying Your Freedom

December 1987

WHAT does it mean to enjoy your freedom? It means to be conscious of it, to be aware of it, to make use of it. "Enjoy" is in many cases like "employ." How are you going to enjoy your new hammer? By finding something to hammer. How are you going to enjoy your new car? By going out for a ride. You enjoy something by using it, by employing it. That is what enjoying means.

So you're free, you just haven't enjoyed that you're free. If you believe you're in a cell, and the door is unlocked but you believe it's locked, that doesn't mean you're not free. You're free, you just don't believe it. Now consider if the door is unlocked and now you know it's unlocked. Now you know that you're free. But if you stay in the cell, would you say that you're enjoying your freedom? Only if you knew that you were staying there by choice.

You can enjoy your freedom by reminding yourself, "I'm here because I choose to be. I'm doing *this* because I choose to. I'm doing *that* because I choose." And walking out of the cell from time to time would really be no different than walking back in or out or whatever, because the enjoying is in the appreciating, the understanding and the realizing of your freedom and that you can count on it.

If you know something is true, you count on it. If your car has gas in it, you counted on that this morning. You go to all the trouble of getting dressed and showering and going out to the car and starting it up because you are counting on the fact that you *are* going to be able to start it and take off and go where you want to go. You will do all kinds of things when you can count on something that you wouldn't have done otherwise. If you thought and you believed that your car would not start no matter what you did, you wouldn't have bothered getting dressed, you wouldn't have showered, you wouldn't have done all the things you were going to do in order to come here.

You probably would have just picked up the phone and said, "By the way, I'm not coming today because my car won't start."

When you know that something is true, enjoying it is living and knowing and counting on the fact that it is true. For instance, when you know there's nothing to be afraid of, you can actually live as if there's nothing to be afraid of. If you know you're free, you will then live as if you knew you were free, because you *are* free. You will live counting on that. When you drive over a bridge, you're counting on the fact that it's going to stand up, and because of that, you're going to use that bridge—and that is not as dependable as your knowing you're free, which you can count on even more.

You can count on that how you feel is *not* one of the things that happened to you. So you can always count on feeling good. That would be called enjoying your freedom. If you are unhappy, you're not counting on feeling good. You're believing it's uncertain.

Somewhere along the line, you say, "Well, unhappiness is going to happen to me anyway, even if I do count on feeling good. If I counted on feeling good, what good would that do me, because I could wind up not feeling good anyway?" That's not called counting on feeling good. If you actually counted on feeling good, you would *really* be counting on feeling good.

What you've been doing all your life is counting on feeling good, but only for a while, not forever. You go to a party, you're counting on feeling good for three hours, and tomorrow you are going to work, and are not counting on feeling good then.

Consider two people in an open jail cell. One says, "I can't leave," and you say, "But look—the door's open." "No, no, no, I can't leave. I can't leave." Is that person free? They're free, and they're liars. They're still free, they just don't believe they are—they don't even believe their own eyes. My definition of a liar is somebody who doesn't believe their own eyes, and claims to not have the power to leave the cell, even though they know they do have the capability.

You can do anything you can do. Whatever it is you can do, you can do it. You're able to do whatever you're able to do. You're allowed to do whatever you can do. You're allowed to do what you're able to do. You're able to do what you're allowed to do. You can do what you can do.

You can also pay the consequences for what you do. And most of the times when people say they can't do something, they mean they don't want to pay the consequences, but that doesn't mean you can't do it. That just means you don't want to do it. The consequence is just the reason you don't want to do it. It's not true you can't jump off a bridge. You can, and don't want to, because you don't want the consequences. That's knowing your freedom.

When you start to feel good, you ask, "How can I keep feeling good?" And if you have used fear to get what you want, you have a paradox. Fear of not feeling good in the future is not going to work anyway to help you keep feeling good. Why worry about yourself if you start to feel really, really happy and you're appreciating it, reflecting on it and being aware of it, and then you got involved with something else or you weren't paying attention? That doesn't mean you're not happy. Someone could say, "Well, how do you feel now?" "Well, I don't know how I feel. Let me see." And you could start feeling happy again. So really, what you call feeling happy is a kind of awareness.

Maybe the feeling high is a kind of an excited feeling and you had relaxed from it a bit, but there's nothing wrong. When you start letting off a little bit, then you're worried, "How can I keep it up?" As if you should. Why should you? What's wrong with letting off a little bit? You're not going to unhappiness. You're experiencing happiness. Different physical feelings of it, that's all. Happiness is excitement, but happiness is also peace. Happiness is knowing that you're happy. Not believing you're unhappy. Not believing there's a problem. Not believing that something that's happening is going to affect your happiness.

You're asking "How can I stop having problems?" and you are *having* no problems.

Miracles and Happiness

January 26, 1991

WHAT is a miracle? A miracle is a creating of something from nothing. In the act of this creation (the miracle), knowledge is created (where there was no knowing) of the fact of the miraculous event. The knowing and the event are the same miracle.

The true knowing of happiness is the miracle.

A miracle can make a person realize he or she is happy and realize that they are allowed to be happy forever. A miracle cannot make a person admit that he or she now realizes he or she is happy, nor prevent the person from insisting on being unhappy; but it shows that unhappiness is always and forever unnecessary.

A miracle cannot make a person stay happy nor prevent the person from being unhappy again; but it shows that unhappiness is always and forever unnecessary. It shows that only people who believe that happiness is wrong are the ones to get unhappy. People who do not admit they are happy when they experience a miracle know they are lying, and are insisting—against their own experience—that they are not allowed to be happy. A miracle humbles believers and such liars. It makes them know that reality is not as it should be and they are not as they should be, because they know then that they no longer "know" what should be. It is awesome and confounding. It could change their lives. They usually see to it that it doesn't—by calling the miracle not a miracle, and by the realization that it is truthful to be happy (not a true realization).

A miracle cannot make a person be happy (that is already true) nor prevent one from being unhappy (that does not exist); but it shows that unhappiness is not real and is always and forever unnecessary.

A miracle does not make unhappiness impossible (it already is), but knowing what the miracle means makes it impossible to ever be unhappy.

The miracle means that there is nothing wrong; that there is no need for worry about unhappiness, and that happiness is the only reality. The miracle means that there is more to truth and happiness than what one merely believes.

The miracle shows that it did not need to be. What does not exist cannot bring itself into existence and has no need to exist. It would have to be created from nothing, independent of what is. It is an act of defiance of the beliefs about what is allowed, what is possible, and what should or should not be.

What is the greatest miracle? The revelation that happiness is all that is, and unhappiness is caused by merely believing it is wrong to be happy. To question why a person believes they must, or should, or needs to be unhappy is a miracle.

What is not a miracle? Any event that does not proceed from, nor demonstrates, or even contradicts the truth of happiness is not a miracle, no matter how many believe it is. That truth is, of course, that all people have the right to be happy and it is not necessary to be unhappy, it is only believed to be.

Any so-called miracle that purports to reveal an angry or sad god or other some other unhappy heavenly being is merely the same old deception of unhappiness. Likewise, any messages from "hell" or warnings of "evil" are also not truth. There is no evil, since nothing causes unhappiness. People merely believe in evil: something that supposedly, ultimately, causes the unhappiness of the innocent. All are innocent, since no one can cause that which anyone must be unhappy about. The most that can happen on this earth, or in this universe, is something that people do not want; not something that should not be, which is what is meant by evil. That is simply impossible.

What is the value of a miracle? The wondrous opportunity to admit the truth. The opportunity to respond. We can have the happy response of being awed and glad for the chance to experience the miracle, and more: the chance to admit it. It is the opportunity to praise the perfect knowing of the truth that created it. Our decision, as in all things, decides the value for us. That is the miracle which is created for us. It gives us the chance to show or become who we are and want to be: Happy.

Feeling the presence of the knowledge of happiness is a miracle.

Knowing of the miracle of happiness is in itself a miracle.

Being healed from all illusions of unhappiness is a miracle.

These make us know that we are involved in a miracle. We may have thought we had "gained" a merely ordinary, intelligent understanding of unhappiness, but now we are aware that we are knowing an extraordinary miracle.

Everything Is Good

November 11, 1995

You don't confer goodness on God's world. It's all good. Even those things you've learned to hate, they're all good. And you like some things better than cancer, fine. But don't tell me that cancer is bad. Where do you get off? Or perhaps you're going to try to make it be okay. You can't make it be okay. It already is. You can't make things okay. If you think that's your job; you're in trouble. You've gotten the idea that you cause your own emotions confused with God. You can't make things okay any more than you can make them bad. You can't do that either. All you can do is delude yourself that they're bad or enjoy that they're good. So what's the answer to having cancer? Not being unhappy about it and knowing that it's good, and desiring and knowing that health is something you like better. That's something you want better, and something you call better and something that *is* better. Why is it better? Because it's what you want. The only reason being healthy is better than having cancer is because it's what you want. And what other way is health better than cancer?

I'm making the comparison between what you want and everything else that you don't want. That's everything else, right? You just only know what you want. You don't go around un-wanting or dis-wanting. That's unhappiness, feeling you have to dis-want things.

You can know you don't prefer cancer. And there's lots of reasons why you're not welcoming it or wanting it, in the sense of inviting it or wishing you had it. You don't want it for the inconvenience. You don't want it for the pain. You don't want it for the cost. You don't want it for the family issues. You don't want it for the shortening of life. You can't go to the movies. You don't want it because you can't drive your car anymore. Whatever reason you don't want it.

But remember, I told you that nobody's afraid of cancer. You're only afraid of the unhappiness that comes with it. So if we're talking about bliss and joy, there are all kinds of things to want. And you don't have to hate anything to give yourself permission to want something. There's a little metaphor, a little parable I tell called "spitting in your blueberry pie."

You're at a friend's house and out of the oven comes a nice, fresh-baked blueberry pie. And your mouth is watering. And you love it. And she says, "Would you like a piece?" And you say, "I'd love it. I'd love a piece." So she cuts you a piece of blueberry pie. She didn't mention it, but she then goes back to the oven and takes out a second pie, which is an apple pie. Steaming hot apple pie. And that is your favorite pie of all time. It has the right amount of cinnamon. You can smell the allspice. You know exactly that you would love this pie more than anything else in your whole life. But "Uh-oh. I'm eating the blueberry pie." So what you do, since you don't feel free to ask for the apple pie; you say, "Oh, gee. Excuse me but there's spit in my blueberry pie. Can I have a piece of apple pie?"

You make it be what you believe is disgusting to allow yourself to choose what you really do want. And you never had to do that. But the truth of the matter is it was only your spit in the first place. It never really makes it disgusting, you know. It's really only your judgment in the first place. That really doesn't count. The truth of the matter is, you still like blueberry pie no matter what you say. But you'd rather have apple pie.

And you didn't automatically start hating blueberry pie, no matter what you say. But you felt you needed to do that. You had to find something repulsive about the blueberry pie to be allowed to ask for the apple pie. And people live their lives that way.

Are You Good? Are All Things Good?

July 23, 1993

In the moral sense it would have to follow that everything that is, including yourself, is truly good, in that nothing is bad (unhappiness causing).

Your very being is the cause of your happiness—your right to be yourself is happiness. It is your nature to be good. It is evident that you have the right to be happy, always. You are made that way and have no choice. Since your very self desires happiness above all, and since nothing has the power to deprive you of happiness, you have the ability to be happy always, because of your right to be happy, because you are allowed to be happy.

You have no choice but to be yourself. Your self can not be other than good for you, nor can your self act other than in your best interests. Your best interests are anything you want them to be. Your self defines your best interests in the way that you are best satisfied is best. You will always agree with your self as to what your best interest is, and will always be motivated accordingly.

You always agree with yourself, perfectly, and never do not. You have no choice. Don't be ashamed of anything you are. You are in perfect conformity with the cause of your being. In religious terms, you are exactly the way God wants you to be, and you need not, nor cannot, be otherwise.

Do anything, or don't do anything, now or at any time. You can never harm or diminish the happiness in your future. You can always expect to be happier and happier.

All people are good and can do no evil (can cause no unhappiness against their will), but all believe otherwise.

All have the right to be happy. They have no choice. To live in joy and peace is the happy reality.

SECTION II

Practical Enjoyment

I Am Not the Cause of Your Happiness

WE'RE talking about our clients, now:

If you decided that you had to be unhappy, then you are unhappy freely and for your own sake. If you decided to seek me out, then you sought me freely and for your own sake. If you decided to ask for my help, then you asked for my help freely and for your own sake. If you decided to try to motivate me to help you, you tried to motivate me freely and for your sake. If you decided to meet my conditions, then you've met my conditions freely and for your own sake. If you decided to let me try to help you, then you let me try to help you freely and for your own sake. If you decided to listen to my questions, then you listened freely and for your own sake. If you decided to answer or not to answer, then you answered or not answered freely for your own sake. If you decided to disclose your beliefs to me, then you're the one who decided to disclose your beliefs freely and for your own sake. If you decided to discard a belief, then you decided that freely and for your own sake. If you decided to choose to be happier, then you chose to be happier freely and for your own sake.

I am not the cause.

You did this all for yourself; it was all *your* choice for *your* sake, not for mine. I didn't make you choose anything. This started with you deciding that you had to be unhappy for your sake, and if you choose to be happier, you choose to be happier freely and for your own sake. It was a total freedom on your part throughout the whole thing. I take no credit any more than I would take the blame.

The guide does his best guiding when he knows he is totally non-responsible. It is only possible to really be involved with helping another not to need help to be happier by not laying trips and by not accepting trips being laid on you by the other. If you have no axe to grind, no need for that other to believe this or that, no need to change them, no need for them happier, then you will help them best.

If you need them for anything during the session, you are subject to blackmail by them. You are subject to agreeing with them that they are not responsible for their feelings. It is most loving and freeing for you to be totally not intimidated by their unhappiness. The greatest love I might have for you is to tell you that I am not afraid of you and you are nobody to be afraid of.

You owe nothing to your clients, they owe you nothing. When you are in sessions with your clients, you are there for your own sake. You do not have to be there. They are there for their own sakes. They do not have to be there. I want to stress the truly free relationship that's involved. Each one decided for themselves that they wanted to be there. Nobody had to be.

You are not helping them, and you're not deluding yourself that you're helping them because they need your help. They don't need your help. You do it for yourself. They seek help for themselves. Now, they may say they need your help but you know that they don't.

I am being paid to do my thing.

You owe no explanation for what you do in a session or for what you don't do. They may come or not come to you, as they wish. If they don't want to be with you when you do your thing, they don't have to be with you when you do your thing.

In my practice I find that some clients demand certain things as their rights. They have no rights over me any more than I have any rights over them. I do what I wish, they do as they wish.

Some think that they are buying or hiring me according to some traditional or mythical rules. They are not paying for anything except for me to *do my thing*. They're not buying or hiring me. If paying is part of it, they pay for me to do my thing. They are free not to do that. They are not paying for 50 minutes; they are not paying for me to wear a tie or not to smoke or to smile or not to smile, or to feign sympathy or whatever. They're not paying for anything other than for me to do my thing. I do what I want. I conduct my business, my sessions, however I want. They are totally free to do their own thing. I will appear eccentric to some, selfish to others, messed up to some others. But I will do my thing, and they will do their thing.

Unless I am in touch that I am freely choosing to be who I want to be, how could I ever help them to know that they're freely choosing to be what *they* want to be? I can charge $1.00 or $100.00 and I can use whatever criteria I wish. I could charge $5.00 for every letter in their name, or double on rainy days. I can show up for sessions or not. I can make my sessions for five minutes or five hours. I could not be a therapist; I could move to the mountains and contemplate a flower for the rest of my life. I can tell clients, "Go away," or I can ask them to stay. They are always free to decide, I know that. They are always free to decide what they are willing to do for my help. Just as I will decide what I am willing to do in order to help.

The more you're in touch with this true freedom, the more you'll be able to help others. If I ask them these questions and they decide freely to answer them, and then they decide they don't have to be unhappy, that is their choice. I became the stimulus that they sought out as part of helping themselves.

You are free. Your client is free.

Some people think that I could help them best if I gave them 50 minutes, for instance. That's kind of arbitrary. Maybe I would be more in touch; maybe I would do a better job if I stopped the session at 30 minutes. It's really quite possible, and maybe really a bad decision on their part to decide that I should go for the full 50 minutes, the last 20 of which I may not be with them at all. I'm usually able to be with them for whatever full time that I give them—but it is certainly not to their benefit to know or to say what it is that I should do, because what they really want me to do is what only I can decide that I can do best. What they want me to do is to help them. They have to decide if that's what I'm wanting, too.

You could tell them to go away if you wanted. That is not to say that anything that I might do or everything I would do is going to be inherently helpful. Not at all. But I am totally free not to be helpful.

Many of you may find that you set yourself 50 minutes to help somebody, but in that 50 minutes you really only were doing therapy for 5 minutes. The other time you might be worried about whether you're actually doing therapy or not, so you're not doing it.

Okay, fine. But see, they have that right to decide to pay you even for those ten minutes. If they feel that they can get better elsewhere, they're free to do that. But meanwhile you're doing your best; and if your best is ten minutes they may still decide that that's much better than none of it from anybody, that they can't get it anywhere else, and that maybe even your fumbling is well worth it for whatever they do get from it. So they're free to decide that. You may be that kind of a therapist.

For instance, Wilhelm Reich used to get up in the middle of the session and say, "I'll be right back," and not come back.

People would have to travel hundreds and hundreds of miles just to get a session with the master, and they'd be in the midst of a session and he'd say, "Gee, I'm going to look up that word," and he'd go off, ostensibly to go to the dictionary; and in 20 minutes he wouldn't be back, and the patient would get up and go out and find him out in the garden gardening or something. If they didn't like that, if they weren't glad for whatever minutes they had with him, they never had to come back. But apparently what he gave was worth coming for, even if they thought, "Maybe he won't even give it to me today. Maybe he'll be so crazy that he won't even remember that I'm here." And he was prone to do that. And he might go off to chase a flying saucer or something and leave you sitting.

I don't know that you're going to make the decision that that's good business. But if you decide to do what is not good for business, then you're doing that freely for your own sake. And if you decide that the average person is not going to put up with that or tolerate it or want it or be able to see how good you are in spite of your eccentricities, then you may decide that freely, on your own, you will keep certain hours, certain times, charge certain prices, and be consistent, and all the things that you think you need to get what you want. You're perfectly free to say that: "This week if you want to see me it'll cost you $500. If you wait until tomorrow you only have to pay me $10." That doesn't mean you will. You may also decide that that's not in your best interest and do otherwise. But what I'm talking about is to know that you're free.

The client does not buy the right to see you alone for 50 minutes. They buy nothing. The worst that happens is you leave people where they want to be. You don't have to sanctify it by saying, "I'm really doing something." You're not doing anything.

You can even sit with a patient and wish that they weren't there, and know that it is perfectly all right for you to do that. If you don't know you are free, you're going to face all kinds of hang-ups: "Oh, my God, I'm not helping them over this." I can only tell you from my own experience, if I don't have the attitude of freedom I'm not going to be able to do my best.

I had a patient this week. In the middle of the session I decided that if I wanted to listen and really wanted to help them I was going to get up and go to the toilet to urinate to relieve my bladder, so that that wouldn't distract me, so that I could do a better job for them. And the patient deducted the minute that it took for me to do that. They were conscious that it cost them a dollar while I went to piss. That comes from the minute-by-minute, dollar-for-dollar kind of evaluation. Not that I was there to do my very best for them and that I could have stayed there and not urinated and just ignored them for twenty minutes. To take a minute from their time in order to give them better minutes later didn't quite make sense to them. But again, if I were to fall for that, I couldn't really help them, I wouldn't be helping them.

The length of the session is fairly arbitrary. I think that some people could really profit a lot more from longer time and others could do well with shorter periods: for example, every day for a half an hour. The schedules are concessions to finances on most people's part. If ten people want to see you in a given day, how do you tell them when to come so that they are not backed up in the waiting room? You just have a standard session length for scheduling convenience, and so basically the session lengths are maximums rather than minimums or exact amounts.

I didn't used to do this, but I tell new patients now—they ask me how long the sessions will be and I say, "I don't know, anywhere from about a minute up to no more than 50 minutes." And if they're willing to come under those conditions, they do and I just have the 50 minutes as a maximum.

Being in Society

In these two essays, Bruce Di Marsico considers two complementary issues:

1. Day-to-day life in a society where conventional symbols of unhappiness are the norm.
2. Acknowledging to oneself that to be happy is not the norm.

And offers two happy choices:

1. Choose to no longer show the conventional symbols of unhappiness.
2. Act unhappy, knowing that it is only an act, and that you are truly happy.

Relative to the conventional symbols of unhappiness, language is a primary sign (though not a cause) of unhappiness. Below are some examples of how language is a sign of unhappiness.

These words are self-contradictory when used to mean "necessary for happiness." Since nothing is necessary for happiness, they are impossible and meaningless words:

should, must, need, have to, obligate, owe, duty

These words are self-contradictory when used to mean "affecting happiness." Since nothing can make you happy or unhappy, they are impossible and meaningless words:

right, wrong, good, bad

These words are used to describe behavior as "unhappiness-causing":

fault, sin, evil, immoral, inappropriate, crazy

These words only have a sense when referring to a demonstrable capability. For example, a "power" that cannot be demonstrated is no power at all!

rights, power

These words describe specific actions as "unhappiness-causing":

theft (unhappiness-causing taking), *murder* (unhappiness-causing killing)

These words are personifications of "unhappiness-causing":

devil, demon

On Fervor

June 22, 1992

THE symbols and styles of other belief systems, religions, philosophies, etc. are not necessarily well-suited for our quest for a satisfying self-image and behavioral style that would signify our new life.

The language of other people is replete with the meanings inherent in their belief in unhappiness. We have gladly dropped much of our old vocabulary of unhappy judgment and fear, and we have no need for new jargon. Yet, some of us do want ways of reminding ourselves that we, indeed, do know the truth. We want ways of appreciating that we are happy and new. The idea of being constantly in touch with our new identity as happy people, we realize, is the same as joy for us.

Many newly happy people do not hesitate to continuously reflect on their good fortune in discovering the freedom of happiness. After a while the initial fervor wanes, and we feel we fit in normally with our unhappy society. We want to *seem* normal, but do we want to *feel* like their kind of normal?

One cause of this feeling of tepidness, which opens us up to relapses of old unhappinesses, and feeling unworthy to be special (in the sense of our relative rarity as happy people), is a certain belief about "relapse" itself. If you believed you would never get unhappy again (since you saw how real it was to be able to not be unhappy), you would not be wrong to believe (or know) that.

The fact that you got unhappy later doesn't mean that you were wrong or did something wrong. That is a belief of unhappiness. If you got disappointed that you got unhappy "again," you did nothing wrong. You just merely got unhappy *about* getting unhappy, instead of just wanting to be happy (as you would really like to be).

When you got unhappy (if you did), you were believing you were supposed to get unhappy, even though you have no liking for it. When you treated yourself as if you failed at something you were also supposed to be (in this case, happy), you were being unhappy about your failure. The truth is that you love happiness more than *anything*; you would never give it up unless you thought you had to. When you realized that you made a mistake, the mistake was over. Nothing had to be done. Nothing. You didn't have to even bother being disappointed, as if your original unhappiness still existed. It didn't.

Once you believe or realize that you *have* been unhappy, since you don't want to be, and you don't believe it is necessary, it is over. Now, you may be unhappy about *having been* unhappy. That's a new one. You are unhappy because you believe something must be done. That will make *anyone* unhappy. It doesn't matter how noble or important the cause. The belief that something must be done to be happy is, in itself, unhappiness primeval.

Once you realize that you don't want to be unhappy, you are still happy. Your original happiness has not left you. You just were feeling it was gone. You can continue appreciating your happiness, and continue appreciating that you don't value or need unhappiness.

Many newly happy people accept the unhappy belief that we shouldn't feel specially blessed, or special at all, especially if we "failed" to be always happy. This egalitarian false-modesty stems from the old belief that since all people are sinners (or some modern version of imperfect), none have any special claim to happiness or wisdom. This fear of being "holier than thou" is everywhere promoted by the fear and jealously of believers who remain faithful to their notion of the universal lowliness and wretchedness of humanity in this mortal world.

Do we want to learn from frightened people what happy people "should" be like? Does true happiness consist of denying our incredible gratitude? These fearful people believe that it is crazy or wrong to even *hope* to be happy always. They would not even dare to admit that they would love to be happy, no matter what happens. For those who do dare to want happiness, are they honest enough to see themselves as no luckier than the others who don't? Does wanting to be always happy become invalidated by mistakes? Does the desire disappear, or, rather, are we ashamed to admit we still want it?

The freedom to be always happy is the right of all people, and all other unhappy people deny that. You are the ones who know that.

This is most relevant and pertinent for those of us who got unhappy after knowing better.

The freedom of happiness also means that there is not a way you should not be. You are free, especially, to know that you are happier than those who believe they must be unhappy. That's obvious. You would have to lie to say otherwise. "Happier than thou" is not a petty, fearful attitude, nor an attempt to denigrate another's right to be happy, far from it. If you think you are happier than any of your acquaintances, then that is not a rebuke, but simply an honest opinion, and an invitation. You are not feeling that others are bad, but only that you are grateful to be lucky to now know that unhappiness is unnecessary.

Acting Unhappy

THE difference between acting as if you were unhappy, for whatever reason, and being unhappy is that acting does not include believing that it would be bad or wrong to be happy. An actor doesn't believe he is not really happy. He denies his happiness to another but not to himself.

When you are done being unhappy you can just admit that you made yourself "feel" that you were, and are not really unhappy. There is no being really unhappy. There was only believing it was wrong to be happy.

"Wrong" is a model word meant to be equivalent to any concept that means bad, crazy, contradictory, insincere, lying, immoral, inappropriate, undeserving, no right to be, unworthy, sinful. All these ideas mean "bad for you to be happy." The implication is that you will be more unhappy later if you're not unhappy now (because you are not being the way you should—unhappy!). But that only repeats the imperative that you not be happy in the future after being happy now, when you should not have been.

There Are No Emotional Problems

November 11, 1995

A LOT of people know they want a divorce. But they're not miserable enough yet. I mean it. People don't think it's fair or right to seek a divorce unless they're terribly miserable, not just simply because they no longer want to be married to this person. So usually divorces are between somebody who's tremendously unhappy and somebody else whom they're hoping to make tremendously unhappy, so that they will then agree to the divorce. I don't really mean these as jokes. These are the things that people up the ante for to feel allowed to do what they want to do. And happiness would question the fear that you have of doing what you really are attracted to. And ask you to examine why you're afraid of that, if that's something you want to look at. If you say to me, "I'm really attracted to something but I'm afraid to move for it or towards it," I would understand immediately because you've added the pros and cons and this is the way they fall. Now, what about the way the pros and cons add up would you like to question? So which is it that you don't like? So the person would say, "Well, I don't like that I want a divorce," or "I don't like it that I feel like I should stay." So in either case we'll help them look at why they feel there's something they must do other than what they want to do. Sometimes really the truth in a lot of these things is that people just don't have enough facts to make any decision. And they just really want more facts. And the situation is not bad enough to be sure they want to leave. Given the current situation, I may not leave—and rather than feel I have to become more unhappy, I could just see that I'm talking about practical matters and stop worrying and thinking that I'm not unhappy enough to leave. You don't have to be unhappy to leave. And perhaps they could see that they could make the decision without being unhappy in either way. And that they want some facts, some more experiences, to make decisions. And once they know that, that feels real good. Oh, it's just a practical matter, which leads us to an axiom of The Option Method: There are no such things as emotional problems.

There are no emotional problems. There are only practical problems, which people are afraid they have emotional problems about. And people get emotional about them because they believe that they're *emotional* problems. How many people think the idea of whether to stay married or not is an emotional problem? How many people think that whether to get a job or not is an emotional problem? Or whether to have children or not? There are lots of things people believe are emotional problems. How many people believe that their not having enough money for their operation is something that really makes them unhappy and is an emotional problem? No, there's a practical problem: how to get the money? And until you focus on that there is a practical problem, you're going to be really stuck in a non-problem. People can take years trying to deal with an emotional problem before they ever get around to fixing a leak. You don't need therapy to know your shoes don't fit. And that you don't have to adjust to the shoes.

On Being Private

June 22, 1992

To have happiness, there is only one thing necessary: to have happiness.

It is not necessary to deny in any way that you are happy. You may gladly deny that you are happy to others, of course, if you wish; but you never have to believe that you are wrong to be happy.

The realization, or even the suspicion, that we may not be serving our desires by exposing them to others does not mean we must be believing that they are wrong or dangerous in themselves. The issues of privacy, protection and finding a better means to get what we want may be more relevant considerations. To be an object of ridicule may or may not be useful in our lives. We may decide on that basis how best to achieve our goals, whatever they may be.

We may not express to the world what we know about happiness. We may have decided to be more private. That does not mean we are afraid, or are actually against happiness in our lives. We may not receive the praise of others for our happiness, or even the simple agreement that it is desirable to be happy. So what? Happiness is personal, only personal, and intrinsically personal. What would the approval of others, or the "sharing" of happiness with others, do for us or for them? Nothing. At most, it is our self-expression in the presence of another. There can be no true sharing of happiness, in the sense that our happiness is *our* happiness, and that a portion of our happiness can never be experienced by others as *their* happiness.

Rather than lose our enjoyment of our own happiness for want of camaraderie, we can look to ourselves as sources of inspiration and affirmation. We know we do not *need* to do this, but we may nonetheless enjoy doing it.

The only thing necessary for your happiness is for you to know (or experience) your own happiness.

Trusting Your Learning

January 19, 1992

Do you go from believing one thing is true, to believing another thing is true? When you do this, that's how you know you can trust yourself. You know you can change your mind, and will always go to what you believe is true.

Now, you have believed that changing your mind means you shouldn't trust yourself. Parents try to do that to children. "I know better. You can never trust yourself, you must trust me."

When you bump into a wall, you now realize that what you believed wasn't true. And what do you use that for? To show yourself that you are growing, learning, taking on new truths as you find them? Or, that there was something wrong with you for not knowing these truths before you knew them?

SECTION III

You Are Your Happiness

The Two Principles

March 10, 1977

1 Happiness is yourself:

Nothing causes unhappiness. All unhappiness symptoms are caused by the belief that some things cause us to feel bad.

We have only just believed that there are events, phenomena, people, attitudes, behaviors, etc., that we must (should, ought to) feel bad about.

2 Enjoying choosing your desires:

To desire to do something (or have something, etc.) is the only emotional prerequisite necessary before the attainment of the goal, and *we* choose the goals.

If we have the desire to do or be something, we do not need any other emotional preparation. If we are happy enough to want it, we are happy enough to do it. If the task takes more than attitude (which is desire without fear), then we will see if we still want to do it. We can decide if we want to do the necessary preliminary preparations for reaching our goals. These intermediate requirements are never a "better attitude" or "stronger desire" or "lesser desire." These requirements are always just something else to do or have. If we want them, then we are emotionally prepared to acquire them if possible.

When there is no fear, desire is the only attitude and personal experience necessary.

Some things only require desire and no fear, and insofar as they do, they shall be done.

The belief that they require other attitudes or emotional states is a mistake. This belief can make an otherwise happy person fail to achieve what they are able to do. To believe that we cannot do what we can do, that we want to do, is often based on the self-image that since we lack experience, we lack the ability to try or lack the right to desire. This is because we have believed we need more happiness (or another attitude, etc.).

To believe that you may not be happy enough (or have the best attitude) to "handle" something is the cause of unhappiness. E.g., to believe that if you got what you wanted you would not have the right attitude to keep it (or you would not be glad enough, which is the same) is to experience yourself as against yourself. This is unhappiness—fear of self, lack of confidence, etc.

To not realize that desire is the best and only necessary condition for achieving or keeping what we want is unhappiness. From desire flows the practical actions we believe necessary.

If we find that we used the wrong tool to do a job and do not get afraid that we lack the best attitude, we will search for the right tool. If there is a right tool and we find it, we will be glad. If we do not find it, it is not because we lack the attitude for it—unless that is lacking desire.

Perfect Happiness Moves You

PERFECT happiness is knowing that you are perfectly happy and that perfect happiness moves you: gives you breath and life, desire and all you have, awareness of what you have; awareness that your desires are not met; awareness that you want others to know what you know about happiness, and to know you are perfectly happy.

All you do, you do on behalf of perfect happiness for all, for you, on behalf of your own perfect happiness.

You do what you want. What you want is from your happiness. You go where your happiness leads you. It leads you where you want. Your happiness serves you by your serving it.

All that you imagine and
All that you feel and
All that you desire and
All that you do and
All that you are and
All that you have
is your perfect happiness manifesting itself
is you perfectly manifesting your perfect happiness
is you perfectly manifesting yourself
is you as you are
is perfect
is happiness
is manifestation
is you!

ALL that you imagine:

going somewhere—upstairs, outside, visiting, vacationing, driving, into a sewer, into a cloud, into someone, to Mars, to a field, into a grave, to a movie, to a restaurant, etc.

going nowhere—(staying where you are)

doing something—walking, eating, flying, digging, loving, killing, moving mountains, having sex, having wild sex, cooking, building, smiling, etc.

doing nothing—(staying with what you're doing)

having something—money, cars, lovers, enemies, pots and pans, flowers, sunshine

not having something—(losing what you have)

being something—healthy, diseased, beautiful, ugly, bald, short, stinking, wise

is from you: perfect, perfect happiness, manifesting you
to you: wonderful, awesome, ordinary, perfectly happy.
Everything that you imagine is perfect for you to imagine.
You are you.
You are who you are.
All that you feel
in your head: sinuses, forehead, ears, tongue, teeth, eyes, nose, etc.
in your neck, and shoulders, and back,
in your arms and hands,
in your chest and gut,
in your groin and butt,
in your hips and legs,
in your ankles and feet,
on your skin and under your skin,
heat and cold, hunger, thirst,
tingles and vibrations, palpitations and stiffness,
movements and lack of movements,
the new feelings, the old feelings,
dizziness and nausea, elation and
buzzing in your ears, that funny feeling, that deep feeling—

All physical sensations are from you; you know what you're doing, your happiness is giving you the awareness of what you are doing from your happiness, for you.

Everything that you feel is perfect for you to feel.
You are you. You are who you are.
All that you desire:
from what you imagine
from what you do
from what happens in you
from what happens around you

from yourself and others.

Anything whatever that you want to be, to happen, not be, not happen, to have, not have,

is you.

ALL, each and every whim, desire, wish, want, hope, dream, etc. comes from your perfect happiness for you—for all that will be; for all that you want, for all to know what you know.

Everything you want is perfect for you to want.

You are you. You are who you are.

All that you do:
to the world
to yourself
to others
to what you have
to what you want to have
with everything, everyone
near anything, anyone
away from anything, anyone
that you first think about,
that you don't think about,
that you enjoy,
that you ignore,
inside you, on you, outside you,
is you.

YOUR imaginings, feelings, decisions, desires, behaviors are you being you, perfectly.

Eating, sleeping, walking, smiling, farting, urinating, breathing, thinking, having sex, giving, taking, talking, listening,

is perfect happiness in the world.

All that you are: skillful, unskillful, joyous, not joyous, healthy, unhealthy, wise, ignorant, fat, skinny, wanting to change, not wanting to change, blonde, bald, nearsighted, old, young

is perfect for you to be now
is from being perfectly happy
is being you
is perfect for the world
is for you, for what you want, for others to know.
You are you. You are who you are.
All that you have:
as a product of your doing
as a gift from others
that just happened to be there for you
that is what you want or
that is what you no longer want
that is exactly what you want or
that is not all that you want it to be
is what you use to do what you do
is for you to be aware of being happy, and getting what you want
is for others to know what you know.
Perfect happiness is what is.

You have what you *don't* want, in order to be aware that you want others to know what you know about happiness, and to know you are perfectly happy. You *don't* have what you want because you want for others to know what you know about happiness, and to know you are perfectly happy.

You have what you want in order to use it, however you want, to do and get what you want, because you are perfectly happy and perfectly wanting.

You have you in order to use you however you want, to do and get whatever you want, because you are Perfectly Happy and Perfectly Wanting and Perfectly Being You.

You are your happiness's gift to you. You are your gift to yourself. Use it however you'd like it. You are yours.

There's Nothing Wrong with You

November 11, 1995

We are exactly as we wish to be and we choose to be. We're exactly what we're glad to be and we can't do anything about it. You are the way you are, and that's the way you want to be. And you can't do anything about that. You wouldn't want to, and you don't need to. It's meaningless. We simply won't or can't want to be anything other than ourselves. And unhappiness is believing, nonetheless, that we ought to, that we should.

If you're ever unhappy right now, it's because you are believing you should be different in some way or another. And when you described yourself as an unhappy person who is seeking help, you weren't an unhappy person. You were a person who described yourself that way. But you're exactly fine. You just didn't believe it.

There was nothing wrong with who you ever were, whoever that was. And you wouldn't have been that way if you knew that. In other words, if you were very bitter and very angry and very sad, if you really realized that there was nothing wrong with you being that way, nothing whatsoever wrong with you being that way, you wouldn't have been very bitter, very angry and sad. If you knew that it was really okay for you. That you really did approve of yourself.

What you believed was that you didn't approve of yourself. People who seek help from me believe that there are certain areas in their lives that they're not approving of themselves. And through The Option Method, people can see that they really do approve. And then all the changes are automatic. You just are happier to know that you don't have to be different. How many here knew that if they never, ever have to work on their unhappiness again, they would be happy? But what if you could find out that this is true: you don't have to work on your unhappiness ever again, and you are perfectly all right the way you are. Whatever you feel, whatever you judge, whether you like, or you don't like.

When you don't like something, you like that you don't like it. That's the way you identify yourself. You know, you're glad that you don't like liver or you don't eat meat. You're glad that you disapprove of this or that. Now if you really knew that that was really okay and you weren't hurting yourself, how would you feel?

What Is Happening?
Four Questions and Four Answers; or, One Question and One Answer

September 8, 1975

FOUR QUESTIONS AND FOUR ANSWERS:

1. **What is happening in you?**

   What are you feeling?

   What are you thinking?

   What do you want: want to have, to do, to think?

   What is causing all that is happening in you? There isn't anything wrong, is there? All within you is perfect and from your happiness, because you are happy, because you were created happy.

2. **What is happening outside you?**

   What do you see?

   What do you want now?

   What do you want to do now?

   What is causing all this?

   All that is happening outside you is for your future happiness, because you are going to be happy always, because you are created for being happy.

3. **What is happening *as* you?**

   What are you doing?

   Where are you going?

   What are you going to do now? What do you know?

   All that you are doing and being is being directed by your happiness toward your perfect happiness. You are becoming more aware of your perfect happiness.

4. **What's missing? What do you want to happen *as* you, that you think you don't know?**

What do you want to be that you feel you aren't?

What do you want to be aware of, that you are aware you are *not* aware of? What is perfect happiness? What is perfected happiness? What *is* your doing? What is it that you can do to perfect all that is? What can you do to perfect all that you have been given? What is it that you can do to be perfectly aware of all that is from and for your happiness? What can change all that is happening to you, in you, as you, into your perfect doing? What can you do to make all there is be perfect? How can you be perfectly happy? What is it that you want to think, do, feel, be, more than anything else? What do you really want to know and be more aware of?

Know that you love happiness. Know that you are glad that happiness is really for you, that you are glad to know that happiness is where everything is at, that you are glad to consent, allow, permit, and let happiness do everything for you that it naturally will do, and does. Know that you are glad that happiness loves you, and directs you and everything there is toward greater awareness of happiness, and that you are glad to concur, glad to say "Do it, Happiness!"

You *can* know, and *want* to know, that you can make it true that you are glad to let happiness do its thing. Then you can enjoy everything that you do and are. You trust happiness and you love doing that. You love knowing that you *are* doing that.

Perfect happiness is knowing you trust happiness gladly. Perfected happiness, realized joy, is knowing that you gladly consent.

Perfect happiness is perfect consent.

Perfect happiness is a perfect partnership.

Perfect happiness is a perfect alliance with your perfect ally. (That you really love happiness and are glad to trust it. That you are glad to give happiness freedom to do its thing. That you are glad to consent and glad to continuously consent and glad to realize that you are doing so.)

R ONE QUESTION AND ONE ANSWER:

What is happening? Happiness, and the chance to say "Yes!"

SECTION IV

A New World

The Future

August 2, 1975

No more predicting that my future will not be what I want.
I don't like that.

I never did.

No more believing or acting as if my future may not suit me. I don't know about any of that stuff.

Wait, Watch, and Enjoy What Happens in You and Around You

January 1987

WHAT we're really doing and all the ways we have of saying it and everything we're after basically boils down to trying to help people to discover why they're not allowing themselves to be happy and okay in certain circumstances.

And as simple as that is, that's really where it is at, too. It seems to me that there might be other ways of saying it, but that's basically what we'll be saying. So that's probably the single most important factor involved.

If there are other factors, whatever other factors there might be, they couldn't possibly be as important because they would only be means or leading to that basic fact, that basic goal.

Now what would be uncovered would be some fear, some kind of fear that amounts to something like this: "If I'm not unhappy, then I will have to have more fear somehow." The basic question again being, "Well, why aren't we okay in certain circumstances?" Because if we were, we'd somehow have more to fear or would have something more to be unhappy about. And it usually expresses itself this way with my patients.

"If I don't feel bad about not having what I want, then I may not want it enough to be motivated to try to get it." Very frequently that's pretty much the way it's verbalized. Somehow, there's an intrinsic recognition that wanting it is the only way to get it, and by motivating oneself is the only way. And the fear is that there wouldn't be enough motivation.

Now this is the fear that I might find myself in a position where I don't want something enough, because I want to be happier and I can't be unless I have X. I want to be happier and I can't be unless I have more good, more good things, more good whatever. This dynamic applies to both happy and unhappy people. For the unhappy person, the desire to get something better would be used as an antidote to unhappiness. "If I had that, I wouldn't be unhappy. If this happened, I wouldn't be unhappy." And for the happy person, it would be very similar. It'd be a happierness. "If I had it, I could be happier."

So the whole process of desiring to motivate oneself is based on some kind of feeling of lack or deprivations. So the person is going to wind up saying something like, "Unless I feel some lack or deprivation here, here now, I won't be motivated toward anything there, then. I sense that I can only move through a sense of lack."

Even the happy person will have beliefs, though these beliefs are not making them unhappy. They may not be saying, "I'll be unhappy unless I get it." What they are saying is, "I will be happier. My reasons for wanting are to be happier, so I'll be happier if I have this and I'll be happier if I have that," all somehow based on, "If I don't, I won't be." There's some lack. "There's something lacking to me now. What is it? More health or more wisdom or more money, more freedom, more whatever."

These same basic beliefs are approached in two different ways. They're approached by the happy person with the confidence that they're not wanting something in order to make themselves happy. They want it in order to be happier. They're okay now. They just want to be happier. The person who is being unhappy in that situation is basically saying, "I'm unhappy now and I need it in order to be happy." But in either case, it's kind of an antidote. It's a kind of filler-upper.

So the statement we find here is, "Unless I feel some lack or deprivation here and now, I won't be motivated toward anything there and then." The ultimate fear behind all other fears around everything else that we seem to find is this: if I find, if I know, if I allow myself to know that I will be happier always under any circumstances, then how will I decide what to do? How can I answer the question, such questions as this, "Okay, what'll I do next?" or, "What would I like to do?" How could I could even answer those questions if my happiness isn't somehow hung up on it, if it's not going to make me happier, if it's not going to make me happy if I'm unhappy?

In other words, it sounds like this: "Once the big question is answered, my happiness is assured. My great goal in life is provided for and there's no room for the question of my happiness. What do I do now? If I were to really allow myself to believe that I would be happier no matter what I do, then what do I do?" I suggest this. Wait, watch, and enjoy what happens in you and around you.

Since the big question is answered, my happiness is assured. My great goal in life is provided for. Everything that I've ever done anything for is really okay and it's taken care of. And there really, really isn't any longer any question of my happiness involved in anything I do. The things I do really have nothing to do with my happiness. Then I can wait and watch. I can enjoy what happens in me and around me. Enjoy what you do.

If you find that you make up reasons for doing things even, enjoy that. You don't have to fool yourself, though, that these so-called reasons are anything more than made up. You don't have to say, "Therefore my happiness or happierness depends on this, my happiness or happierness depends on that." If you find yourself making plans for the future, well, you could enjoy that game. You don't have to pretend that you have a reason to do that.

You don't have to pretend that your reason has anything to do with happiness. If you do make a belief, if you make up a belief, if you make believe somehow that the reason for your behavior is to make you happier, you don't have to pretend that you aren't believing that. But you could know that this made-up belief is only a made-up belief, and you could reaffirm your knowledge that the question has been settled once and for all, that you've settled it for yourself.

So do you see that if you continue investigating the basic goal, the basic question for The Option Method is: "Why aren't my clients, why aren't the people that I'm trying to help, allowing themselves to be happy and okay in certain circumstances?" Then all the right questions will come if that's my goal, that's my mind. Somehow they're going to be devised just to fit that ultimate question, "Why aren't you allowing yourself to be happy in these situations?"

I said we have been asking it, knowing that they have other fears. That, ideally, is the best question. For somebody who is into Option and knows what we're talking about, if I were to say, "Why are you not allowing yourself to be okay in these circumstances?" you would know what I'm talking about by "not allowing themselves." But because we know the fears that other people feel that don't allow that, we have very special, appropriate questions taking their fears into account.

So since that's what we're after, we're going to find answers basically that amount to: "If I'm not unhappy, if I don't make myself unhappy, then I'm going to have to be afraid more, because I'm not going to want what I want. I'm not going to be believing that I need it." It might even boil down to: "Hey, if I can be happy now without it, then why do I even want it? Why should I want it?" So I have to kind of believe that I need it on some level, even as a happy person. I need it to be happier. I need it to be happy.

In the happier person there tends to be a difference. The unhappy person tends to need it and only it. That's the big difference. The happy person says, "Well, I don't need it, but I need something like it." Maybe its much wider net is cast for things you believe you need. "Well, if one doesn't make it, so what. I'll have this. I don't really need it to be happy. But it would just help me to be happier."

And so that kind of an attitude is not fearful. There's no horror. There's no pain in not having it, and wanting something else instead. But there's still that kind of belief that things will make them happier, to be wanting of something, to be lacking in it.

You may have questions in your mind, such as "How do I determine how to do that? How do I decide how to do that? I've been sitting all night with a cigarette, should I or shouldn't I? What reasons do I have to light it? What reasons wouldn't I have to light it?" You may be needing reasons because you have got to try to hang it on your happiness, but yet you know your happiness may have nothing to do with it.

I've always found my experience has been that if I'm not really happy, I want something that I'm going to do. I want it before I do it. When I'm happy, I'm doing what I want to do. There's a different thing. Then, what I'm doing, I'm wanting.

There is an experience of wanting; but it's so congruous and identical to doing, so that I'm doing what I'm wanting, and there isn't a question of "will I do what I want, or what will I want, and will I do what I want to do," because there's no distance between my wanting and doing.

That would hearken back to the example last week of no child wants to walk, in itself. Instead, he wants to get something, and walking seems the best way. Now if he's really happy, he will be doing and wanting at the same moment, and there wouldn't be a question. He'd be wanting to walk as he's walking, but he wouldn't want to walk before he walked.

Wanting becomes obsolete as you are doing. If you put clothes on yourself, all of the things that you have on, you wouldn't think that you want to wear them. It's not necessary to want, desire. It's obsolete. It's irrelevant. Wanting was only to go the next step.

Do you want to breathe? Or do you just do breathing? There is lots that you neither want nor don't want, you just do, and it's not relevant and you solved that question a long time ago. And yet we can get hung up and have lots of feelings about: "Will I do what I want to do? And if I'm not unhappy, will I really do it?" There are lots of things we do in our life without being unhappy.

Once the question is solved, if I know that I will be always happier under any circumstance in the future, what will I do? If that becomes a question—and I don't know that it *has* to be a question for us, that we *have* to ask ourselves, "What will I do?"—but if we do, if we find ourselves in the course of where we've been and for whatever reason asking ourselves, "Okay, what will I do?" I don't know that it has to be answered by saying "this" for happiness or "that" for unhappiness.

One could just simply make up a belief. If you equally like vanilla and chocolate ice cream, how do you make the decision that you like vanilla or chocolate? We resort to the most absurd distinctions in order to make that decision. But we feel we have to have some kind of a reason because we can't decide. You can resort to such things—and people do—"Well, last time, I had vanilla, so this time I'll have chocolate." And all of a sudden you've created a system, a standard called "variety," as a means by which to judge things. "Last time I had vanilla. Oh, so that's my reason this time for not having chocolate or for having chocolate." They don't have anything to do with each other, as if somehow the vanilla ice cream is still in the stomach or still in their taste buds or whatever.

And some people wouldn't even attempt to say things like, "I'm sick of vanilla. I think I'll have chocolate," and they wouldn't have to go that far to be able to choose between two equals. Up rises the god of variety. And now when everything else is equal and you've got no other basis to make the choice on, you could always make the choice and claim variety as your reason. And there may be lots of things like that. *Sameness* becomes another basis for criteria. We have people who will choose because, "That's what I did choose. I'll choose the other this time because I chose it last time." So sameness becomes the reason. And all of the so-called virtues are ways of making distinctions for happiness; somewhere, it has to have something to do with my happiness.

Now if we do that there, why would we have to fool ourselves into thinking that that's some kind of rational, logical, real distinction? Why can't we be content to know that it's a game we play in order to make the distinction, in order to make the choice? I just go for vanilla, and somehow I let my liver say that, or somehow my ingrown toenail could say chocolate. But I don't have to know what my reason was for whatever just came out of my mouth.

We can remind ourselves, "I don't need to know the reason because my happiness is not at stake." The question of our happiness being at stake is really unnecessary because our happiness is not really at stake unless we make it at stake.

Questions for Reflection

Here, the questions are offered by Bruce Di Marsico in the original talk.

Perhaps an exercise that vocalizes the belief or the knowledge that "I am happy and will be happier" would be for us to get in touch for ourselves—wherever we are and any time of the day or night—that "I'm happy and will always be happier."

When we say that, what might happen is that certain objections will come up with inside us, and our fears will bring up suggestions like, "Oh, no. Remember this?" or "Aren't you afraid of that?" Because whatever is preventing us from truly believing that and truly knowing it may very well come up, come to mind. So now if we expose each of those fears as they come up, we could expose then some verbalization, saying it and hearing ourselves using the sentence. And so we can tune in to ourselves.

The idea is to vocalize and verbalize that we are happier and we will always be happy. As the objections come up, we refuse them. We can rebuke. We can challenge in a way that we've never bothered to do before, when we've ignored them, when we've made believe that happiness is really being threatened by that knowledge that I have nothing to fear, that I'm really going to be happier.

And the big question that you all ask me all the time is, "Bruce, how come I know that my happiness is not at stake, but I don't *really* know?" We may find that this is going to answer that question. So now if a belief comes up, you could always verbalize, "That is a lie, a myth, a false belief."

Our happiness is not at stake. I am going to be happier. It's a mistake that I believe it's just not true or it's unreal or it's bullshit or it's merely an unnecessary caution. I don't need it. Or, it's an excess protection. Somehow, it's unnecessary.

As each belief comes up, it gets the opportunity to be rebutted—if we simply refuse to give these beliefs credence, and recognize them as myths—if we simply refuse to give them credibility, if we say, "I don't have to believe that," they can't survive.

I am not denying that there are many things that I believe I have to be unhappy about. I am denying that I need to believe that. You understand the extension? I'm not denying the fear's existence. I'm not denying that it exists. I'm not denying that I believe it as a reason to be unhappy. I'm not denying my own beliefs. What I am denying is that I need to believe that.

The beliefs don't have to be denied. But we can see them as lies in a very special way. Because, see, the reason I say it's a lie is important. It's not the same as saying I shouldn't be unhappy. When I say it's a lie, my reason is that it's refuted because I know that I really am happy and I really will be happier. Now if it was refuted because I should be happy or I should be happier, *that* I could deny. But it can't be denied and can't be suppressed if I'm refuting it because I know I'll be happier.

The belief cannot survive if you really believe that it's not necessary. You will never hold onto a feeling that you don't think you need. Every time we've ever explored fears together, every time we've ever looked at our fears, as soon as we saw we didn't need it, we let it go, right? We only held it because we felt we needed it to be happy. You're not going to wear any more armor than you think you need.

I don't need to fear that I'm going to forget. That's excess. I don't need that fear. I know, because I know I'm going to be happier. So what's my forgetting and remembering have to do with anything? Now what if you forget to play the game? What if you forget to refute? "Okay, that fear is unnecessary because I'm going to be happier."

I know that I can refute it, because I am the greatest authority on myself that there is. Each of us will become the greatest possible authorities on our own happiness.

And we have the right to say to ourselves that that belief is nonsense. We have that right because we know the truth because we're the authority. I know that I make myself unhappy, so I have the authority to tell myself that this is unnecessary.

Happiness Opens Up a New World

December 12, 1992

UNHAPPINESS can only occur by believing something should or shouldn't be. Unhappiness about yourself is believing there is something that you need to be or not be, a quality you should or shouldn't have. Unhappiness doesn't come from wanting. It never comes from wanting, but by believing that what is wanted should be. Not by believing that something is good, but that the good should be, should be wanted, should be done, should be desired. That's what causes unhappiness. This is the whole truth, which is The Option Method.

This is the reason why unhappiness is untrue. It hasn't got any truth in it whatsoever. Unhappiness is a belief based on a false belief that things should be, ought to be. And unhappiness has no truth in it whatsoever. The truth is that nothing should or should not be. Just like you don't need anything, you don't have any right to anything, nothing needs to be, nor is anything needed for happiness. That's just simply the whole truth: nothing is needed. The belief that it is, causes unhappiness. Without that belief, there could have never been unhappiness.

Now you are learning how and why people have gotten unhappy. But that doesn't mean you have the full understanding of it. And you don't need to. When it comes to your happiness, there are things that have nothing to do with it . . . or have everything to do with it.

I really want to say this: what happens, is none of your business.

What happens in the world, and why it happens is really none of your business. Be happy, and just do whatever you want to do. You don't need to understand in the sense that you intend to judge things as bad or not. What is, is.

Change it if you want. When I say it's none of your business, that doesn't mean you can't go change it if you want. You just want to be happy, first and only. This is the truth I'm trying to share with you, that I want you to realize about yourself. This is not something I'm offering you as a way of thinking. You do, first and foremost, want to be happy. If you just spend a couple of minutes looking at yourself, you'll know that. Everything you've ever wanted, you've wanted in order to be happier. Everything you've ever wanted to avoid, you've wanted to avoid in order to be happier.

You just want to be happy, first and foremost. And this is your experience. Everything else just happens. There's you, and then there's everything that's happening. Well, I suggest that you just watch *yourself* happen.

This may sound like it's a hard thing, like it's something to do, there's a switch to turn. Just hear the words.

Just watch yourself happen. What you want will happen or not. You will make choices, or you won't. Enjoy yourself happening. Be where your choices lead you. You will be anyway—but actually *be* there, where your choices lead you. And if you make new choices, see yourself making them. See yourself making choices, see yourself not making choices. See yourself going where you are going, and go with yourself there. Do this, and you will have more than you could have ever thought to want. You'll find things you never realized you were seeking, until you found them. And this will be your actual experience.

Everything that is perfect for you is becoming apparent to you. It's all here, and you are allowed to see it. When you do see it, be glad for what you have allowed to happen to you.

When you realize that unhappiness is an illusion, you're living in a new world with a new life. You are new and everything in your experience is new. You may not appreciate this, you may not realize it, but you can come to realize it. What you are experiencing is not like you used to experience things. This knowledge is new to you, but it's also new to the world you were originally born in. What you are knowing now isn't what you knew when you were born. And you can appreciate that difference.

Not one single thing is what you used to think it was. Nothing. This comes from what you already know.

Now, begin to see what is really there, what was hidden, while you lived in a nightmare of the illusions of truth. What seemed true isn't true, not one single bit. What was impossible, and what is possible, you can now know. It's not what you thought it was. Not the illusions of the impossible but the actuality of it: unhappiness is really impossible, but it had the illusion of existing, when it was never an experience, but an interpretation, of the real.

Unhappiness was never really an experience. It's the name you gave to it, but it was an interpretation of reality, and a belief that, by its very nature, made you experience it as not impossible but inevitable. What you know now is that unhappiness is really impossible. You never experienced it as impossible. You experienced it as inevitable. The absolute opposite of what is the truth. So it wasn't experience, it was interpretation of your experience.

But now, the impossible might manifest itself. And it won't be the illusion of the impossible as it used to be, as unhappiness was, but the real presence of what you used to think was impossible, of what your mind can't anticipate or understand or justify in the old sense. But the body will react precisely *not* because of a belief.

When you now know that unhappiness is impossible, there are many things you used to think were impossible that you can now actually experience, once you are open. And you won't be experiencing them as illusions. And you are not necessarily going to understand in the old sense of explaining and justifying what they are and what they mean. And it may at first seem impossible, but that's not true.

What's going to happen is that, as you open up and as you are clear, you don't really believe in the impossibility, in the magic, the superstition of unhappiness, that thing that can't be that you thought was real. You may experience things you never used to experience. Your body may very well experience things precisely because beliefs are not interfering.

Because you don't have an unhappy belief, then whatever it is you experience can be a real stimulus, and can have a real effect on the whole new person that you are. What I'm describing is a kind of knowledge. Knowledge can come to you which doesn't come in words, doesn't come in descriptions; it doesn't come in old-fashioned justifications. You can just start experiencing it. Not necessarily know the words for it, but allow it to run its course, to manifest in you, in a wordless way, but in a very real way, that there's no doubt in your mind.

Awesome vs. Awful. If you judge the experience as a bad experience —that's an illusion, and you are going to deform the experience. You can be awed by it, and allow the real of truth of it to do its job, which you have nothing to fear from, which is everything you really want. It is the truth of you knowing something you want to know, and experiencing what it is you are knowing. But if you judge it as bad, you've deformed it, and not only can you not know it, but if you did know it, you would probably know it as evil or bad, or something like that.

Once you take away the beliefs of unhappiness, the beliefs of evil, the beliefs of "should" and "supposed to," and you are no longer looking through those glasses, what's left? What's left has got to be what's true. What IS true, not what you assumed is true. And you can only do that by letting yourself do that. There is nothing to be afraid of. Why? Because nothing can happen to you that can ever make you unhappy. Why? Because nothing ever has the power to make you unhappy.

SECTION V

Perfect Freedom

The Freedom Not to Change

January 19, 1992

CAN you ever do something you shouldn't have done? Will you ever do something you shouldn't have done? Could you ever "play" yourself wrong? How could you not be perfect?

Perfect people aren't wedded to anything, except what they feel like being wedded to. Since I am perfect, I could never change, or I could always change. It is not imperative for me to change anything, so I could continue exactly the way I am, and that would be perfect, and it would be perfect, also, to change.

Real freedom doesn't mean change. Real freedom means the freedom to not change as well. Isn't it true that nothing needs to be different? Then everything's perfect, right now, already. The difference between feeling the whole world is perfect, and not feeling it, is feeling that something needs to be changed ("feel" means "believe"). There are things I want you to change, but to believe they need to be changed . . .

That's perfection, to want things to change. To need things to change is not—that's the same as saying that they are not perfect.

We're dealing with the fundamental freedom of the whole universe. Nothing *needs to be* in the whole universe—I only know that because I know nobody needs to be unhappy. You are at this moment everything you need to be. If you stop at this moment and call it an end product, it is exactly what it is supposed to be, because it was necessarily caused by the history of the universe up till now. So for people to believe that they are not what they are supposed to be seems very contrary to all reality, because everything that is now, had to be because of the history of the universe.

So it's very strange to have a world based on "I'm not the way I'm supposed to be and people aren't acting the way they are supposed to act." It's so obviously impossible. That person who just offended you, you say they shouldn't have been that way. How in the world could they have not been that way?

Doing Nothing

If you could personally recognize that "All that's happening is I'm not getting what I want," that could clarify everything for you. That's all that's going on. You're not getting what you want, and you think that needs to be different.

You're not getting what you want. Now, what do you want? Do you want to do something about that, perhaps? But nothing needs to be different for you to have the right to *want* it to be different. You notice if what is going on is what you want. If not, what do you want to do about that? Or even, merely, what do you want to *do*?

Sometimes, doing "something" about something is not doing *anything* about it, it is just being aware that you are doing what you want. For example, trusting yourself if you just don't want to think about it right now. Some people believe they ought to do something about a situation, not realizing that to *not think* about it is doing something about it. Do you know how much trouble we can *not* get in, because we didn't do something just for the sake of doing something?

When you don't know what to do, to do nothing can sometimes be the best thing to do. It is a prejudiced idea that you are supposed to do something about a situation. You don't have to. Go get a drink of water. Have lunch. Take a nap. Have sex. Do anything you want—and that may be the very thing to do. It is perfect for you to do—and *not* do—whatever you are doing.

We cannot understand the hundred trillion things we are *not* doing in any moment, except to be aware that whatever I *am* doing is what I *am* doing instead of a hundred trillion other possibilities. And the perfect reason to do anything is: it is what you are doing.

SECTION VI

The Experience of Happiness

On Quiet

Monday Night Study Group, 1973

We have the opportunity to be quiet together. And by "quiet" we don't mean silence. Quiet, inside. It doesn't mean to whisper. Quiet doesn't mean to not rattle. It doesn't mean rattling or not rattling, it has nothing to do with any of those things.

Quiet is letting yourself be done with things for a little while, just be done with things for a little while. Everything could all be suspended just for a couple of minutes and you could allow yourselves to indulge in the opportunities that will be there in quiet that are not there other times. We don't have to play games to say that quiet is better than not quiet or that one is better than the other. One has opportunities that the other doesn't have, and in being quiet there are opportunities that aren't there in not being quiet. Not better or worse opportunities, different ones.

It is possible, certainly, for any of us to be quiet in some way in the midst of a riot; we can have that in ourselves, we don't really need the environment to be perfectly conducive to such a thing.

Don't deny your specialness. That's not modest. You have within you the seeds for a very beautiful garden and you can let yourself know that. You could spread them fearlessly. These seeds that are within you will never grow a bitter plant but only sweet fruits. Some seeds will not seem to grow; others will seem to need extra care, and others will disappear to grow where you may never see the fruit. For wherever they take root and for however short they seem to grow, you can know that there was at least that chance for something that there never was a chance for before. You are the nucleus of a future that depends on you. The best way to spread happiness is to live it. And be conscious of the fact that you are living it. Be happy and be at peace with all around you. Change what you want, do what you wish, but in all things be happy, live it, and let this place here be a place where you will live it.

Live it with each other and be patient if you are not yet sharing all you can. You are not yet as happy as you will be. As you grow in happiness, so will your thoughts and actions reach others who are waiting. If you grow in happiness, they'll ask you to help them. Many will come to you from what seems like nowhere, and you and they will be ready at that time to go on being happier. Help one another to be happy, each of you. Help each other to be happy. Unless you help one another here, now, how we help others? You can't always say "Tomorrow, tomorrow, after I learn more, after I experience more, in time." Some day, if you were to be happier, you will say, "I will, *now*, I will, *now*."

Love each other right now, love each other more. You don't believe in the world's cop-out that says, "Time will help me to love more. Time will help me to love more." You may not have a lot in common from your pasts, but you have the most in common that any people ever will have. Are there any reasons why you really must be aloof from each other?

Are you going to really carry out the world's myth that we are not yet friends? Some of you may even believe, and some of you do believe right now, that there is no real advantage to loving some others of you. Do you really need such a delusion? Is there really no advantage to being happier with all people? Is there really no advantage to *really* being with anybody?

Stop all the pretending that you are significantly different from each other. You are denying yourself a great peace. Those of you who love the others most will be the happiest among you.

The Story of Boris and Gleb

Happiness in the face of trials and disasters seems so incomprehensible to people, seems so extraordinary, that it's been the custom of the Catholic Church for the last 2,000 years that pretty much whenever it has come to their attention that someone's managed to be happy, they declare them a saint. And I was thinking of three brothers that lived in ancient Russia: the names were Boris and Gleb. They had a third brother, Sviatopolk.

Their father was a czar, and when the czar died, as was the custom of the time, his domains would be split and the revenues were to be split among the surviving sons. The third brother decided that he didn't want a split with Boris and Gleb, and that he wanted all of Russia for himself and all the income. And so he started out on a scheme to kill them, to assassinate them. He didn't even try to justify it by saying, "I have to get them before they get me," because they were both very, very happy people, Boris and Gleb, and they weren't going to be out to do that to him and he knew that. He just simply decided that he would take advantage of them since they were so happy; it would be pretty easy to take what was theirs from them. So he got henchmen together and planned the scheme. Boris and Gleb both found out about it and they were going about their business, and they decided to do what they could to stay alive but they wouldn't resort to killing their brother.

And when the time came, the one was out for a walk in the woods and he was waylaid, captured, brought to his brother. Meanwhile the henchmen who had captured him delighted in torturing him and doing whatever they could to him. They brought Gleb to his brother to kill him, and Gleb did what he could to talk his brother out of it. He used different reasons he could think of, he appealed to every emotion he could imagine, and he couldn't talk his brother out of it.

The other brother was pretty much in the same position, except he was much more frightened; and when they got him he was on a boat somewhere. And his brother faced him and he cried and it didn't do any good, and he threw himself into tantrums and it didn't do him any good. He pleaded, he offered everything that he had—none of it did any good.

And what's recorded about each of those brothers is that after they did everything they could do—one used unhappiness and fear, and the other didn't—they both resigned themselves to it and said, "Well, if you are going to kill me, you are going to kill me, but you are not going to make me unhappy." And each of them decided that they were going to love him. They loved him. They saw his fear, and he murdered them, each of them.

They henchman and the others who were around the time they were murdered were really struck by the happiness that Boris and Gleb allowed themselves in their last days and their last moments—so much so that the words spread and the Russian people wanted them to be canonized as saints. The archbishop of the Metropolitan of Kiev said, "They don't fit into any category. They are not really martyrs of faith, they didn't die for their faith, they are not confessors of the faith, they are not priests, they are not widows." And they canonized them anyway and they're known today as the Saints Boris and Gleb.

Sometimes, in our lives, there is just no more time to wait to be happier.

Peace and Joy

May 4, 1979

THE only repetition people desire is that alternation of joy (active involvement in unfolding) and peace (restful satisfaction in completion).

These desired emotional states are not dependent on external events or an internal secret.

The secret may be that there is no secret, just a universal belief in one.

Can a person be bored if they don't fear it? Does a person need to seek entertainment if they naturally will fluctuate between peace and joy?

Peace is boring when it lasts too long. Too long for what? Joy is boring when it lasts too long. Too long for what?

A child is not necessarily experiencing boredom when it throws down a toy it is "satisfied" with just having explored. It is done with it for now (or always), that is all. It may now be feeling satisfied and peaceful or it may be "turned on" to something else. There is always peace or a new joy. There is always happiness. There really need not be a belief that we need to escape peace or disturbance. They are unhappy problems when we believe that the timing "should" be different. How long "should" a child be interested in something? How long "should" a child be uninterested in something? How long "should" you or anyone? How long should it be before you are free to drop something or pick up something else, or both, or neither?

Excitement versus peace, activity versus passivity, consciousness versus sleep—something is always happening, whether to the mystic or to the frantic. All is life, living, motion, feeling, being.

Peace is when changing does not seem dramatically important. Joy is when changing seems dramatically important.

There is no principle of Life, Change, Happiness, Joy, Peace or Anything. There are only things that happen to or occur to or affect a person. There is no Reality, only each person's reality! There is no Great Secret hidden from us. There is a drama of the moment or not. Drama is the unfolding present. Drama is the personal perception or judgment that something is indeed unfolding. Boredom is the belief that something should be unfolding, dammit!

Impatience with self or others or the world or God or children or governments or anything is the belief, judgment, decision that now is the time for some good thing to happen. And it doesn't seem like it will happen.

Boredom is the need for drama while believing it probably won't happen.

Gladness

EITHER be glad for what will be or be sorry for what was.
Whichever you do, is now what is.
When something is not what you now want,
be glad for what could be,
or
be sad for what could have been and isn't.
Be glad for where you're going
or
feel bad for where you've been.
Each choice will be now.
Sad or glad.

Being Grateful without Reasons

Monday Night Study Group, 1973

It's now that you can feel grateful. Feel grateful to be happy. Feel grateful to do anything you feel like doing. Feel grateful to do whatever you want to do. Feel grateful to do everything you want to do, and be happy.

You don't need reasons anymore; they don't have to be your motivation. Everything you do, you can do out of love—that can be your motivation—and use your mind for what it was intended. Your mind is to help you figure out and to decide things, not to make emotional judgments and feel bad. Only to *help* you to decide things. Not to convince you that you don't love. Not to make you feel that you're unworthy of all the good that there is for you.

In the end, there's no way to understand it. You just know. That's all. All labels can do is limit you and make you afraid. All labels can do is give you implications you don't need.

It's everything you've ever wanted, that's all. Let your minds be at peace. Let them rest. You don't need them for what you are doing.

Questions and Answers

Questioner: *When you say there are no reasons for our being happy or unhappy, that scares me.*

There are only reasons for being *un*happy. If you are unhappy, it is because you believe there are reasons to be happy and because you believe there are reasons for being unhappy—but all you can really do with your reasons is be *un*happy.

Questioner: *What's the point of wanting something specific? Is it believing that if I had it, I would be happier?*

You think it's possible that you might want something other than what's really best for you. It's not a matter of believing. You know what you're tending toward. You tend toward food when you're hungry. You tend towards your bed when you're tired.

Questioner: *Would it be good to let yourself tend towards whatever you're tending toward, even if it's out of unhappiness?*

You've got to start where you are. And if there's any unhappiness or there's any fear in your life, its cause is going to be in your wanting. You're going to think that you're wanting it from your unhappiness. And so in trying to put down your unhappiness, you put down your wanting.

Questioner: *So if I'm tending towards having a drink, then the best thing to do is to let myself have a drink?*

If you're not aware that you don't want *more* not to drink. It just depends on what you want more. The only reason people could perhaps not know that they want more *not* to drink is because they use all kinds of beliefs to get in the way of what they know.

Questioner: *When I get what I want or I see the possibility of my being likely to have it in the future, I feel happy about that. And I'm saying to myself, "I'm happy now because I have a reason to be happy, because I'm getting what I want."*

That's because you believe you need help to be happier. What if you knew you were going to be happier, then would you have to make up that game: "If I get *this*, I'll be happier, if I get *that*, I'll be happier"? What if you *knew* you'd be happier? You say to yourself, "Well, what would I do if I really knew I was going to be happier?" Well, what are you doing right now? You really do know you don't need help to be happier. It doesn't prove that you don't know that, just because you're acting as if you don't.

You can know something and act as if you don't know it. It doesn't mean you don't know it. You can feel something and act as if you're not feeling it. It doesn't mean you're not feeling it. You know it whether you admit it or not. You feel it whether you admit it or not. So that's all irrelevant. Somehow acknowledge that you consent to be happier, that you know you're going to be happier.

You have to admit, "I know where I'm going and I'm open to it," not " I wonder where I'm going, I don't know where I'm going and what could it lead to and could it be bad?" That's acting as if you didn't know where you were going. All you need to do, when real happiness presents itself to you, when you come to know what it can really feel like, what it really means, is to somehow consent to it. "Okay, I consent to it. I'm not going to act as if it doesn't matter. I'm not going to act as if I don't know."

You can only *act* as if you don't know. It doesn't mean you don't know. You can drive it so far back in your mind and out of your experience that you could walk around all the time as if you never knew it, and cover your knowledge over by believing that unhappiness is possible.

Questioner: *What messed it up?*

There's nothing messed up. It's just not admitting what you know.

Questioner: *I have this experience of being coerced into being happy, like I'm supposed to be happy.*

You're the only one who can give the consent. Who else can? You're just feeling like you're not consenting to what you want. That's all.

Questioner: *You were saying, we all want to be loving. And I don't feel loving or happiness. That's what everybody talks about, loving and happy, but I don't experience that. Maybe it's because I want to experience a relationship with other people but I don't experience it.*

You're talking as if you don't want to feel loving, but have to feel loving against your will. You're talking as if you could feel loving without wanting to feel loving. You're talking as if it was possible for someone to make you feel loving if you don't want to feel loving.

All being loving is, is a nod of the head. All loving is, is a consent, an awareness and a being glad for what you've got. That's all it takes to be loving. And you want to prove that you're free to not do that. You've been proving that all your life. So you've proved it.

There's no pressure. Your feeling loving isn't going to do a damn thing for any of us. So stop fooling yourself. It's only for you that you would feel loving. Nobody's pressuring you. You feel loving for your own sake. That's all. Right? That's really what it amounts to. *We* don't need you to feel loving. And you're just kind of robbing yourself of that feeling that you want so much, and instead, you've become afraid that you're not going to do what you want to do and that you'll go away from what's good for you and that you're being coerced into being happy, as if you didn't want to be happy. As if you could be coerced.

Why would you be afraid of being happy? Are you afraid that then you'd be unhappy? What kind of a circle is that? Then you're not talking about being coerced into being happy. Then you're not talking about being happy.

All there ever was for you is happiness. Whether you consent to it or not, it's there. All you were able to say about it is, "I consent. I'm glad that I'm feeling so good." Nobody's making you be that way and your past is not making you be that way right now. Nothing is. You want everything you've ever wanted—you could just admit it. "I want everything I've ever wanted. I'm glad for getting everything I've ever wanted." That's all. It doesn't cost you anything. You're not giving anything to anybody else that you need for yourself. You're just diving into what you are and who you are and what you've got. That's all. That's all there is. It's very simple.

Now, you can feel whatever you want to fear in your judgments, and you can make yourself feel sick. But the thing that would get rid of all of that, all the other feelings, would be to just consent and be glad for what you're feeling. Be glad for feeling happy. Be glad for feeling good. Be glad that there is peace for you. That everything you've ever wanted is at hand. Nothing to be afraid of.

Questioner: *My confusion is that I know that I am capable of loving because I have experienced that. But not all the time. I feel happy when I feel that way. Or maybe I feel that way because I'm happy. Whatever comes first.*

Loving and being happy are the same thing. It's being glad for what you have. It's being glad that you're happy. It is just the opposite of depression, which is being unhappy that you're unhappy. Real love is being glad that you're loving, being glad that you're happy. That regardless of what somebody else is doing, you know you are. You may feel hostile. That doesn't prove you don't love. And the more you know that, the more at peace you'll be.

You are not the cause of your life. But you can consent to it or not. You are not the cause of your happiness. You can consent to it or not. You know where the real true cause of your happiness is.

You can consent to it or not. Would you refuse to be happy because you don't know where it comes from, you don't like where it comes from, or it doesn't fit your rules? All you need to know is you cannot create happy feelings in yourself. You can only consent to them. They don't come from you. They're everything you've ever been destined for. They're everything and more than what you've ever wanted. All you can do is consent to it or not.

COMMENTARIES

by Aryeh Nielsen on

"Enjoying Your Happiness"

The Worst of Humanity

This commentary is a synopsis of ideas that Bruce Di Marsico expressed in many writings or talks, but did not express summarily in a single writing or talk.

THERE is nothing wrong with you, and there is nothing wrong with anybody. But perhaps you disagree with somebody's actions, perhaps very intensely, and wish to act strongly against them. There is nothing wrong with that.

Is a universal morality necessary as a support to condemn and oppose the actions of those who oppose you? Let us consider those who are often called "the worst of humanity," "evil," "completely inhumane," such as dictators who attempt genocide, serial killers, and predators.

You probably don't like it when people try to kill you, those you love, or have sympathy with. And, publicly, an appeal to universal morals may coalesce forces to oppose these actions, whether via war in the case of genocidal dictators, or jail in the case of serial killers.

But all you really need to know is that you don't like what these people are doing. Other people also don't like it. You can work together to oppose these actions.

Here's what this has to do with happiness and unhappiness: to believe that anybody or anything is wrong in the sense that it can cause unhappiness against your will, is the root of unhappiness. Happiness has been attacked as problematic by some who fear it because they believe that a happy person would passively allow their interests to be violated. But you don't need to know that a genocidal dictator is wrong to oppose him. You don't need to be unhappy to oppose him. You can be perfectly happy, and know that you don't like the actions of a genocidal dictator, with a passionate intensity. The dictator is no more wrong than a tiger that wants to eat you is wrong. You merely have diametrically opposed interests.

Practically, fearing evil has led to many questionable actions in opposing what is intensely disliked; for example, taking punitive actions against a population that become the seed of further hatred and opposition. Happiness is the best position even to fight against "the worst of humanity," knowing that even "the worst of humanity" is good—in the sense of not being able to cause unhappiness against your will—*and* you will do everything in your power to not let them have their way.

Option and the Play of Existence

This commentary is based on the editor's understanding of Bruce Di Marsico's teachings.

THE Option Attitude has some basic similarities to unstructured play. The two most fundamental aspects of play are:

1. Make believe, or the making of beliefs that are the basis of actions. For example, children might "play house," making believe they are their parents.
2. Freedom to quit. If there is no freedom to quit playing, then it is not play anymore. To play at cleaning house implies the player knows that they are choosing to do the activity, and could choose not to. To toil at cleaning house implies that the person feels they are not choosing the activity, and could not choose otherwise.

> Reasons are a game we play in order to make a choice. You don't have to pretend that your reason has anything to do with happiness, but you could know that the belief is only a made-up belief, and you could reaffirm your knowledge that the question of happiness has been settled once and for all.
>
> BRUCE DI MARSICO

Option recognizes that no beliefs are necessary to have or not to have for happiness. Any belief can be held without impeding happiness. Any belief can be quit. A person could even make believe that they are obligated to be unhappy against their will. Those for whom there is a tacit awareness that there is no ultimate necessity to such a belief can trust themselves to stop playing at unhappiness if it really matters.

From that fundamental knowing of non-necessity, then, even apparently unhappy beliefs can be held with no ultimate detriment to happiness. Hence, someone who has fully realized the Option

Attitude does not necessarily appear to be any different than anyone in any way. The only difference is their knowing of their own perfect freedom.

> The feelings of happiness are the feelings that we are feeling while not "knowing" necessity. Because I know I have my own peace, I can kind of act crazy. What's the difference? Because you are really happy, you can do everything you're doing. You could also act unhappy, and you could make believe you're unhappy, and you can make believe you have all kinds of reasons to be unhappy, and you can act as if you are unhappy, because you really are happy.
>
> BRUCE DI MARSICO

Emotions Are Happiness

This commentary is a synopsis of ideas that Bruce Di Marsico expressed in many writings or talks, but did not express summarily in a single writing or talk.

> You can only get unhappy by believing your emotions are bad for you.
>
> BRUCE DI MARSICO

It is commonly believed that unhappiness is an emotional state. But what are emotions? Emotions are the whole-organism orientation toward well-being of the organism. Unhappiness is *predicting* (believing) that emotions experienced *now* (which *are* the bodily orientation toward well-being) will be against *future* well-being, as if somehow your present orientation toward well-being did not fully incorporate all predictions of the future.

So unhappiness is believing in what is not so, and what can never be so, in the context of emotions. That unhappiness always arises in the context of emotions has led people to believe that unhappiness was emotional.

> Unhappiness is believing in the "not-me" me—which doesn't exist.
>
> BRUCE DI MARSICO

You are always perfectly oriented toward your well-being. A "you" not perfectly oriented toward your well-being doesn't exist—it is *not* you. How could you ever feel about things a way that you don't feel about things? Unhappiness is believing you are *not* you.

> Unhappiness is disowning your feelings.
>
> BRUCE DI MARSICO

Believing that what you feel about something is, somehow, not truly indicative of how you feel about it is the root dilemma of unhappiness. Our own feelings are believed to be not our own.

> Emotions are happiness. Judging your own emotions as bad is unhappiness.
>
> Bruce Di Marsico

PART VI

Option Mysticism

On God

Monday Night Study Group, 1973

INTERPRET this question for yourself. How many of you believe in God, and to how many is that an irrelevant question? Irrelevant to you, to your life, to anything. I would probably raise my hand on both the questions.

What I am interested in is those who don't believe in God or believe that there is no God. How do they know what I am talking about that they could answer? Now, what you might be saying you don't believe in is the God your mother and father told you about, but you don't know what *I* am talking about. Interpret it for yourself, and that's what I am trying to point out now: that somehow you had to interpret it to be something that you objected to, or you could interpret into no meaning, as into a meaningless Name. How many of you believe in "photo"?

Now the next question is, how many of you *know* that there is a God, as opposed to those of you who believe in God? I am with those people, whoever they are. And for those of you who can't answer, okay, how many of you know there is no God?

You don't have to know what everybody in the world calls God, you only have to know what *you* wanted to call God; and the only way you could say that you could know there is *no* God is to make it a contradiction. You'd have to define God as an impossible, and then you could say you know there is no God.

You can define God as a non-existent, but you cannot believe in that which is both not existent and substantiates itself, for instance as a square circle. I do not believe that there is a square circle. It is a contradiction by definition, but it's truly irrelevant whether there is a square circle or not; there is nothing I could do with one if there was one. By definition, it's non-existent.

Now, I think that you are going to find that the question of God has got a lot to do with your own happiness, and a lot to do with the society around you and its happiness and unhappiness and its beliefs. God is very frequently defined by most theologians as, first of all, indefinable; God is ineffable and indefinable . . . and then they go on to define him.

I had a theology professor who said to me, "You can't draw a picture of a soul; there is no doubt about that. By definition a soul is an immaterial thing." But then he proceeded to go to the blackboard and drew a circle, which he then divided up into sections, labels, and everything else which to him was supposed to be meaningful to us, and then from there on acted as if there was such a thing as a soul.

Freud did the same, with such terms as id, ego, super-ego, libido, etc. These were constructs, as God is a construct for most theologians and psychologists; it's a construct which is an explanatory principle. As an explanatory principle, one can talk about it, relate to it and understand it. If you stop understanding it as an explanatory principle but believe it to be an existent, a thing with existence and substance and reality, then you start treating it as if it weren't an explanatory principle any longer—which leads you into a whole other thing, which is people can talk about forces inside themselves for good and for evil just as freely through psychological jargon as they can with theological jargon. I'd like to point out to you that they are both very much the same, the history of psychology and the history of theology. They've been dealing with the problem of God and the problem of evil and man, and the problem of forces unseen by man that determine men's behavior.

An explanatory principle is meant to explain something. As an explanatory principle, I have no difficulty in talking about God. I think that the problem very frequently is "How does that affect me if I want to treat it as a subsistent? Can I make it subsistent for purposes of my own life and happiness? Can it mean something?"

So now, for instance, a lot of you who object to all the traditional interpretations of God, you are probably also intuitively objecting to something that you just can't conceive. You might be stymied by statements of like that of St. Gregory of Nyssa who says that God is beyond that which can be known, that God is beyond what we can know, so it's impossible to say it doesn't exist if you define it as beyond what can be known. But then it's totally irrelevant, unless it taps you on the shoulder. Something beyond knowing is, as far as all practical concerns, non-existent.

There are probably quite a few hundred very good proofs of the existence of God, but none of them propose a God that, for instance, you would pray to or blame in the theological definitions. So that when you get into the existence of God as the prime mover or the cause of the universe or the thing that sets order, that might be a fun idea to play with, but that isn't necessarily anything to relate to.

God can be something to relate to in your lives. Many of you here have made a God out of happiness. Now, I don't mean a false idol. I mean that what you have understood as Happiness with a capital H may very well be, and probably is to the best of my knowledge, what everyone else has ever meant by God, what they really mean by it. There is an unknowable that we will profess to know, and that's, for instance, perfect happiness. Striving for happiness with a capital H—if you are striving for it, it proceeds somehow from the premise that you don't know it, you haven't yet experienced it, you are not experiencing it, and that hasn't stopped you from striving for it. You haven't even got any evidence somehow, and yet that doesn't stop you from striving for it.

Everybody in the world can give you very good arguments that God does not exist or that happiness does not exist, and that does not stop you from striving for it. That is very in alignment with certain saints who say, "I don't know whether it's possible for there to be God or not, but I don't care. I want there to be, and there is for me"—and that's the same thing with happiness. Who cares if it doesn't exist, I am still going to have it. Who cares if it's impossible, that's what I still strive for, and somehow it would be really okay even if pure, perfect, absolute happiness were never reached, as long as you constantly got closer to it. And if we don't object to that concept, we understand what many people mean by God in terms that we might be able to understand. That although God is unknowable, unreachable, unattainable and ineffable, that has never stopped us from anything.

It becomes kind of a thing to fix one's focus on that which can never be in perfect focus. It becomes that which is at the end of a road, when we can't see the end of the road, but we can see the road.

Happiness can be described as an explanatory principle and not a substantive thing. It's that beyond which we are constantly striving for, that which even after we are happy we are still striving for, that which explains everything that we do. We have often talked about it that way: that even after we are happy we want to be happier and that is the ultimate reason behind everything that we do, joy, peace. It's the ultimate reason for our actions and our motives.

Well, some people have been calling the ultimate reason for what we do God. I always say in my classes that you could even call it happiness, but it is that beyond which we always strive for. Understood in that way, there isn't anything to object to. The problem is when all of a sudden God becomes personified and says, "You shall not do this and you must not do that and you ought to do this," when that starts saying you should feel bad, then it becomes a contradiction and it no longer is a explanatory principle. When *that which is beyond* becomes personified so that it could feel hurt and feel bad itself, it becomes a contradiction.

No true theologian in their right mind believes that God could be hurt or offended. They find it very hard to talk about sin against God as having any meaning whatsoever, because all sins can be only be against your own happiness. They have been saying that nobody goes to hell who doesn't want to.

The Episcopalians have a funny thing. In the beginning of the service, they recite at the beginning of the book of Genesis that everything that God created was good and constantly "and it was good and it was good, it was good"; but yet as soon as that was over, "I am no good. Everything is good but me." Within religions, many of them have theologies that do not use guilt or fear. In Christianity, that is called *mystical theology*. Mystical theology by definition has never had anything to do with unhappiness, guilt or fear or sin, and it never even admitted the concept. Mystical theology is a theology that always taught that if you loved God you could do anything. If you loved God, it was impossible to sin and it made no difference what a man did; no man could ever be judged. That's as the old as the Christian church, but many people don't consider themselves mystical theologians and they prefer the dogmatic theology which has existed side-by-side with mystical theology. And they both have had their adherents. Mystical theologians tend not to become bishops and popes.

So what I want to present to you is the possibility to consider that the concept of God, or the term God, can a useful concept and could perhaps be a useful concept for us, and could be meaningful. It is by no means a necessary concept, but as we are speaking English, it is a term that already exists.

Just as people can say, "What do you mean, "happiness"? What if it makes a person happy to kill? Why do you want to help them to be happy?" there are meanings of God which we can't possibly be talking about.

Why even bring this up? What does it have to do with anything? Why should we even be talking about it? Why can't such terms as "happiness" suffice? Well, simply because they don't suffice. They are not really sufficient, and maybe the term God isn't sufficient either. But there is a concept there that perhaps you can open yourself up to seeing as a relationship that in some way you can elect or choose to concretize, to give it meaning and relevance to your life, to try to strive for it.

For instance, we could describe a person at prayer this way: a person at prayer is talking to a projection that they see as the fulfillment of themselves, and what they are doing is they are putting themselves in touch with all that they hope to be and somehow relating to that, and they are getting in touch with their desire to be one with that. What is called "the person in prayer who is relating to God" sees God as love, and in so doing is desiring to be more and more in union with that love. It's not any different than a person who was wanting to be happier, but one of the values it has for us, in terms of the peace and joy that it gives, is that it helps the person to be in touch that they are good for themselves and that they are striving and that they are reminding themselves of what it is they are really after. And so what they do is incarnate, made tangible, something that up to now has been very intangible: the question of perfect happiness. It's to make it present to themselves and that the major function of religion is to make something ineffable somehow effable, tangible and present to you to remind you; so religion develops lots of rituals, buildings, symbols.

We've seen people's reluctance to refer to happiness as what they are striving for and everything that they want. So they call it God, but they can't avoid it; everything they are doing, they are doing it in order to be happy, and they will naturally come together and form religions. And just as you will find a temptation to say that other people should be happy, should have straightened out their beliefs, etcetera, so have these other religions that have come together had a tendency to do that. From such practices as Option have sprung established religions with laws and commandments, in the contradictory idea of "what you *must* to do be happy."

Sin in almost every theology is the turning away from that which is your perfection. Sin is "Thou shalt not turn away from what is your perfect good" and making it a law, as if that was necessary! Even the idea that you would want to turn away from your happiness in order to help you not to turn away somehow assumes you would like to turn away from what is your natural fulfillment.

We can understand the happiness as that which is perfect in the universe, and that insofar as we are not coinciding with ourselves, we are unhappy. That unhappiness is somehow not coinciding with myself, not being at peace with myself, not being in harmony with myself, not being at one with the universe, and such things as that. Then you can talk about personifying the concept of order in the universe. There is a principle involved there somehow, and there was a principle involved with you before you were ever created, and when you came to be that, what you are calling happiness has somehow already been determined. It's like in your very nature. We talk about free will and free choice all the time, but there is one thing that we can never choose to not choose and that's to be happy. Some people refer to that as divine compulsion; other people have referred to what is the natural order; but nonetheless there is one thing that we all agree on: there is that which we all strive for—willing or not.

Happiness is something that we all naturally go to, and the whole question of wanting it, willing it, choosing it, desiring it, are irrelevant questions. We can play around and we pretend to want it or not want it, or choose it or not choose it, but everything within us is geared toward our being happier. If you explore yourselves and you are patient, you'll see for anybody to ever choose anything that they don't believe will lead to happiness is totally incomprehensible, impossible.

Hell will have to be in terms of somehow an afterlife. See, the idea of an afterlife is, then your vision is clear, and now you can see clearly what you are all about. All that held you back—which supposedly was your body, your materiality, which held you back from seeing things clearly—is now gone, and there is no obstacle to what you are seeing anymore. You see God, and you have one of two choices. You can be fantastically happy about that, and that's called heaven; or you could say, "Oh my God, had I only known" and you can spend an eternity saying "Oh, what did I do, being unhappy," and that's called hell. I am not so sure your vision isn't clear now. I think the whole idea that your body stood in your way is only an explanation for why we haven't chosen now, but I am not so sure our vision isn't clear—that we are not doing right now the very same things that some of us would do for all eternity if we were given eternity to do it.

Why would it be any different if I said to you, "You will never die; you will live for all eternity?" Would you really be any different or might you, for the rest of all eternity, still choose to be unhappy in order to get something done? It ultimately still comes down to the future us.

"Everything is good" can be a very useful attitude. I say useful, if we understand what we mean by it. Everything that *is*, is good in the sense that nothing is bad, or in the sense that no particular thing is bad (unhappiness-causing).

Option Theology

October 23, 1993

Option Mysticism

In the following, "he" in any form (him, himself, his, etc.) means he and she (and all their forms) when used in reference to humankind. He, in reference to God, does not refer to any limiting sexual role or gender identity. It is a convenient personification. "God" does not mean either male or female. "Man" means each human.

Introduction

Option Mysticism is based on the following fundamental apprehension of the meanings of the terms, and the relationship of God, man, and happiness, without which there could not be fruitful discussion, study, and ultimately, true contemplation. This basic apprehension is not limited to learning from this treatise, and may not, in fact, be grasped here, but of course may be known though a simple knowing, a remarkable personal experience. The ability to see the "face of God" and the fruits of such intimacy are intrinsic to enjoying Option Mystical Pragmatism, or Option Pragmatic Mysticism.

To be able to rest in the breast of The One Who Knows and Loves You—The One Who You Know and Cannot but Love—is the joy of life. To live by letting God live as you is the true self-abandonment of all fear and care, which self-abandonment is the goal of true selfishness and the highest fulfillment of self. To act in any and all your actions enveloped and suffused with the total protection of the Author of All Acts, to be truly invulnerable to any fear of doubt, punishment or mistake is the gift of the Option mystic.

To be a true contemplative or a true mystic, in its fullest meaning, is to be perfectly happy, a lover and the possessor of True Wisdom Itself; not a seeker of perfection or a meditator, as many have believed. To be absolutely happy is to know yourself as only Happy, no matter who or what else others think you are.

About God as God

God creates and causes Himself, the world, and man because of, and for, happiness, which is the same as the Presence of God. In God, creating, knowing, deciding, and choosing are the same. The knowing and deciding the truth of happiness is the sole creative act of God—God deciding to know Himself is the happiest of all choices He could make. It would be His expression and experience of perfect happiness.

This decision to reflect upon Himself is a creative act (in man, it would be called consciousness), and necessarily creates the necessity for an "other," which starts the ball rolling as creation unfolding. Ultimately, this will produce a way for God to know Himself as the Happiness he is for Himself. God knowing Himself would be His primary, and only, goal, and will be His first in primacy creature. This creature for consciousness would be made in the image and likeness of God in that only it could truly encompass, apprehend and appreciate the glory of the essential Happiness of God. He (man) will be created to know this happiness in its fullest. Man will experience it as himself and his own; thoroughly and perfectly. This knowing of happiness creates God in relationship with man, which is the same as "God is happiness for man." Knowing Happiness is the same as knowing God.

That feeling of happiness is the feeling of God. That is what God "feels" like. That is what the real God, the relevant and pertinent God, feels like. An experience which is so congruent with self is what we always mean by knowing something perfectly. Man is the way God knows and feels happiness. Man is the actual (realized) happiness of God.

God is not to be known, nor can He be known, as a distinct being, but is known only and precisely by the name and nature of His role. The term, God, is a description of a relationship, like husband or wife, mother or son; not an unrelated person distinct from the relationship. The name, God, is the name of a profession, like healer or teacher; known by what he does. With God (or Godness, if you will), the relationship is the person and the only thing to know of the person. An example of this understanding may be that whenever Jesus referred to God, he would usually refer to their relationship and call it "Father." Or for the Jews, he would refer to "The Lord," another relationship term they always used, rarely calling on the ineffable "God."

God is only known as what He does: happiness or knower of happiness. What else is done or created is done by that happiness. God really means The Creator of Happiness for Man, The Cause of Happiness for Man, The Purpose of Happiness for Man, The Reality of Happiness for Man, All that is Meant by Happiness for Man.

The name of God is My-Happiness. God is a "person" because "He" has a personal meaning and relationship intrinsic to our very idea of personness.

Happiness is at the same time the Creator of Happiness, the Created Happiness, and the Creating (the effective action of creating) of the creation. All the same God. An analogy would be like the knowledge or decision to heal, which is really the same as the act of healing, which is really the same as having been healed. A *fait accompli.*

God's Happiness . . . . (God's knowledge: the "Father"; as a role)
decides . . . . (creates)
His Happiness . . . . . (knowing God the "Son": HimSelf known)
is man's happiness . . . (man's Knowing God)
by means of Happiness (God's Knowing Action: the Holy Spirit)
in man.

Another way of saying it is that since God knows Himself as man's happiness, so therefore man can only know God as his own happiness or know his happiness as the only God. In fact, all men worship or love their own happiness more than any god. When any love God above all, it is precisely because they believe God to be their greatest happiness.

All you can know of God is His/your happiness, which is your aware response to His and your knowing that you need nothing to be happy. That's all that you do know or can know. You are capable of believing (but not knowing) anything else—even contradictions, like "God allows evil." Since evil means "causes unhappiness against one's will," it is impossible. God allows things which you believe you don't like, but never what can cause unhappiness. To believe God could want someone *to* be unhappy would be the same as believing

God doesn't know what happiness is. And yourself not knowing what happiness is.

Everything that can be said of happiness is exactly said of knowing, or realizing, God. If happiness is praised, so is God. If happiness is feared, or ridiculed or rejected, so is knowing God. The only relevant meaning of God for man is whatever there is about God that is Happiness. And it just so happens that that is all there is about God and all that is known. Any other theology without God as Happiness is irrelevant and flawed in its inception and premise. Any understanding of man is flawed without understanding man's identity as a happy person. Man wants only to be happy and would be happy if he did not believe he wasn't.

God knowing Happiness is the same as realizing Himself; that is, being real and present to himself. Man knowing Happiness is the same as realizing himself, realizing God, and experiencing himself as an act of God, who knows him perfectly.

What God "wants" is perfect for each. To be perfectly known by God means that knowing oneself, who God knows, is realizing your real self. To comprehend God is to experience perfect happiness. To experience God and accept God's perfect happiness is to understand that it is true that there is nothing to fear or be unhappy about, ever. Then, to want what God wants is the same as wanting what you really want. Then, all actions and desires come from God and knowing God and God knowing you.

The knowing and deciding that happiness is imminent (inherently present within) and can only be imminent, is the same as deciding and knowing that God is imminent and can only be imminent.

Say "Yes" to happiness! Always, only say "Yes!" to happiness. Say "Yes" to happiness at all times in all places, and bring all the blessings of happiness forward that will well up within you. Happiness is always present to you. Just say "Yes." A nod will do.

Do not worry. None of these truths needs to be known or understood by anyone who does not know them, but they are the greatest joy for those who do.

Ancient Wisdom

1994

From the ancient wisdom of the book of sayings of the Preacher called Ecclesiastes *(The Assembly)*:

> I know for sure that there is absolutely nothing better for them than being happy
> and making for themselves the best life.
> This includes each and every person:
> Eat and drink, and see how truly good are all your efforts—
> this is a gift from God.
>
> Ecclesiastes 3:12–13
> Translation from the Hebrew by Bruce M. Di Marsico

Option Mysticism

In Option Mysticism, Bruce Di Marsico summarizes the wisdom of the esoteric religious and spiritual traditions of Mysticism.

The summary theological argument of Mysticism:

God wants our perfect happiness.

Any "God" that does not want our perfect happiness could not really be the God we are seeking.

Whatever God wants, is.

Therefore, we must be perfectly happy.

Why, then does it appear that we are not perfectly happy?

God has granted us the freedom to pretend not to know that we are perfectly happy. We are in heaven now, and are aware of that when we stop pretending we are not.

In the following essay, "You" refers to God.

ALL we really want is for You to have everything that You want: our perfect happiness—Yourself in us, perfectly and fully.

If You only knew that we were everything You wanted, we would all know it too. How could You want us to be perfectly happy without Your already knowing that we are? Why does it seem to us that You don't know? We are mistaken.

If You knew there was a rosebush blooming here, we would all know it too. If You knew it was visible, tangible, and aromatic, we would too.

It seems that I want You to know what You don't seem to know. Because we can think it seems to us that we are not yet perfectly happy and it seems to us that we can worry and fear losing happiness, we feel that You are not all we want You to be and we are not all You want us to be. If we knew that You knew we were perfectly happy, we would be.

What more do we need to know in order to never be unhappy? Nothing, it seems. Only to remind ourselves.

What more do we need to know in order to always be happy? Nothing, it seems. Only to remind ourselves.

Whenever we believe that we may be unhappy, we are believing that it is possible that You may be unhappy. If You can be unhappy, then You are not who I want You to be and You are not what I mean by perfect. Since You *are* perfect, why are we not believing *we* are perfect?

When You know something about us, we know it too; we can only pretend not to know. We are how *You* can pretend not to know. We are the pretending part of You. By being in us, and by being us, You can pretend You don't know. If one of us will only stop pretending and will believe that You are really not unhappy, then You will believe we are perfectly all You want us to be, and we will finally believe that You are really what we know You can only be—perfect.

You give us knowing. We give You believing—that is, deciding that we really do know. You decide that You know by my deciding that I know. You can only know what is. I can *decide* that I know what is or what is not. I can only *really* know what is. If I decide I know what is not, then that is what will seem to be. If I decide that I am not yet perfectly happy forever, then that is what it seems. You and I can know that that isn't so, but so what!

Why don't we believe we are in heaven—happy forever? We are not aware of Your knowing any such thing. We "know" that You don't know—until we know You do, and heaven is known again.

God's Prayer to Man

God says,
Happiness says,
Nature says,
Let go. Let me have my way with you. My power is in your heart, your mind and in every cell of you.

All that you do is for happiness. That is why you exist—to have happiness.

I am the cause of your very life, and awareness of me is my goal for you. It is your goal.

You are made of life materials passed on by your parents and the whole chain of parents before them. You have many parents, but I am their parent. It was I who began this whole process, and awareness of me is what it is all for. It all tends toward me. I, Nature, Happiness, God, whatever name you give me, am tending toward greater awareness of me.

With awareness you shall have more and more signs of my presence and power and love. You will have gladness.

In a way, you have been blind to the signs of me, and in a way, you have not been blind to the signs of me. You have been arguing with the awareness of me. You are trying to fight or avoid unhappiness. I have already taken care of that. I am here now. There is no unhappiness. It has been vanquished. It never existed. You have been waiting for awareness of me. Let me give it to you. Let go. Submit, gladly. Let me, your own happiness, fill your life. Let me direct all your movement and thoughts and awareness. Let me have your body. Let me have my way, for your sake. I am your happiness and all that that implies. I am perfect for you. There is nothing better than me for you.

All seeking of other things that you want in order to be happy is missing the point. I am available without your needing or having anything else. I will guide you. In truth, everything you seek and want is what I am prompting you to want, so that there will be more and greater signs of me. I want to manifest myself in you and in the whole world. In fact, I will manifest myself to you in the sky and on the earth and in all that I have caused to exist. I want to be seen for the perfection I am. I am perfect for you and I want you to have great signs of it. I am your own personal happiness, not a theoretical god or concept. I am your happiness. I am who I am. Anyone who thinks I am other than who I am, other than real happiness, is mistaken.

All that *is*, is either a sign of me or a manifestation that I exist, or else it is a sign of unhappiness, which does not exist. There is no devil, no evil, no sin, no wrong, no unhappiness. I am the God of all Creation and Life of Your Life, Heart of your Heart, Desire of your Desires. I am real happiness. Let me have my way. Only say yes. Always say yes. Say yes by letting go. Let go of all your rules other than the law in your heart, which I put there. Your heart cannot deceive you, neither can your mind. You are perfect for me, because of me.

Unhappiness only seemed to exist. The belief that it existed was for you the so-called proof of its existence. In truth, the fact that your hearts hated unhappiness, felt sick with it, was the real proof that it couldn't exist. It couldn't be natural or else you would have loved unhappiness. Since you believed it was natural, you tried to find some value in it. Do you see how much you naturally love nature? You naturally didn't love unhappiness and when you thought that was unnatural of you, you tried to love it. I am so glad for you to see that you never really succeeded. You couldn't ever succeed at that. You just are not made that way. You just can't love unhappiness in you, no matter what. How perfect. In fact, the name you give it, Un-happiness, showed how Un-natural you knew it was. Un-happy means un-wanted.

I direct your desires. You can only desire me. Have you noticed? You wanted everything you wanted, whether it was money or health or beauty or truth, so that when you had it you would not be unhappy. Well, now you don't have to avoid unhappiness. You do not have to protect yourself against it. I am here. I am the only one. There is no other besides me. I am your real happiness. We belong together. Let me serve you. Let me do it for you. That is why I am. I will serve you. That will be your perfect service to me also. That way we can see great signs of my existence, which is for you. I am for you. You are for me. Let me have my way with you. Have your way with me. It is what you really want. Have what you want from me.

Now you are allowed. You are allowed (by me) to trust me and abandon yourself to me. Follow your heart. Let go. Let me have my way. Let yourself have your way from now on.

You know me well. I am in your heart. I am behind the next thing you do or want or think. I am the impulse in your body. I am easy to find. I am what you love most in you. I am the cause of your desires, which are to manifest me. Don't question them or me. I am your happiness. There is no such thing as being hurt by your happiness. In fact, there is no such thing as getting unhappy anymore.

I Am Your God

I AM both immanent and transcendent. I am immediately present in you as your desires. I cause them. I am always with you. I am the life of your heart. I am the yearning behind all desires of your body. I am more than your life; I am the meaning and the cause of your life. I am the impetus that sparks your thoughts and actions. I am the life that your living is from. I am behind your seeking to be satisfied. That is me seeking awareness of myself with you, in you, for you, from you. Together we shall have joyous awareness of me.

I am also most transcendent. I am what is always promised. I am beyond the next moment. I am in the future, as greater awareness of me, more of me: more of me in the senses. That is where we are going. That is our future. Since I am the cause of your desires, awareness of me is the goal of your desires. I am alpha and omega, the cause and the goal, the first and ultimate, the primary and the eventual. I am the goal of your goals. I am the fulfillment of all your desires.

My immanence is cause and desire for my transcendence, my transcendence is greater awareness of me. There are signs of both my immanence and transcendence. Signs of desires and signs of more than you hoped for. Signs of desire for manifestations of me. All you want is to see me in everything, to see me everywhere, to always be aware of me. That is my doing. You will have great gladness whenever you see manifestations and are aware that they are signs of me.

I am the satisfaction you want. I am the justification for everything.

Awareness of me is the most perfect goal for you. It is the most perfect reward for desiring the goal. It is the most perfect reward for achieving the goal. I am the perfect reward to be aware of having. I am what makes you happy. I am what makes you feel lucky or blessed. I am what makes you feel whole, holy and completely yourself.

I am your god. The only god you'll ever want. The only god you ever wanted. I am everything to you. I am your happiness and I am here now. I live. Live with me.

Your awareness of me and all that I do is all that I want. Your awareness of my reality is all that you want. I am everything for us. Your awareness of me is everything for us. Together we make a perfect union, a perfect partnership. Together we are perfectly happy. I am glad that I exist for you and am your happiness. There are no other desires pre-eminent to your desire for me. I am jealous, but I don't have to be, for you could never want anything more than you want what is so perfect; happiness, perfectly.

Contemplation Is Joy

May 1990

On the subject of: Relief of Earthly Ties, Life Free of Care, Detachment and Spirituality:

Contemplation is reflecting on the fact that you really do know that the truth is happiness, and the enjoyment of realizing that what that really means is that you are happy.

A life of contemplation is constantly and habitually remembering that this truth is always true and you are always allowed to be happy and are indeed happy. You can allow all things to remind you of this. The contemplative life is the source of great joys and miracles.

Wisdom is the act of being contemplative and allowing yourself to say, do, or feel, or know whatever follows from that state.

The rewards of a contemplative life are greater than can be imagined. The peace that does all things, greater than love can even foresee and intend, is the natural action of a contemplative. The bliss that is contemplation is your very life.

A happy person is spiritual. Spiritual does not mean love of nonexistents or invisible "entities" (in short, not what is usually meant by God, angels, magical powers, etc.), but the lack of fear of real things, matter of whatever form, lack of need for anything of the world, lack of fear or need of anything of the Universe of "All-that-Is or Will-Be."

A spiritual person does not need anything to be or not be. He or she does not believe that anything should be or should not be. That is a happy person.

COMMENTARIES

by Aryeh Nielsen on

"Option Mysticism"

Option, Mysticism, and Pragmatism

This commentary is based on the editor's understanding of Bruce Di Marsico's teachings.

Mystical Pragmatism

One way that Bruce Di Marsico described Option is as "Mystical Pragmatism." This description can be illuminated by exploring the traditions of Mysticism and Pragmatism. Both of these traditions have many aspects and schools; as discussed here, the focus is only on those aspects that are closely allied with Option.

Mysticism

Mysticism is a mode of experience that has arisen within most cultures and religions. The strain of mystic thought most relevant to Option is Catholic Mysticism, in particular the thread following from St. Thomas Aquinas's Via Negativa (Negative Theology): theology that attempts to describe what *is* by negation, speaking only in terms of what *cannot* be said about the perfect goodness that may be called happiness, reality, existence, or God. St. Thomas Aquinas: "In itself the proposition 'God [happiness] exists' is necessarily true, for in it subject and predicate are the same [i.e., to exist is to be happy]."

Mysticism as a religious practice focuses on the individual experience, as opposed to institutional practices or theoretical knowledge. Some branches of mysticism proclaim that nothing can be said of what the mystic experiences. In the negative theology tradition, terms such as "happiness" and "God" are references to what is fully known beyond illusions, but can never be fully described. There is no knowledge to be gained, only occluding "knowledge" to set aside in order to see the reality of happiness clearly. In this tradition, Option Mysticism focuses on dissolution and deconstruction of beliefs, not on their acquisition. In some schools of the Buddhist tradition, this is summed up as "Wanting enlightenment is a big mistake," meaning that the illusion that you need to become enlightened is, in itself, un-enlightenment.

These are some traditional descriptions of the experience when all apparent "knowledge" of unhappiness is set aside (using "happiness" interchangeably with "God," "reality," "existence," etc.):

* Happiness is perfectly simple.
* Nothing is evil.
* The knowing of happiness is unique to each consciousness.
* What makes Option Mysticism unique is its rigorous lack of providing frameworks of myths and metaphors to describe the indescribable, and an avoidance of prescribed rituals to facilitate the experience of happiness (such as prescribed forms of meditation, prayer, or behavior).

Pragmatism

* Pragmatism is a tradition that first rose to prominence in 19th-century America, developed by, among others, Williams James, who taught that "a belief is a proposition on which a person is prepared to act." Functional Psychology, an outgrowth of pragmatism, developed the idea of Stimulus-Organism-Response, in response to behaviorist models of the human organism as a Stimulus-Response mechanism.
* Some relevant tenets of classical pragmatism are:
* That which is known to be true is what we believe; it is not objective.
* Beliefs are a model of a reality that may exist objectively, but objective reality is not knowable to us except through beliefs. Knowledge is true for us until it is discovered to be false by failing to match our experience.
* We needn't have justifications for what we know.
* Values are hypotheses about what action is useful to an organism.
* It is worth noting that the Mystic and Pragmatic traditions use the word "Knowing" in very different manners. In Mysticism, "Knowing" refers to that which is known natively, *prior* to beliefs, and has no object. "To know" is an intransitive verb

that takes no direct object. In the language of Mystics, happiness is the only thing truly known by anybody, and is known as inherent knowledge.

* In Pragmatism, that which is "Known as True" is that which is known *by virtue of* beliefs held as true: "To know" is a transitive verb that always takes a direct object. In the language of Pragmatists, what is known are facts about the world, which are only ever known provisionally and tentatively.

Option

In summary, Option can be described as a form of Mysticism because of the axiom that happiness is known whenever unhappiness is not "known," and Option can be described as Pragmatism because it takes the "knowledge" of unhappiness as a belief—that is, a predictive basis for action, with no inherent truth value. Together, they reveal that happiness is always known when it is no longer believed that it is necessary to be unhappy.

PART VII
Practicing The Option Method

SECTION I

About Practicing The Option Method

Learning the Practice of The Option Method

October 24, 1992

THE Option Method is the procedure of questioning the belief (or seemingly, beliefs) that is the real cause of all forms of unhappiness. The proper (i.e., effective) application of The Method assumes an understanding of the principles and reasons for The Question (or seemingly, questions).

The implications and the further derived insights of these principles and insights are called the Teachings of Option Method (O.M.).

The integration of the principles, insights, relevance, the basic understanding, the reasons wherefore and, of course, happiness, is called the attitude that determines the behavior of a practitioner or adept. Simply, The Option Method in practice comes from the knowledge which creates the attitude of a happy person.

Even minimal practice of The Option Method cannot be accomplished based on classes, lectures, memorization of principles and the like. Only as an expression of the Option Analyst's own continuous experience of consciously, deliberately wanting to eliminate his unhappiness can there be any meaningful attempt to practice O.M. Only the person who diligently questions his own unhappiness is at all suited to help another.

An unchallenged unhappiness of our own does not prevent the use of The Option Method for another. It is still an opportunity to affirm that we have our reason for believing we must be unhappy, and the other person has his. That there is no objective cause of unhappiness is the great truth of Option. Knowing that another does not have to be unhappy is a great reminder. Yet recognizing our unhappiness, and not realizing that it is possible to eliminate it, is an unhappy attitude that does prevent the correct practice of The Option Method.

The requirements for a successful learning of The Option Method are exactly the same as for a successful life by any standard. Happiness first, not second. No tolerance for any unhappiness as if it were necessary. No fear of anything. To fear unhappiness is the biggest mistake and self-deception. It is denying that all our previous unhappiness was anything but self-chosen. Unhappiness never "happened." So, to fear that it will (as if it did) is simply to reflect that denial.

That fear of unhappiness is exactly what is wrong with the thinking of other people. Unhappiness just never happened. This is the main teaching of Option and upon which all other insights are based. People got unhappy because they believed it was good or useful to future greater happiness and therefore wanted to be unhappy. Unhappy means to fear happiness as bad for future happiness.

How to Do The Option Method

1993

The First Question: "What are you unhappy about?"

Why would you ask this question?

This primary question, of course assumes that the person being asked may be unhappy about something. In practice it is usually only asked of a person who has first specifically complained of feeling bad. It might be considered intrusive if it were not for the fact that the client has come to see you with the understanding that you try to help unhappy people with their unhappiness.

In order to not make unwarranted assumptions, and to start off on the right foot, which is to speak to a person where he/she is right now, you might initially ask, 'Would you tell me in your own words why you are here?" or "How may I help you?"

Alternatively, you might introduce yourself by telling the prospective client what it is that you do. By making it clear that your only function is to deal with his or her unhappiness, it allows the client to decide whether he/she will tell you that he/she is indeed worried, bothered or otherwise unhappy and wants help. After telling him/her what you do, you then might ask, "Is there something you're unhappy about that you would like me to help you with?" or some such.

What are you unhappy about? (*Identify* the complaint.)

This question seems forthright and simple enough, but certain conditions apply to the proper use of it.

1. "Unhappy" means anything that the person might indicate as feeling in a way they don't like. It is merely a model word. Any description that the client uses is usually the best word to use. For example: worried, annoyed, feel bad, bothered, angry, etc.
2. "About" is not as simple as it seems. What a person claims they are unhappy about does not mean they are actually unhappy about it. For example, they may just use another word for a kind of unhappiness: "I feel bad that I get nervous when I meet new

people." Before you go on to the second Option Method question you would clarify this answer. You will now use the word "nervous" as the unhappy word.

What do you mean? (*Clarify* the complaint.)

This question, or a version of it; such as, "What do you mean by 'he is unfair to you?'" This is a way to ascertain more precisely what the person is actually believing he/she is feeling bad about.

What about that are you unhappy about? (*Further Identify.*)

This question can have many forms, some more useful or pertinent than others. One is "What about that are you most bothered (worried, frightened, angry, sad) about?" Another might be "If that were to happen, what would you be most afraid of?" or "If that were to happen, what would be the worst thing about it?"

Your main emphasis is to keep the focus on the unhappiness of the person, not on anecdotes or the history of details that are irrelevant to what he/she is unhappy about.

"Unhappy" means any bad feeling. Use his or her own vocabulary. Vulgarities and Anglo-Saxon are, in fact, desirable when used first by the client.

This process of *further identifying* the unhappiness is, of course, used in conjunction with *further clarifying* when necessary. Whenever you don't understand anything relevant to the person's unhappiness, it is usually an essential part of the Method to ask for clarification. For a simple and honest approach to helping someone, you will rarely ever hesitate or shirk from asking "Could you explain that?" or "Excuse me. Could you tell what you mean by that?"

On the other hand, it is not *further identifying* nor *further clarifying* to be curious or nosy. Never ask for personal or for selfish information. The important reason for this is not especially out of respect for decorum, but most relevantly to not distract from the subject at hand, the important and personal unhappiness of the client.

The Second Question: "Why are you unhappy about that?" (Identify the belief or reason.)

This question really means, "Why do you believe that you have to (must) be unhappy about that?"

This is part of the Method that begins the enlightening, and is really a teaching and revealing of an Option truth about unhappiness. It presupposes that each person has a reason and is not an unwilling recipient of "natural or supernatural" unhappiness. This question is even more personal than the preceding ones. It asks the person to realize that he has his own very personal reason for being unhappy about whatever it is. The question can have many forms. The various ways of asking are meant to approach the most direct way of asking "Since you don't want to be unhappy if it's unnecessary, why do you believe that it is necessary in this case?" For example:

(*Identify*)

"What is your reason for feeling bad about not having a boyfriend?"

"Others will think I'm a loser."

(*Clarify*)

"What do you mean by a loser?"

"Someone with no self-respect."

(*Further Clarify*)

"What do you mean by no self-respect?"

"Someone who doesn't care enough about herself to get and keep a boyfriend."

(*Further Identify*)

"Why would you feel bad if others believed you had no self-respect, which means you don't care enough about yourself to get a boyfriend?"

Why? means "For what reason of yours?" or "For what purpose of yours?" or "Of what is the value or use to you?"

"Because I do care, and don't want to be seen as a loser."

(*Further Clarify*)

"Even though you *don't* want to be seen as a loser, why does that mean you have to be unhappy if they *do* see you that way?"

"Because I am a loser."

(*Clarify*)

"What does loser mean in that case?"

"I'm a loser because they don't like me."

(*Identify*)

"So, are you saying you are unhappy because they don't like you?"

Continue as above.

When you arrive at . . .

"Even though you can't have what you want unless people help you have it or give it to you, why do you have to feel bad when you know you still want it, and don't know how to get it?"

"What?"

Repeat the question. When you arrive at . . .

"I should have it," or "I should know how," or any version of should, must, ought to, etc., or a form of "Anyone would," or "Wouldn't you?" or "Everybody knows that,"

ask the most direct form of the why question, which is,

"Why do you believe that?" or "Yes, maybe I or anyone would be like that and we would have our reasons, but what is your reason?"

The answer is some version of "I must because my happiness depends on it," or "If I don't, I have to be unhappy."

Now ask again.

"Why?" or "Why do you believe that?"

When you arrive at any answer which indicates that the client has no current real reason, such as "I don't know," or "I always have," or "I just assumed it," ask the *third question.*

Unhappy reasons to be questioned:

Should, Must, Need To, Have To, Ought To, It's Natural

Helpful explanations or insights: "Not everyone would be unhappy about that. Why are you?" "Since you believe God wants you to be unhappy in order to really change, why can't you change for God without being unhappy?" "Do you really believe that, or do you just think you should?"

The Third Question: "What would it mean if you were not unhappy about that?"

The purpose of this extraordinary question of The Option Method is to help a person see that he assumed that being unhappy was the only way of caring; really caring. In fact, this question and its answer disclose that people assume and are afraid that they are not on their own side, do not act in their own best interests, and are intrinsically motivated by unhappiness and undeserving of happiness when they find the unhappy evidence which they believe proves they are wrong or bad for themselves. The answers are usually a form of . . .

"It would mean I don't care about myself," or

"It would mean I don't want what I want," or

"I'd be crazy."

This Third (Reverse) Question is meant to reveal what all people are basically afraid of: finding proof of being bad for their own happiness or self-interest.

Respond in some fashion with this summary, ultimate question: "Why would it mean you were bad for yourself or your happiness if you were not unhappy?" or the longer version:

"Since you know that you want what you want, don't want what you don't want, care about what you care about, don't care about what you don't care about, approve of and/or don't approve of what you choose, how or why does anything mean you are the opposite of what you choose and decide about you?"

The Frequent Interjection

"*How do you feel?*"

Throughout the use of The Option Method, it is useful and helpful to both you and the client to frequently reassess the mood of the client. Such questions as "How do you feel now?" or "Are you unhappy about *that* (the discussed unhappiness) at the moment?" will help to keep your questions relevant to the most current feelings of the client. What frequently begins as a questioning of one fear often becomes a reminder of another, more important (to the client's) unhappiness.

When the person seems to be feeling better, double-check. When the unhappiness changes, start with "What?" again.

There is no greater kindness nor a more loving vocation than to question unhappiness!

Helpful Reminders and Affirmations

"How do you feel right now?"

"Of course you want that, but why are you feeling bad . . .?"

"Others have their reasons for feeling bad about that, but what is your reason?"

"Just a reminder! You would like to feel less unhappy, wouldn't you?"

"Do you want to be unhappy about this?"

"Why does that mean you don't want the best for yourself?"

'What's wrong with that?"

"I am really just asking a question. There is no right answer, only yours."

"Why does that mean you are unhappy?"

"If that symptom did not mean to you that you were unhappy, how would you feel about it?"

The Practice of Option

Monday Night Study Group, 1973

TONIGHT I'll say some things about the actual practice and the actual use of the method, step-by-step and in terms of the "do's" and "don'ts" of working with a patient.

The way to help people to be happy in the purest form would be to strictly ask questions while making very few, if any, statements. The reason for that is: you're not going to tell someone *what* they *should* be feeling, or *how* they *should* be feeling, or that they *shouldn't* be feeling the way they are.

So one of the "do's" is: you *do* ask questions about how a person is feeling. And one of the "don'ts" is: you *don't* suggest how they should feel.

Although the question itself *may* suggest how they *could* feel, you *never* suggest how they *should* feel. You never imply that they shouldn't feel bad, and you place no "should's" on them and no "should not's" on them.

You help them to see *what* reasons they have for feeling bad. You are *not* trying to help them to see that they have *no* reason for feeling bad. It's an important difference. To do so is a judgment. To do so is to assert that they shouldn't feel bad. Just that orientation will make a whole difference in your tone of voice, in your perception, in your attitude, in your questions, in their answers, and in their response to you. Even so, they will most likely lay it on themselves anyway that they should not be unhappy, or that they should be happy.

The line of questioning can be formalized, and the actual session in its simplest form would sound something like this:

The person would tell you something. They would tell you anything.

First, you decide whether what they've told you or not is something that they're unhappy about. If not, you ask them what they're unhappy about, approximating whatever language they use.

So with one person you might say, "What's bugging you?" With another person you might say, "What's bothering you?" or, "What is there that you're feeling bad about?" or, "Why are you sad?" And you go with their language.

You pick up on their vocabulary. If they say "I'm bothered by this. I'm bothered by that," their word is "bother," so use that. If they say, "I'm uncomfortable about this," their word is "uncomfortable," and so on.

The reason we don't use other words is twofold. First, they will very frequently have a different meaning for another word, and second, they will think that your use of another word is some kind of a judgment on the word that they were using, and that you perhaps have a reluctance to use the word that they were using. You might very well be reluctant, if you're avoiding their words and using your own.

The model word I'm going to use here is "unhappy," but that's in quotes because that's only the model word. Substitute any other word for that.

So you've asked "What are you unhappy about?" and they've answered. The next question to ask is, "Why are you unhappy about that?"

The second question is also a model question. Some other forms it could take: "For what reason does that bother you?" Or, "What is there about that?" The first few times you ask, they're going to give you a belief, a further explanation of *what* they're unhappy about.

Imagine a situation where a young person says, "I'm really feeling bad." And you ask, "What are you feeling bad about?" or "Why are you feeling bad?" He responds, "Because my parents are so strict." You ask, "Why do you feel bad because your parents are so strict?" He responds, "Because they won't let me stay up to see the late show." He's further explaining *what* particular thing he's unhappy about, not *why*, yet.

You ask, "Why are you unhappy that they won't let you stay up to see the late show? Why do you feel bad about that?" He responds, "Because if I can't stay up and see the late show I feel bad because all my friends are going to be staying up to see it." You ask, "Why would you be unhappy if you didn't get to see the late show, and all your friends got to see it?" He responds, "Because the next day they're all going to be talking about what they saw on that movie and I'm not going to know what to say." You ask, "Why would that make you feel unhappy?" He responds, "Well, because then I feel stupid."

So you started off with him saying, "I'm unhappy because my parents are strict." But what he's really unhappy about, or *why* he's really unhappy that his parents are strict, is because their strictness makes him feel stupid, and you only get to that by asking, "Why?"

"So I'm unhappy that I feel stupid." Now this is a point at which many of you run into a problem. Do you ask the person why they're unhappy if they feel stupid, or why do they feel stupid? The reason there is a question is because you don't know what he means by "stupid."

So you clarify by simply asking, "What do you mean by stupid?" "Stupid" could simply mean "I feel bad." It could mean that, "My friends think that I am ignorant because I can't talk about the late show, and I don't really want to tell them that my parents won't let me stay up, because then they'll think that I'm a baby," or almost anything.

So you have to find out what "stupid" means. And then the session could go in the direction of peer group approval and concern about whether people are going to like him or not, and what that means, or it could go in the direction of his own relationship with his parents, or his relationship with his friends or, in fact, even how he feels about himself.

You may be feeling that he has no reason to feel stupid, but you don't know what he means by "stupid," and so the best thing to do is to find out.

Many words that people will use (they get good at it) are just other words for being unhappy, like "stupid."

"I feel dumb. I feel silly. I feel foolish. I feel stupid." But all these words could also be practical descriptions: "I actually do have difficulty thinking, and I feel like I can't learn anything and I feel like I don't know anything." And the next question might be, "Why do you believe you should know something?" or perhaps "Why would you be unhappy that you don't know?"

So the practical, strictly simple way of using Option is to continuously ask why, or what "why" really stands for—"for what reason." You can ask in any way. You can say, "What is there about it that you're unhappy about?" or "For what reason does that bother you?" or "Why does that bother you?"

Your questions needn't be strict and rigid, but in a sense it's always the same question and that's very formal. And when you ask the question, the person will come up with some answer. So in terms of the "do's" and "don'ts," you *don't* say anything. You only ask *why*.

Sometimes you will find yourself talking in order to clarify: "Well, is *this* what you mean?" or, "Is *that* what you mean?" or, "If I get you right, *this* is what you're saying"; you're trying to sum up and to clarify further. So insofar as there are statements, they may be like: "Is this where it's at? Is this what you're saying and why are you saying that?"

Now the question, "Why do you believe that?" There are very clear times when that is *never* to be used, and there are very clear times when it *is* to be used. You *never* use it when there's a matter of fact involved. If a person believes that taller people die sooner than shorter people, it isn't going to really matter whether that's true or it's not true. What you're concerned with is *why* they'd be unhappy about it if it *were* true.

You'll find that if you get into *why* they'll be unhappy about it, if it *were* true, they may very well come to why they believe that's true. But your position is not to challenge, "Why do you believe that's so?" The question, "Why do you believe?" is "Why do *you* believe you'd have to be *unhappy*? Why do you believe that that is something to be unhappy about?"

You use, "Why do you believe?" not when there's a question of fact, but when there's an emotional contradiction. An emotional contradiction is such things as depressions. You will use, "Why do you believe?" quite a bit perhaps when you're really in a clear case of depression.

For example, a person says, "I blush because I'm afraid of these people." You ask them, "Why are you afraid?" and they keep saying they don't know. The question that's called for is, "Why do you believe that you blush because you're afraid? Why did you make that deduction that the reason you blush is because you're afraid, when you say you don't know why you're afraid?"

The patient who says, "I don't know. I don't know. I don't know." may seem to have the perfect system to beat you at your game. That's not so. Because when the patient says to me, "I don't know why I'm unhappy about that," I ask them, "Why, then, do you believe you are unhappy?"

They may say, "Because I feel unhappy." I ask, "And why do you feel unhappy?" They say, "I don't know." I ask, "Then how do you know that what you're feeling is unhappy?" So that's why we use the question, "Why do you believe?" or "How do you know?" or "What makes you think?" These questions are used only when you have a contradiction.

When are contradictions an option? A contradiction is a person saying, "I'm unhappy," which means, "I have a reason to be unhappy," and then saying, "But I don't have a reason to be." So that anything in the form of: "I'm unhappy, but I don't know my reason," is a very clear contradiction. You question the belief of why they believe that that contradiction is even possible.

You'll find the person is going to have to say something like, "What I'm unhappy about is I'm afraid I'm going to be unhappy" or that, "I'm afraid I'm unhappy."

And so we find that the person who says, "I don't know" all the time is depressed. That's why they say, "I'm unhappy and I don't know why." It's because they're *afraid* that they are unhappy, and they look for every reason in the book, and they quickly sort through them all in their heads, and they know that none of them are really reasons.

They don't trust any of those answers. They have 50 things to choose from, 50 reasons, but they know that's not what is really bothering them. What's really bothering them is that they're afraid they're going to be unhappy.

Again, the "do's" and "don'ts." You *do* ask a person why they believe what they believe, when they are involved in an emotional contradiction. You *don't* ask a person why they believe what they believe when they're involved with a disputed fact, something that you think you disagree with.

By observing that guideline, I have found out some very amazing things from my patients. When I didn't challenge or question why a person believes such-and-such a thing, we really got into some real things about why they were feeling the way they were, that showed me that what I had believed was a fact wasn't indeed a fact.

You can let them tell you more about where they're at: "Why do you believe that when such-and-such a thing happens to you, another thing can happen? How could that be?" Sometimes this can be heard as a challenge, as if you asked "Why do you believe you're breathing?" Frequently the kind of answer you'll get is, "Why are you asking me that?" And you'll find that you won't have a good reason for asking that. If they believe that Paris is the capital of Russia, who cares? You want to know why they are *unhappy*.

A lot of people have dire predictions, and if their predictions are from unhappiness, you'll be dealing with the unhappiness; and if their predictions are just because they're in the know and you're not, that's your problem, not theirs.

To reiterate, some of the basic questions are, "Why?" or "For what reason?" and then you clarify, "Do you mean this or do you mean that?" and from time-to-time, "Why do you believe that?"

By and large, when they're just talking about how they feel such-and-such a way, they will respond with, "Because. . ." When you get a contradiction, you ask them why they believe that contradiction is possible. How do they know this? You'll find that they may answer that they're deducing it by certain signs, or they may tell you how they know. If they tell you how they know, then you have something to ask them.

Here are some examples of emotional contradictions: "I feel such-and-such and I don't know why," "Other people make me unhappy," "If it was okay for me not to have it, then I wouldn't want it." You ask, "Why do you believe that?"

An easy guideline to follow could be, when it would seem absurd to ask, "Why would you be unhappy about that?" then you ask, "Why do you believe that?"

There's another question that becomes very important. When you've traced down the beliefs, and the person says, "I'm unhappy for this reason, that reason, the other reason," and you ask, "Well, why would you be unhappy if that happened?" and they say, "I don't know," what they are really saying is "I can't think of a reason but I still would be unhappy, I don't know why." The question that you ask at that point is, "Well, what are you afraid would happen if you weren't unhappy?" because the unhappiness has got its own reason, which is *motivation*.

When there is no other reason for being unhappy (and there is always a point at which there's no other reason to be unhappy), and you've gone through every reason they could have to be unhappy and then there *finally* is no other reason for being unhappy, the reason for being unhappy then is a motivation. "Because if I wasn't unhappy I wouldn't get what I wanted." "I wouldn't want it." "I wouldn't care." Care becomes a very frequently used word at that point. It would mean, if I wasn't unhappy, it would mean I didn't care about my happiness.

"Why do you believe that if you didn't need it anymore you wouldn't want it?" is basically a way of saying, "Why do you believe if it didn't make you unhappy not to have it, you still couldn't want it?"

They start with, "I'm unhappy with my spouse. She's always —" and you work all the way down to, "If I wasn't unhappy with her that would be the same as saying I didn't want her to be happy, I didn't want her to change. I didn't want her to be happier."

I might ask, "Why do you believe that if you weren't unhappy with the way she was that it would mean that you didn't want her to be different with all your heart?" And then you get into the question of how we use depression as a way of motivating ourselves. "Why would you believe that you wouldn't want what you wanted if you no longer feared not having it?"

When someone says, "Because of who I am, people get unhappy with me. I make so-and-so unhappy. I make this one unhappy," a question I ask at that time is, "Do they have to be unhappy with you?" Which is the same question as, "Why do you believe that they would have to be unhappy with you?" That flips it back to them and they would tell you why they believe they would have to be unhappy with somebody like them. So when people are talking about making other people unhappy, they often feel bad because they believe that *they* made somebody *else* unhappy.

If I really believe I've made someone unhappy, I have to feel bad because I am believing that they have reasons to be unhappy with what I've done, and that there *are* reasons to be unhappy.

If I believe that there are reasons to be unhappy with something, I'm unhappy about it. So the question I often would ask deals with the emotional contradiction that I could make someone unhappy. That basic myth (if you want to call it that rather than "an emotional contradiction") is, "Why do you believe that they would have to be unhappy if you did that?"

I ask such things as, "Why would anyone have to be unhappy with you? Would anyone *have* to be unhappy with you?" Most everyone I've ever asked has said, "No, no one *has* to be unhappy with me." That's why I say things, like, "If people loved you, would they be unhappy with you if you did something like that? If someone loved you couldn't they understand? Would they *have* to be unhappy?"

Almost invariably, people I've asked have said, "No, of course not." If I ask "Why would they be unhappy about that quality in you?" the answer very frequently is, "Because *I* would be" and then I ask, "Why would you be unhappy about that quality in yourself?" That's a "Why do you believe that?" question.

More sophisticated people might say "No, of course they wouldn't have to be unhappy, but I know their beliefs and I know they believe they have to be unhappy, and I know if I do it, they *will* be." I then might use a question like, "Why are other people not allowed to do what they have to do?" Which brings up the question, "Why are *you* not allowed to do what *you* have to do?"

"Why aren't people allowed to be unhappy if they have to be? Why aren't I allowed to be unhappy?" When we're very unhappy or if we're unhappy about other people being unhappy, what it boils down to is, "I'm not allowed to be unhappy," so it's a depression, again.

If you're unhappy about someone else's being unhappy, it's just simply because you're not allowed to be unhappy. How else could you ever be unhappy about someone else's being unhappy?

For the patient who comes into your office, though, the very first question you're going to ask them is *not*, "Why do you believe you ever have to be unhappy about anything?" because they will hear "Why the hell do you believe you have to be unhappy?" In a particular *situation* you say, "Okay, what is there about what that person does that makes you unhappy?" They'll get to, "Okay, I don't really have to be unhappy about it." In time, you will ask, "Why do you believe you have to be unhappy?" And that's basically the whole Option Method!

Misapplied to ourselves, we ask, "Why would I have to be unhappy? What is there *ever* that I would have to be unhappy about?" and each of us answers to ourselves, "Nothing. There's nothing that we ever *have* to be unhappy about." And then we deduce that we must *like* being unhappy, which becomes depression. Once you've deduced, "Oh, there's nothing I have to be unhappy about, but I must like it," you're depressed instantly. How could you believe you *like* being unhappy, and be happy?

"There's something wrong with me because I have a tendency towards something I don't like. I tend to do something that I really don't enjoy." (In fact, "don't enjoy" means "unhappy.") "I'm wanting to feel a way I don't want to feel."

The only reason a person has a fear is that they'd be more afraid *not* to have that fear. So the greatest of all fears is the fear of not fearing. We have both a tremendous desire to stop fearing, and at the same time a great fear of not fearing; and so when we ask a person, "What are you afraid would happen if you weren't afraid?" you'll get their answer, whatever it will be, and it usually takes the form, "I'd be more afraid that . . ."

For example:

Practitioner: *What are you afraid would happen if you stopped feeling bad about that? If that was okay?*

Client: *Oh, that'd be tremendous if I stopped feeling bad.*

Practitioner: *You would* really *feel good if such-and-such a thing happened?*

Client: *Oh, no.*

Practitioner: *Okay, well, what are you afraid would happen if you didn't feel bad?*

More specifically:

Practitioner: *Why would you feel bad if your wife is unhappy with you?*

Client: *I don't know.*

Practitioner: *Well, what are you afraid would happen if you didn't feel bad every time she got unhappy?*

Client: *That'd be great. That'd be fantastic. Our marriage would be better, everything would be better.*

Practitioner: *You mean it would* really *be okay with you if she got unhappy?*

Client: *Oh, well, no, it wouldn't.*

Practitioner: *Okay, why? What are you afraid would happen if it was okay with you?*

Client: *But then I'd have no problem.*

Practitioner: *If you really believed you have no problem you would be choosing that. You'd want to feel that way. So why wouldn't you want to feel that way?*

Sometimes I use "What would be the disadvantage to you of thinking it is okay?" Or, "What would be the threat to you to think it is okay? And if there was something to be unhappy about, what would it be, if you felt it was okay for your wife to be unhappy and not to change?"

And you keep going until they come up with something. Usually what they come up with is, "Well, if it was okay it would mean I didn't care. It would mean I didn't want it to be better."

It's the first time in their life that they've ever heard that question. We feel that all the questions in the world have been asked, but this is the very first time in our lives that such questions have been asked.

And so I have patients who frequently say, "I don't know" and then answer me. Their initial response is always, "I don't know." Yes, *of course* they don't know. Up until then they've never been asked such a question. Then they think about it and they answer. And if you're using these questions, you're asking questions of people that have never been asked of them before—ever.

And so such questions are what they call "mind-blowers." A mind-blowing question is just simply a question that's never been asked, that is being asked seriously now.

SECTION II

The Option Method Questions

Introduction to the Questions

November 11, 1995

So what we start with is a person who says, "I feel bad and I don't think it's physical." Here's what I say: "Insofar as it's not physical I might be able to help you to not feel as bad, if that's what you want. What are you feeling bad about?" And that's the beginning question of The Option Method.

Then the person says whatever they say. There's no right answer. There's no wrong answer; or every answer is the right answer. It's whatever they say. Then they tell me what it is that they're unhappy about. I ask them, "Just go a little more into that." In other words I'm still asking, "What are you unhappy about?"

I say to them, "What about that are you unhappy about?" Or I say, "Well, what's the worst about that that you're imagining?" or "What's the worst you're afraid is going to happen? Why are you unhappy about it, basically? What do you believe? What do you have?" And at some point people usually respond to what they're unhappy about and they tell me.

Then I go a little bit deeper and ask them, "What about that are you afraid of?" At some point I ask them, "What about that are you afraid of?" or "What about that would you be unhappy about? Are you unhappy about it? Would you be unhappy about it if it happened?"

"I'm afraid my wife will leave me," or "I'm afraid my children will go to jail."

"What about that are you afraid of?" They stop, because they didn't think that they were going to have anything to do with this. They are the same people who believe that there's somebody out there who's going to make them happy or make them not unhappy, supply them with what they need to be happy or give them the perfect advice on what they need to do to not be unhappy.

Give them an insight, like they've always received. Show them in some way that this isn't something to be unhappy about because it doesn't exist. "You're just mistaken. They're not coming to take your house away from you. They're just going to fine you $300."

"Oh, I feel better."

That's the kind of answers they're looking for. "No, you're not totally crazy. You're just a little worried sometimes."

"Oh, thank you for saying that."

But I have no problem saying that. Nobody who finds their way to me is totally crazy and anybody who wants to not be unhappy can be totally crazy—simple as that.

"Why would I be unhappy about that? Wouldn't *you* be?" Ah, first belief—they believe that their unhappiness is universal; that anyone and everybody and anybody with good sense, anybody with an honest heart, anybody with any love in them or any compassion, anybody with any brains, etc., etc., whatever model they're fitting me into would certainly be unhappy about that.

And in line with The Option Method—which is what? That each person believes what they believe and that causes their feelings, right? The cause of their feelings comes from what they believe.—I would say to them, "Well, I would have my reasons for being unhappy about it if I was, and you have yours. What are yours?"

I don't deny or accept that I would get unhappy about it. I reaffirm the truth that I'm operating from, which is that if I was unhappy about it, I would have my reasons. What's your reason?

Then it comes down to, "Gee, I don't know. Isn't everybody?" Or "I just always was." Fine, good; that's your answer. Remember, that's your answer. There's no problem. That's it. That's the cause of the emotion. You feel bad about it because you believe that everybody does. Okay. Well, everybody who does has their own reason. I lied again because there's a good chance their own reason is the same as this.

But nonetheless, if they are unhappy they do have their own reason. They have their reason. Do you believe it for the same reason they do? How do you know? Well, they have a reason for believing that this is something to be unhappy about.

"If you don't have a reason for believing it's something to be unhappy about then let me ask you, do you right now honestly believe that it's something to be unhappy about?" Universally they say no—universally! I've never had a person not say, "No, I'm not unhappy about it now." But—okay, we'll get into that—but they quickly want to remind me that they're merely human, they didn't just become saints, and I mustn't have too high expectations of them. I accept that. See you next week.

We go on from that. Okay. "Right, I don't have any real reason to be unhappy about it. I don't see any real reason to be unhappy about it. Then how come I don't give it up? Why don't I just stop being unhappy about it?" That's easy.

"What are you afraid will happen?" This is the third question in Option. "What are you afraid will happen if you stop being unhappy about it?" And whatever their answer is to that is really their reason for being unhappy about it.

So although they've never spelled out their reason in English and verbally before, they still have a rationale. It isn't just mere mythology, not usually for the things that are most crucial to them, for the most terrifying complaints that they come with, not for the things that are really ruining their lives. That's usually not just based on an awareness of theirs that they're just believing a myth of some sort and here's their answer. They are believing a myth, but they didn't realize it until now.

"Well, if I wasn't unhappy it would mean . . ." and then here are the answers, whatever they are. "It would mean I don't care. It would mean my life has all been a lie," etc. I don't have to add them in. There are various things, but they all amount to pretty much the same thing. "I don't have any real reason for believing in this unhappiness anymore, but if I stop I'm afraid I'll be in trouble. I'm afraid it'll mean things that I don't mean."

And the ultimate answer that we get down to after the "I don't knows, I don't knows," is that by using The Option Method a person winds up usually saying, "I don't know why I get unhappy about it, but the only reason I can think of for what I'd be afraid of if I was not happy about it is that I'd wind up somehow denying that there really is something to be unhappy about even though I don't know what it is." Why? "Because I've always believed it." Now we go back.

Because yes, but that's what you've always believed. It is something to be unhappy about even though you didn't know what it was. You see, that's what we found out ten minutes ago. They think they came to a big realization right now, but they didn't.

They just went around and expressed it in terms that they can hear.

I heard them before. Do you understand me? That they were saying that they believe they have to be unhappy just merely because they're afraid not to believe that they have to be unhappy because everyone else believes that this is something to be unhappy about and they're afraid that if they're happy they're just pretending to not be unhappy.

So now, what do you do with somebody who's afraid that they're just pretending that they're not unhappy? You give them their money back? Well, seriously. You tell them to go out and have a good meal?

Or if you want to go on with this, there's a couple of ways to go, but they have now just realized at least that they personally don't have a reason for being unhappy, and that's very important—that they don't have a rationale, they don't have a belief, they don't have a fact, they don't have a premise.

They're just supporting—let's say—this unhappiness about losing their wife with their general belief that if they weren't unhappy about losing their wife, they'd still be unhappy about losing their wife, but not admitting it—whatever that means.

Now we're into some kind of philosophy stuff. We're not into human beings' feeling anymore. It's like, "Where have you been before here?" And they've been somewhere. Oh, believe me. I don't have to ask that question. They've been somewhere else to come up with that defense for their unhappiness.

Freud said that people will defend to the death their neurosis and psychosis and that they set up all kinds of defense mechanisms. You've heard the term. It's totally misused by the public, but they will set up defense mechanisms which are natural—unconscious because they're so natural—mechanisms, meaning dynamics.

The modern term is dynamics for making their beliefs understandable—which means, translates into human feelings.

If you can't follow it, okay. I can't repeat it. That's the best I could do for one shot. Basically I'm saying that they've tried to show you that they can paint themselves in a corner, and I'm saying yes, they can. That's all.

But now I'm willing to go a little further, but not necessarily forever. I'll ask them why they believe that if they were happy, it would mean something they didn't want it to mean. Why would it mean that they're against what they're for or that they're for what they're against? Why and how could it ever mean that?

You understand it because that's what they were saying.

You're looking at me questioningly, but actually that's what they were saying. See, what they were saying is, "If I stop being unhappy I can't believe myself."

But who are you going to believe? All right, dial up somebody every morning and you do it that way.

"What do you mean?"

Do you see?

You're believing yourself when you're unhappy because you're believing that what it's based on is based on something. See, the reason when you're unhappy is you're believing that that unhappiness you're feeling is based on something.

Now that you know it's not based on something, you're telling me you're more glad to do that than to have a happiness that denies an unhappiness that's not based on anything. And this is getting too heavy.

I've had all the philosophy I need. Thank you. But I bear with it and I try to just follow along. Option is not about imposing any logic on anybody. I follow what is going on. That's all.

Dialogue Model

Client: *I feel bad.*

Practitioner: *What are you feeling bad about?*

Client: (Tells practitioner what it is that they're unhappy about.)

Practitioner: *What about that are you unhappy about?*

What's the worst about that that you're imagining?

What's the worst you're afraid is going to happen?

What about that would you be unhappy about?

What would you be unhappy about if it happened?

Client: (Expresses belief that their unhappiness is universal.)

Practitioner: *I would have my reasons for being unhappy about it if I was, and you have yours. What are yours?*

Client: *I don't know. Isn't everybody? I just always was.*

Practitioner: *If you don't have a reason for believing it's something to be unhappy about, do you, right now, honestly believe that it's something to be unhappy about?*

Client: *I don't have any real reason to be unhappy about it. How come I don't give it up? Why don't I just stop being unhappy about it?*

Practitioner: *What are you afraid will happen?*

Client: *Well, if I wasn't unhappy it would mean . . .*

I don't care.

My life has all been a lie.

I don't have any real reason for believing in this unhappiness anymore, but if I stop I'm afraid I'll be in trouble.

Things that I don't mean.

I'd wind up somehow denying that there really is something to be unhappy about, even though I don't know what it is, because I've always believed it.

Practitioner: *Why do you believe that if you were happy that it would mean something that you didn't want it to mean?*

Why would it mean that you're against what you're for, or that you're for what you're against?

Client: *My unhappiness is insurmountable and infallible.*

My unhappiness will always be there, it's invulnerable and can't be beat.

You want me to be happier than I want to be.

You want me to be happier, and I don't want to be.

Practitioner: *Why are you here and what are you here for?*

Client: (Is relieved—was afraid that practitioner was going to start helping them *more*.)

Variants of the Option Questions

Unspecified pronouns such as "it" and "that" are model words for an event. In practice, substitute a summary of the client's actual description of the event, using their own language.

General emotional words such as "unhappy," "feeling bad," "feeling good," "sad," etc. are model words for the client's specific emotional feelings. In practice, substitute a summary of the client's actual description of their feelings, using their own language.

Questions to clarify ambiguous language

"What do you mean by that?"

Questions to initiate a session ("First Question")

"What are you unhappy about?"
"How can I help you?"
"What are you feeling bad about?"
"Why are you feeling bad?"
"Well, what's bugging you?"
"Well, what's bothering you?"
"Well, what is there that you're feeling bad about?"
"Why are you sad?"

Questions to clarify specifically what the client is unhappy about ("Second Question")

"What about that makes you unhappy?"
"Well, what is there about that that you're unhappy about?"

Questions to explore reasons for unhappiness ("Third Question")

"Why are you unhappy about that?"
"Well, for what reason does that bother you?"
"What is there about that?"
"For what reason? Why are you unhappy?"

"For what reason does that bother you?"
"Why does that bother you?"
"Well, why would you be unhappy if that happened?"

Variants of third question in response to "I don't know"
"Why do you believe you'd have to be unhappy?"
"Why do you believe that that is something to be unhappy about?"

Questions to explore the causes of the unhappiness ("Fourth Question")
"What are you afraid it would mean, if you weren't unhappy about that?"
"What are you afraid would happen, if you weren't unhappy about that?"
"What are you afraid would happen if you stopped feeling bad about that?"
"What are you afraid would happen if that was okay?"
"What would be the disadvantage to you of thinking it's okay?"
"What would be the threat to you to think it's okay?"

Variants of fourth question when the presumed cause is other people's behavior
"Why are other people not allowed to do what they have to do?"
"Why aren't people allowed to be unhappy if they have to be?"
"Would anyone have to be unhappy with you?"

Exploring releasing unhappiness ("Fifth Question")
"Why do you believe that?"
"Why do you believe that if you didn't need it anymore you wouldn't want it?"
"Why do you believe that if you weren't unhappy with the way it was, it would mean that you didn't want it different with all your heart?"
"Why would you believe that you wouldn't want what you wanted, when you no longer feared not having it?"

Questions to test whether the client has truly released unhappiness:
"So you would really be okay with that happening?"
"You would really feel good if such-and-such a thing happened?"

The Goal of the Guide

September 10, 1973

THE goal of the guide is to help the clients discover why they are not allowing themselves to be happy and okay in certain circumstances. What will be uncovered is some fear that amounts to "If I am not unhappy, then I will have more to fear (or be unhappy about)." It usually expresses itself as "If I don't feel bad about not having what I want, then I may not want it enough to be motivated to try to get it." This is fearful because "I want to be happier, and I can't be unless I have what is more good (better)."

This can be seen by them as an antidote to unhappiness, for the unhappy: "Unless I feel some lack or deprivation here, I won't be motivated toward anything there."

The ultimate fear is "If I know that I will be happier always under any circumstances, how will I decide what to do? How can I answer the questions 'Okay, what shall I do next? What would I like to do?'"

In other words, "Once the big question is answered, my happiness is assured, my great goal in life is provided for and there is no longer a question of my happiness. What do I do now?"

I answer, Wait! watch! enjoy what happens in you and around you! Enjoy what you do. If you find that you make up reasons for doing things, enjoy that. You don't have to fool yourself anymore that those so-called reasons are anything more than made up.

If you find yourself making plans for the future, enjoy that game. You don't have to pretend that you have a reason that has to do with happiness.

If you do make a belief (make believe) that your behavior is in order to make you happier, you don't have to pretend that you aren't believing that, but you could know that the made belief is only a made-up belief and you could reaffirm your knowledge that the question has been settled once and for all.

Now that you know this, you can help others. The questions you ask them could be designed to help them experience this.

What are you unhappy about?

Why are you unhappy about that?

Why are you choosing to be unhappy about that?

Why do you not want to stop being unhappy about that?

What are you afraid it would mean to you if you weren't unhappy about that?

Why do you believe you wouldn't have motivation without that fear?

If you did not want what you now want, how could you be unhappy, then?

The guide can determine if the response is a circular one or not, e.g., "It bothers me because I don't like it." You could ask "Why do you dislike it?" not "Why does it make you unhappy because you dislike it?" That is like saying "Why does it make you unhappy, when you make yourself unhappy?" The Method principle: "If we see that a fear is unnecessary, we will give it up automatically."

An exercise that vocalizes the belief or knowledge that "I am happy. I am not unhappy and will be happier" will bring up objections from our fears. If we continue to expose each fear with some verbalization when it happens, such as "That is a lie, a myth, a false belief, a mistake, not true, un-real, bullshit, merely an unnecessary caution, excess protection, unnecessary protest," then each objection has the opportunity to be rebutted. If we simply refuse to give them credibility (believableness), they cannot survive. Their only life is in our acting as if they were true or possibly helpful.

As each objection is refuted, it is refuted because I know that "I really am happy and I really will be happier."

I am not refuting that I believe I have reasons to be unhappy. I am not denying that there are many things I believe I have to be unhappy about. I am denying that I *need* to believe that. I am not denying that I believe I am lacking, as a reason to move to what I believe will fill the lack. I deny that I *need* to believe that in order to move or be happier.

Exploring "I Don't Know"

Monday Night Study Group, 1973

There's no mystery about feeling bad. It's impossible to feel bad without knowing why.

Option is the only method that doesn't take "I don't know" as an answer. And everybody else will kind of go for that and accept that.

When people say, "I don't know," there are a couple of responses I might use. "Why don't you know? What are you afraid of knowing?" Or, "What would you be afraid of if you knew?" I have a patient who consistently says, "I don't know." I sit. I count to three. And he tells me.

My technique is first, silence. Then I keep repeating the question. If they're really stuck on it, I ask the opposite. What would they be afraid of if a certain thing happens? Because then "I don't know" comes to, "Why do you believe that that's bad or why would you be unhappy about that?" "What are you afraid would happen if you weren't unhappy about it?" That's another way to get through an "I don't know."

Other approaches: "What if you did know? What would it be?" That, surprisingly, works. Or "What are you most afraid of it being? What are you most afraid of the reason being? What would you be afraid of if you knew?" The compulsive might respond, "If I knew I'd have to give it up." I ask them, "Why do you believe you'd have to give it up if you knew?" "Why would you believe you would give up a behavior that you felt was protecting you while you still believed it was necessary to have?" Each thing that comes up, you work with it. And it's just another thing to be unhappy about, and so you deal with that. You have the person who says "I don't know why I'd be unhappy. I just don't feel right." And what they're constantly afraid of doing is making a decision, even about what it is that makes them unhappy. They're constantly afraid of being wrong.

"Why are you afraid of telling me the wrong reason?" you say. They respond, "If I gave the wrong reason I won't get help." You could respond, "What are you afraid would happen if you didn't get help?"

I might respond, "If for some reason or another I'm not able to help you, why do you believe *you* can't help you? Why do you believe you *need* help?" Then we're off again. Because there are many patients where it really becomes very clear that the place you start is "Why are you here and why do you believe you need help? And what if you don't get what you're looking for?"

There Are No Option Statements

Monday Night Study Group, 1973

THERE should be no Option statements, period. I ask questions that imply absolutely no statements.

Can you see what the tremendous natural resistance to any kind of an Option statement would be or an Option "message" would be? Can you see why it would bring out the greatest insanity and fears of people, if anything you say during your session even implies that they needn't be unhappy without something, if it even implies that you shouldn't be unhappy?

There can be no Option statements, except to people who have already worked with that feeling and are not afraid of that, who are not afraid of seeing that they do want and they do choose to be unhappy, that they are choosing unhappiness somehow, who are understanding somehow that their choices are mistakes, nonetheless, made in good faith somewhere. Because what a person is most afraid of hearing is that somehow they're not acting in their own best interest or they're not acting with good intentions. That would be on one of those lists of "this is what is wrong with me."

What is wrong with me is that I screw myself all the time, that's what's wrong with me. That I want things that are bad for me.

SECTION III

Applying The Option Method

I Am Not the Cause

August 5, 1973

If you decided that you had to be unhappy,
Then you were unhappy freely and for your own sake.
If you decided to seek me out,
Then you sought me freely and for your own sake.
If you decided to ask me for my help,
Then you asked my help freely and for your own sake.
If you decided to try to motivate me to help you,
Then you tried to motivate me freely and for your own sake.
If you decided to meet my conditions and fees,
Then you met my conditions and fees freely and for your own sake.
If you decided to let me try to help you,
Then you let me try to help you freely and for your own sake.
If you decided to listen to my questions,
Then you listened to my questions freely and for your own sake.
If you decided to answer,
Then you answered freely and for your own sake.
If you decided to disclose your beliefs,
Then you disclosed your beliefs freely and for your own sake.
If you decided to discard a belief,
Then you discarded it freely and for your own sake.
If you decided to choose to be happier,
Then you chose to be happier freely and for your own sake.

You did this all for yourself. It was *all* your choice for your sake, not mine. I don't make you choose anything.

The Best Way to Help

THE guide does his best guiding when he knows he is totally non-responsible. It is only possible to be really involved with helping another not to need help to be happier by not "laying trips on" or "accepting a trip laid on you by" the other.

If you have no "axe to grind," no need for the other to believe this or that, no need to change them, no *need* for them to be happier, then you will help best. If you need them for anything during the session then you are subject to "blackmail" by them. You are subject to agreeing that they are not responsible for their bad feelings.

It may seem cold and unloving if you look at it with fear, but it is most loving and freeing for you to be totally unintimidated.

You owe nothing to your clients. You are there for your sake. You do not have to be. They are there for their sakes; they do not have to be.

You are not helping them because they need your help. You do it for yourself. They seek help for themselves.

You owe no alibis for what you do in the session, or for what you don't do. They may come or not as they wish.

In my business I find that some clients demand certain things as their rights. They have no rights over me anymore than I have over them. I do what I wish, they as they wish. Some think that they are buying or hiring me according to some traditional or mythical rules. They are not. They pay me to do my thing. They are free to not do that.

They are not paying for fifty minutes.

They are not paying for me to wear a tie, or not to smoke, or smile, or not smile, or feign sympathy, etc.

I do what I want. I conduct my business and sessions however I want. They are free to do their own thing.

I will appear eccentric to some, selfish to others, or "messed-up." I can charge one dollar or one hundred and I can use whatever criteria

I wish; be it five dollars for every letter in their name, or double on rainy days. I can show up for sessions or not. I can make them wait for five minutes or five hours. I can tell clients to go away or ask them to stay. They are always free to decide what they are willing to do for my services, just as I will decide what I am willing to do in order to be of service.

The more you are in touch with this true freedom to be, the more you will be able to help others.

The Client Is the Expert

November 11, 1995

Not everything you call unhappiness is unhappiness. And not everything you call happiness is happiness. And not everything that you say isn't unhappiness, isn't unhappiness. In other words, diagnosis is not a human being's strong point, especially self-diagnosis and self-analysis. Usually, that's the problem. You're analyzing and diagnosing, and giving connotations to that.

Take something that you have heard is happiness, like say, uncontrollable laughter. No one faults uncontrollable laughter. Well, there are times when that's a symptom of a very frightened person. And they're not happy, although, they don't mind being counted among the happy. There are lots of symptoms that are controversial and up for dispute and that people think is a matter of opinion.

Ultimately, there is only one opinion that really matters. If, in other words, an unhappy person is trying to tell you that they're not unhappy, and you clearly see it as something you would call unhappy, the consensus is: you leave them with their own judgment, with their own opinion. And your opinion? Too bad. Because you're not here, if you're going to try to help somebody with The Option Method, to tell them that what they're feeling is something that could be fixed.

It could be something that they're proud of. For instance, they're really feeling mournful, they're sorrowful over the death of a loved one. You happen to meet them the day that's happening. They don't necessarily want to be tampered with and so an Option Method practitioner would always respect that. We do not tell people when they're unhappy. First of all, it's too presumptuous. You just simply don't know them that well. If you've been doing it for a long, long time and you have some kind of psychic abilities, you might be able to make an honest guess. But, in either case, it's none of your business.

So that even if you could sense it and you could feel it and you guessed that they're feeling a lump in their throat right now and they're feeling tightness in their stomach . . . so you're very sensitive. Shut up. That doesn't help people.

You see, all the other kinds of ways of telling people where they're at, and where they could be at, doesn't help people. Never did. In all of the accepted forms of therapy there's the one-third, one-third, one-third proposition. All people who go for help: one-third get worse, one-third get better and one-third stay the same. And all psychology students are taught that in early years.

You don't learn it in psych 101 but you certainly learn it in personality theory or in abnormal psychology. And those are statistics that are drawn from every mental hospital in the country and every private practice that subscribes to certain organizations and is a member. Are talk therapies better than behavioral therapies? One-third, one-third, one-third. Is medicine better than the talking therapies? One-third, one-third, one-third. And it just keeps coming out that way. Could there be some beliefs involved? I don't know. I wouldn't say.

So unhappiness is a very subjective thing. It often means something that someone no longer wants to feel and doesn't want to feel any longer. It doesn't mean a bad feeling that they feel proud of or a bad feeling that they have always respected in themselves. What we do in The Option Method is we help somebody with the unhappiness that they, themselves, right now want to deal with. Just that and that alone. No matter how small—you may think that it's not important. I don't care if they're sitting there chewing off their toes. We help somebody with the unhappiness that *they* want to deal with.

All we're helping them deal with is what they say makes them unhappy. And if they are not ready to work with it, then it's none of our business. You know why they're not ready to work with it? Because they're not; because for them there's nothing to work with. Now as they stop being unhappy about something, they may notice the other unhappiness that you noticed. And it may even just simply go away the moment they notice it. Or they may look at it and say, "Oh, gee. I've been unhappy about that." And with a flick of the eye it's gone. They no longer are unhappy.

No one needs ever point out to anybody what they're unhappy about. Because what you're pointing out is not worth pointing out. If the person, themselves, doesn't identify it as unhappiness, that they hope they could feel less unhappy about, then there's no need to deal with it. But I would think that people—once they start to know how they can use The Option Method and what an Option Method session is—every time that they think that they're unhappy, they think, "That's something I'll bring up in my session." And that's something that they'll want to stop being as unhappy about or less unhappy about.

But they will find out that in God's world, in the real world that exists, when they get to their session, they'll forget that and deal with what really counts. They'll bring up, only if they know themselves, what they're feeling then and there. And what they're unhappy about then and there. They don't ever have to keep a notebook. We don't ever ask our clients to keep a notebook in any way. We never tell our clients that they're unhappy about anything. We can't.

And besides that, that's not what The Option Method is about. Remember, The Option Method is to help people to not need help, to help themselves, to be less unhappy about what they want to be less unhappy about. And so maybe after they deal with a certain unhappiness and they're no longer unhappy about that and then they're no longer unhappy about another thing, all things about their lives—maybe then they're willing to deal with their homicidal rage, and why they occasionally get these desires to murder the therapist. But we can't tell them that that is something for them to deal with. Because it just won't work.

Why won't it work? Because that's not what works. It just doesn't work. That's not the way they create their emotions. It's not the way emotions work. It has to be an emotion that a person actually starts experiencing as being uncomfortable for them. They wish they didn't shed a tear every time that they went to this kind of movie or that. They wish they didn't get angry so much. Or they wish they weren't so subject to somebody's insults. You know, things like that, little things that real people get unhappy about.

The Option Method Doesn't Call for Repeat Business

So we don't want to ever run the risk of running a school for psychological hypochondriacs. "Okay, see you next week. Okay, see you next week." We want to run a clinic, a self-help program for people to learn how to be their own best helpers. So they can use the same tool that I use to help them to not be unhappy. That's all. And that's it. Not to go through every unhappiness they may have for the rest of their life and help them not be unhappy about it. Because they don't need The Option Method for that.

Remember I said The Option Method is only to introduce you to the fact that unhappiness is not a mystery. It doesn't fall out of the sky. And it's not your fault. And you have to understand both things. As soon as people start believing unhappiness is their fault—that's the danger with The Option Method—then they are only believing what they've always believed. That unhappiness is their fault. Sometimes it used to be the other person's unhappiness. Now it's their unhappiness. But all people have believed, in one way or another, that unhappiness was their fault, too. So that's not new. That's not a special danger of The Option Method. At least, practitioners who learn from me know never to indulge in that.

If a person thinks unhappiness is their fault, well, then we'd have to ask them why they see this as something to be unhappy about. In other words, if I discovered that I give myself that knot in my stomach, I don't really need to know whether I'm unhappy or not. I only need to know that it's true that I give myself that knot in my stomach. And if I want to know how I do that, it may be because that's what I've always done when this kind of thing happened. And it's just a physical response.

I give myself a knot in my stomach. And if I'm not unhappy about that symptom, I'm not unhappy at all. And then so once I've discovered I give myself a knot in my stomach, I no longer give myself a knot in my stomach. But, if I discover that it's my fault that I give myself a knot in my stomach and make that equivalent to making myself unhappy—now I know where you're going to spend your money. But you see The Option Method doesn't call for repeat business. It's a particular problem we have, those of us who want to devote our lives to trying to help people to be less unhappy.

We don't want to engender that constant need for help. It's just the opposite. And so we hope that grateful clients will send other people, who they hope will be helped.

There's nothing in learning that we cause our unhappiness that can, in and of itself, be depressing or can, in and of itself, cause unhappiness. That's a cause for joy. We now know it's not a great mystery and it's not falling down on our head from the heavens. To discover that we're doing it to ourselves is a great joy.

It's like when the stammerer or the stutterer discovers that they're just doing that because they're trying too hard. Oh, is that all? Yeah. If you don't try so hard you won't stutter. You're just trying to do something that you don't normally do. Whereas, speaking is something you can normally do. If you understand that speaking is natural to you, you won't be a stammerer or a stutterer. Because you think that all of a sudden, your talking needs some special attention from your brain or your tongue—not unless you've had a stroke or something like that. That's usually really the only case.

And that's what we're finding out about ourselves—that we create movements in our body, muscular movements, some of which we call unhappiness and some of which we call happiness. The one that makes us want to throw up, we usually call unhappiness. but not always. We mistakenly make all movements about unhappiness.

Everyone Does Not, in Practice, Want Happiness

September 1990

WHILE anyone would probably assert that they want to be happy, in practice they are actually unwilling to be, under numerous circumstances. And that is precisely why they are not happy then.

That people believe it is good to be unhappy is the greatest self-deception they can inflict on themselves. If "good" can ever have any personal, relevant meaning to a person, it could only be as an emotionally equivalent word for "happiness causing," even if indirectly. Happiness is the goal of all human behavior and concepts. Believing something is "good" in a general or moral sense is to believe it fosters happiness in some way. It usually means good for what we want or value. Unhappiness is believed to be good because it "proves" we have our values consistent with our desires. No one questions why this is believed.

Why does being happy mean that my values are not exactly what I chose them to be? My remaining happy does not, of course, contradict what I affirm. My being happy does not mean I wanted or approved of my not getting what I wanted any more than my being healthy does. It makes as much sense to be unhappy when we don't get what we want as it would to make ourselves sick or hurt ourselves in any way. That people say that it does make "sense" is their doom. They are doomed to be unhappy to prove that their loss means loss, their disapproval means disapproval, their not wanting means not wanting, etc., *ad infinitum, ad mortem*.

Getting unhappy is like slapping your hand because the fruit you picked with it was unripe and sour. That will show it. Right? Bad hand! No right to be happy? Besides losing what we want, we must also lose our right to be happy because that is "good" to do. It is not.

The truth is and can only be that I want what I want as long as I want it; and nothing means otherwise. Not my actions, my gestures, my behavior nor my other desires or lack thereof. I, and only I, mean my desires. If someone else says I really mean to do other than I do, they are wrong. I and only I truly value my values and desire my desires. If someone else says I *really* value something else, they are wrong. If someone else says I *really* desire something else, they are wrong. To accept another's belief or opinion that my happiness or lack of unhappiness means that I don't choose to care about what I indeed do choose to care about would be to delude myself along with the other who does not think I should be happy under the circumstances.

Option as Therapy

Monday Night Study Group, 1973

Understanding More About The Option Method Is Not Necessary

I want to say something about learning. Some of you may have the impression that when I'm giving what you might call a "lecture," that's in order to help you learn better. It isn't. You may learn *more* about certain aspects of things as result of what I'm saying. But I'm not sure it has got to do with learning *better.*

I was speaking to someone who felt that she was getting very confused, especially when things started to get very logical and orderly, like outlines and step-by-step descriptions. She believed that was supposed to help her to understand better and it didn't, because she got confused.

But she understood the concepts of what we are talking about as best she could possibly understand. And the simplest understanding is the best understanding. We talked about all the other aspects of Option, but that doesn't mean we're understanding it *better.* We are understanding *more* things about it.

We have discussed that our emotional states come from our beliefs, and that we use unhappiness to motivate ourselves. Some of us just simply know that, and we use the rest of the talking about it to confuse ourselves. If you know it, you know it, and to think that you didn't get all the rest of the elaboration implies some kind of a defect in what you're knowing is not true. If you came away just being more convinced or more aware that beliefs cause unhappiness, that unhappiness does not *happen* to us a result of our environment, then you understand better without understanding anything more.

Some people, because of their beliefs, believe that the more sides they see to a thing the better they know it. It's an illusion but nonetheless it helps them. Learning is beginning to know that there is nothing more that *needs* to be said about something. And we may continue to talk.

Some of you want to look at things from all sides; over it and under it and inside and outside of it, perhaps the motive being to help describe it to others or to defend it, or even to defend it to yourself in times of doubt. There are many people who feel that is useful, but it shouldn't be seen as somehow *adding* to the original information. It can't, if the original information is clear in your mind: our unhappiness comes from our beliefs and not from the environment, not from what happens to us. What better can be said about it than that? What clearer thing could be said? All the intricacies and all the details are not to help you better understand it, if you already understand it. But for those of you who feel that it helps out to know more aspects of it, for whatever purposes they want to use it, fine.

If you don't know the truth of unhappiness, then these details might be ways to help you to begin to know it; but for those of you who know it, you shouldn't feel that you have to know *more* than that. If you understand the basic concept, you've truly got all you really need to have.

What would probably help us to know anything better, is to be happier.

The only times that you don't *know* that you are using unhappiness as a motivation is when you *are* using it as a motivation. And the only times that you don't *know* that unhappiness is a result of beliefs is when your unhappiness *is* a result of your beliefs.

The implications of the truth of unhappiness you could derive on your own, from your own experiences, in your own ways.

Communicating the Truth of Happiness

Questioner: *I'm concerned about how to get Option across to other people.*

The way *I'm* explaining it is *my* style when I explain it to others. It might not be suitable for *you* at all as a way *you* can explain it to others.

Ask yourself, why do you need to explain it to others? Start off with freedom: "I don't have to explain it to others, and they don't have to know what I know."

I've stopped explaining Option just about everywhere except here. People say to me, "What is it all about?" And I say, "You got a couple of days?" What it amounts to is that I don't know how, nor am I willing, to really explain it in just a few minutes, because I find that most any time I try to explain it, I'm more mis-explaining it than anything.

I try to use examples, and I find the best it does is to get people to think. It doesn't prove anything.

This is an example of the four kinds of emotional responses to one single event: a girl's going off to college and standing on her front stoop with her family—her mother, and her father, and her sister—and there is a man passing by. She's going away to college; that's the only single real, objective event. Her mother is feeling very sad about it. Her sister is very happy about it. Her father is kind of mixed about it. And the man walking down the block doesn't think anything about it. Each one, according to their beliefs, is feeling what they're feeling.

The mother is only seeing it as a loss of a daughter. She can't understand why she's got to go away to school. Why can't she go to a college in town and live at home? and so on. And she only sees the loss for herself, so she only sees that it is an unhappy experience. So she's unhappy. The father sees it as kind of good for his daughter to grow up and be away with her friends and at school and to get away from home. That's good; but he's also going to miss his little girl, so he sees it as both good and bad, and feels accordingly. And the little sister is just absolutely overjoyed that that brat is going away to school: she's going to have the phone to herself, and the room all to herself, and her mother and father all to herself. So she's only seeing it as good and she feels good about it. She's really happy. And the man walking down the street doesn't think it is good or bad or anything. He doesn't even think about it at all, so he doesn't feel anything about it.

I like to use that as an example. Do you think it really proves anything to anybody who doesn't want proof?

That really helps people to start thinking. But usually their way of thinking is to immediately make objections from their fears. So then if you're interested in getting involved with their fears and actually doing therapy with them right then and right there, there is no such thing as an explanation. The only explanation is that you are really going to get involved with therapy.

Some people will grasp the fundamental nature of happiness

and unhappiness easily, and their fears won't stand in their way. Perhaps this threatens all of us to some extent. And I think many of us still use it to threaten ourselves, by saying that we should be happy. I think that's the biggest misunderstanding that most people hear. They know everything I am saying but they immediately can go right through it and say, "You mean you are not supposed to be unhappy about anything? You shouldn't be unhappy?" They seem to have the intuition that's it's all very true, but they are frightened of the implication, which, in their fear, they take to be that they *shouldn't* be unhappy.

Every one of you, to one degree or another, says to yourself, "I shouldn't be unhappy." And so we still use the possibility of happiness to threaten ourselves. One of the easiest things, one of the best things to say if you are explaining Option is just that. Even if they are not saying it, *you* say "It doesn't mean that one shouldn't be unhappy." That becomes a very important first statement to me. Because the whole system can be heard as another "should."

Defining The Option Method

Option Method is a process or a method for becoming happier. Now, that definition has got a leak in it, because in a sense making money is a process for becoming happier, some would say. So let me add, a method for becoming happier in every way and in any way without reservations, without drawbacks. It's a method of becoming happier anytime we need to become happier under any circumstances, in any situation.

It's not a way of controlling others. It's not a way of "helping" others to achieve states of mind or forms of behaviors which we have judged to be better than others. It's not a process by which people learn to function better according to some ideals. It is not to prevent thieves from stealing or murderers from murdering, or lovers from loving. The Option Method is not to help students to learn better, or workers to work better, or fighters to fight better. It's to help us to be happier. Although some of the above may happen, it is not because they were a desired goal of ours, but perhaps they were a product of becoming happier. So, students may learn better, or workers work better, or fighters may not fight anymore or they may fight better, or thieves may stop stealing or they may steal better. Any of the changes might be a function of their becoming happier, but those things are not our goal. Our goal is to help a person to be happier.

Not to be happier *in order* to function better. Not to be happier *in order* to change their form of behavior, not to be happier in order to *anything.* They may ask you about that. They may think they want that. But The Option Method is to help them to be happy.

To the best of my knowledge, no other therapy or system defines its goals this way, simply to help people to be happier. Changing behavior seems to happen, true. But The Option Method is not to help people to become happier *in order* to change their behavior; it is to help them become *happy.* As they become happier, they invariably will change their behavior. But the goal is not to stop thieves from stealing. Maybe a happy person would not steal, but who are we to say? We're not going to judge any behavior. Behavior definitely changes, but in a way that people want for themselves, and we cannot predict. We're not knowing better what people should do.

Now, many people seek out the other methods and sciences with the implicit hope of achieving more happiness, although, explicitly stated, they really strive for other goals. Some strive for awareness, integration, normalcy, etcetera, hoping to be more happy as a product of this. A person may go into therapy hoping that if they become well-adjusted that they will be happier. That if they are better integrated they will be happier. But if they are seeking these things primarily as a way of being happy, that, in my mind, is not much different than seeking money as a way of being happy—another tool, of which happiness is sometimes the by-product.

Almost every therapy, every religion that I know, and certainly in the way it's presented, has the point of view that happiness is a by-product of doing this or that, of thinking a certain way. Many even state axiomatically, "Without a doubt there will always be unhappiness in life." So therefore their goal is to help one cope, or face unhappiness realistically, to adjust or function in spite of it, or to function well with it. "Since there is going to be unhappiness in life, therefore we propose this system to help you through it." Their belief in the permanence of unhappiness is so unequivocal that they often have a pervasive despair and a built-in support for the belief that we are victims—victims to our environment and to our past, and something like that—and the idea is to lessen this victimization.

These therapies help people to be happy in much the same way as giving money to somebody unhappy about the lack of it helps that person to be happy.

Removing what makes one unhappy, be it hunger or fear, certainly makes one happy. But if in doing so, the belief in the value of unhappiness is the motivation that's used, one's happiness is delicate, and conditional on the environment. We're always happy *because* of this or that, and it is dependent on this going right and that going right. Unhappiness will be felt to be necessary again each time one faces difficulty.

I'd like to give you an example from traditional psychoanalysis. In psychoanalysis, a patient sees the "reason" that he feels unhappy in a certain way. They see how they began to be unhappy in a certain way in their childhood and then they see that they are no longer really in that situation and they needn't feel the same way as they did in childhood. For example, a man needn't feel about all women what he felt about his mother. And once he sees that he needn't feel about all women what he felt about his mother, then he has a good reason to stop feeling that way about all women.

And the real issue of unhappiness has not been touched. At its limited best, real good psychoanalysis amounts to something like this: since you can now see that what you feared was a castrating mother, you projected this characteristic on all women. In order to better protect yourself in your relationship with them, you can now also see that you don't have to do this in order to avoid castrating women. Now that you see the cause of it, you don't have to project your fear of castrating women on to all women in order to avoid women who are *really* castrating.

My point is that there is no question of not fearing castration; that's not a question. That one shouldn't fear castration, or needn't fear castration, or even if there is such a thing as a castrating female, is not the question.

What is implied and even stated is that not all women are castrating, but only some. That, hopefully, is the more "realistic" approach to life that psychoanalysis would help you gain. Without your neurosis, you can more properly assess who is who. Now you'll only feel fear of really dangerous women, not women whom you'd imagine to be dangerous. Again, there is no question that there are of course some dangerous women and there are really castrating females.

There are many preconceived notions in the process of psychoanalysis, such as what healthy heterosexual relationships are, and what's in it for each sex, and they are all predefined for the person undergoing analysis by the system: what's better, what's bad. What I just stated is an example. It's not a true representation of all psychoanalysis, it's not intended to be. What many other people propose as psychoanalysis is even more obnoxious.

I like the old Greek meaning of the word *therapon*, which is where we get the modern word therapist. The ancient Greek meaning is a comrade in a common struggle. In The Option Method, a therapist is more like that original Greek meaning; it's to be with a client to help him or her to be with themselves.

A serviceable definition of a therapist for us might be helping those who want me to help them to be happier, not to need help to be happier.

Now when you come to me as your therapist, and you ask me to help you to be happier, I want to help you to not to need help to be happier.

The whole idea of mental illness is just unpopular behavior, that's what it means. It's a political designation, and always has been—psychiatrists and all who propose ideal behaviors are being policemen for a higher utopia, to shape people up, as part of a grander scheme to have them be normal and adjusted.

The Option Method is not about fitting people into a society. We're not concerned with that. Go see a society-fitter.

The Four Attitudes

Monday Night Study Group, 1973

In this talk, Bruce Di Marsico discusses the attitude of The Option Method guide.

How do we know that helping is wanted? We know that someone wants help either because they ask for help, or we suspect they may want help and do not refuse it when we offer it.

There are four attitudes which we may proceed with in helping:

Attitude Zero: The non-attitude: we don't want to help. In this case, we do not help anymore.

Attitude Three: We believe the person is unhappy because they have to be; they need something (advice, money, love). In this case, we may give them what we believe they need in order to be happy.

Attitude Two: We believe the person is choosing to be unhappy, and wants to be (the attitude of existentialism). In this case, we do not believe we can help, and return to Attitude Zero.

Attitude One (The Option Method attitude): We believe the person is choosing to be unhappy, only because they mistakenly believe they have to be. This is the attitude that The Option Method proceeds under.

Since we know we don't know why someone is happy, we have to proceed on the basis that they may know.

How do I know that someone wants help to be happier?

Since I defined being a therapist as helping those who want help from me, this brings up the question, "who wants help from me?" I answer this way: "just about anybody," but with this meaning: anyone who is with me when I employ The Option Method, in one of these ways I'll outline, is somebody who wants help. It could be (a) one who asks help to be happier; (b) one who does not *refuse* my offer to help them be happier, and who in some way helps me even passively until they do ask me for help.

There are some people who needn't ask for help but who still want help. How will I know that they are wanting help? I know that they are wanting help because somehow they are not refusing help. They are kind of playing along with me. Even though it might be an air of tolerating what I'm doing, there is apparently some hope there in their minds that they might be helped. I'm thinking of even involuntary patients. I've had patients who have been brought in by family, have been brought in by police, children that are brought in by their parents, forced physically to come, and who insist that there is nothing wrong with them, and they don't need anybody's help for anything, etc.

But nonetheless I have found that if I ask them if they are unhappy about something—and even if it amounts to "I'm unhappy about these bastards who dragged me here"—they are willing to talk to me. They're willing to discuss their unhappiness. They are somehow not wanting to be as unhappy. And then I ask them why they're unhappy, and they tell me—or at least they just don't get up and leave, or do not just start talking about something else altogether—perhaps they also still are wanting help. And then ultimately I find that even involuntary patients eventually (in my case, and it needn't be this way) always ask me to help them. But I can foresee that that might not always be the case, that they might not eventually let me help them, and would eventually just stop wanting help.

But somehow they're cooperating; somehow they're allowing me to try to help. And that is as good as wanting help.

The Four Attitudes

When we ask the question, "What is the method of helping others to be happier?" we have an attitude. This preliminary attitude is "I believe they want to be happier," so everything would be based on that.

There are attitudes that I call "Attitude Zero," "Three," "Two," and "One."

Attitude Zero is simply "I don't want to help them to be happier." It can take a number of forms, like "I don't want to help those who want me to help them to be happier not to need help to be happier." Ultimately, Attitude Zero would be the *non*-attitude: I don't want to help people not to need help to be happier.

As someone who might help, our helping begins when we state to ourselves, "Either I am here to help them to be happier in themselves, if possible, or I am here to supply them with the things or information that they believe they need to be happier."

Whether I believe they *need* to be happier might be the determining factor. If I give them advice, I'm a strategy counselor or a teacher, not a therapist—a therapist meaning somebody who helps somebody not to need help to be happier. If I give them things, I'm their protector, not their therapist. I might be their lover, their friend, their protector, but not their therapist. For example, I might say to somebody, "Don't subject yourself to your husband's abusiveness. If you leave you'll be happier. You have the ability to make it on your own." Sometimes "marriage counseling" is giving a pep talk. That's advice-giving; and if I do that, I'm not a therapist, I'm their protector.

As their protector, I'm giving them or making up for what I think they need, supplying what I feel they need—either the information or the protection. Another example: "You're worried about money? Well, I think you qualify for public assistance, that will solve your problems." Giving information. To give $100 would be the protector. The attitude of the protector or supplier, I am calling Attitude Three. Attitude Zero is: "I'm not willing to help them at all." Attitude Three is: "I believe they're unhappy because they need things. They need information or advice or things to be supplied." Attitude Three can be summed up this way: "I believe they're unhappy because they need."

If I decide that I *will* help them to *not need help* to be happier, if possible, that will be, depending on the details, Attitude Two or One. The question that distinguishes Attitude Three from Attitudes Two and One is: do I believe they are unhappy because they *have* to be or because they *choose* to be? If I decide that they are unhappy because they *have* to be, then I have Attitude Three. I'm their protector and supplier.

If I decide they may be unhappy because they *choose* to be, then I proceed this way: they choose to be unhappy either because they *believe* they have to be unhappy (Attitude One), or because they just choose to be and really *want* to be (Attitude Two). Once I've decided that their unhappiness is a matter of choice, I have to decide which *kind* of choice: do they choose it because they believe they have to choose unhappiness, or do they choose it because they want to? If I decide that they really *want* to be unhappy then I believe that they neither want nor need help to do what they want, and I don't really need to wait on them to choose otherwise. If they do choose otherwise, I didn't help them, and if they don't choose otherwise, I didn't help them. So, I've circled around to Attitude Zero again: I do not want to help, because I understand that there is no help to offer. I can't want to help them, because at that point I'm believing that they neither want help nor need help to do what they really want to do, which is simply choosing to be unhappy.

Attitude One is the Option attitude: they may be choosing to be unhappy because they believe they *have* to choose to be unhappy.

To summarize, Attitude Zero is having no attitude at all. It's not positive or negative. As a therapist, if you take Attitude Zero, then you don't have any concern for helping. It's really not being any kind of help-giver at all.

Attitude Three is a very everyday attitude: people are unhappy because they need to be, because they just have to be. Unhappiness happens, it's the nature of life, it's the nature of the world, it just happens to people. There's nothing that anybody can do about it except to try to make up for it by giving information or supplies, giving them things so they no longer need to be unhappy about not having them. It's just natural for people to be unhappy if they don't have money, so the idea is to give them money. It's just natural for people to be unhappy if they don't have certain information, so you try to give them the information.

Now Attitude Two is a more existential attitude. People are unhappy because they want to be. It's very cynical and hopeless, because you can't help it. People are unhappy because they just simply want to be out of some perversity, perhaps, and they just choose to be unhappy because they want to choose to be unhappy. Attitude Two is the existentialism of Sartre and Kierkegaard, or theories such as "That is the nature of humanity, that's the nature of not being divine, that's the nature of just being imperfect and frail, that's just the nature of life."

I'm not saying any of these attitudes are right or wrong, by the way. We're talking from a purely empirical point of view: Attitude Three is a possible attitude. If Attitude Two or Three is true, The Option Method will have no effect.

If I decide that people may be unhappy because they *believe* they have to be, I can proceed with The Option Method. The attitude from which the Method will flow is that if I'm going to help people at all, what I am helping them with is that they *believe* they have to be unhappy.

The only possible attitude toward helping others in "therapy" is because I have the attitude that they are causing their own unhappiness by their beliefs; that they're unhappy because they believe they have to be. If I believe that they're unhappy because they just simply wanted to be, there wouldn't be any reason for therapy; and if I decide that they are unhappy because they simply had to be, therapy would be of no avail, would make no sense, would be useless. And yet there are people practicing therapy who believe that people are unhappy because they have to be, and there are people who are practicing therapy believing that people are unhappy just simply because they choose to be. But if either of these is true, then they can't help, in either case.

So Option will come from the attitude that "the only way I'm going to help anybody at all is to proceed with the attitude that they may be unhappy because they believe they have to be." Now, if that's not so, if in fact there really was a good reason for being unhappy, okay, then we can't help, if that really turns out to be the case.

When we begin the therapeutic process, in The Option Method, we don't need to make any assumptions. We don't need to know that people are unhappy because they have to be, because that's the nature of things. We don't need to know whether people are unhappy because they simply choose to be; because if that is so, we won't be able to help them anyway, there's neither harm nor good to come out of our therapy.

So we might as well then just simply investigate, and begin with the proposition "*Maybe* you're unhappy because you believe you have to be, and you want to be happier, right?" And look at it and find out why. If you are unhappy because you simply want to be unhappy, then there is nothing we can do for you. If you're unhappy because you really have to be, there is nothing we could do for you.

What I'm talking about is allowing all possibilities in your mind. What I am talking about is you being the most open-minded person who ever approached another person who wanted to help. What I'm talking about is that you be so open-minded that you don't even have to know what the real reason is that they are unhappy. You don't have to know whether they're unhappy because God made them unhappy or they're unhappy because they just decided they wanted to be unhappy. What you'll be proceeding with is, if you're going to help someone, if they're unhappy because they believe they have reasons to be, you can help. If they're unhappy because there's a virus going around that makes one unhappy, you're not going to be able to help them. If that kind of thing caused unhappiness, no therapies would work.

You proceed with an attitude of complete openness, and you will devise The Option Method as a result of that openness. Your approach is: you don't know why these people are unhappy. And you approach them with a total openness. You just simply do not know why anyone else is unhappy. Their unhappiness may resemble yours. It may resemble the unhappiness of hundreds of other people whom you've met, hundreds of other patients. But in this particular case that you're facing, you do not know why they are unhappy. You won't allow yourself to even think that you know that.

Pragmatically, you begin with the proposition "I don't know why they're unhappy. I'll ask them, they'll tell me." Now, if they know, wonderful. And if they really don't know, well then you can't know. So we begin with the question, "I don't know why you're unhappy. I'm really open to it being God, the world, the nature of life, but I'm also open to it being possible that you are unhappy because you believe you have to be." Then I'll approach with, "Let's look at it and see if there is a way out. If, just in case, it may not be necessary for you to be unhappy." And that's what The Option Method comes from. I approach my patients *just in case* if may not be necessary for them to be unhappy, never quite assuming that they may not have good reasons to be unhappy. That doesn't help you one way or the other, that they have no good reason to be.

So I don't approach them saying that therefore they ought to be happy, because I don't know. All I can take is the facts that they give me: they want to be happier. If they want to be happier then we can see that maybe, if their unhappiness is not necessary, maybe they can be free of it.

They may or may not know why they are unhappy. I will proceed *as if* they know why they were unhappy. Even though I have found in every case that *I* have dealt with that unhappiness has been caused by a particular belief, that need not stop us from being open to it being another belief or other reason in any particular case. You can allow yourself to be open to the possibility that the devil is doing it, if you want. And if he is, then you will not be able to help.

So a person may or may not know why they are unhappy, but if I have the assumption that they don't know, there's no sense proceeding. So I might as well proceed on the assumption that they know. That if it is possible for anybody to know, they'll know. That if indeed they are unhappy, it is because they believe they have to be, that unhappiness is simply believing that there is something to be unhappy about. They have to know what that is. That unhappiness would have to be, somehow, something that they decided there was something to be unhappy about, even if that something was being unhappy itself.

So we're going to be really empirical. We're approaching people who are saying they're unhappy and they say they don't want to be. This is our dilemma. If people are going to come to us and say, "I'm unhappy and I don't want to be," how do you approach it? Any other way is impossible except to say, "Okay, you're unhappy and you don't want to be; since you want to be happier, what is it that you are unhappy about?" This will be the first question. Identify what they are unhappy about. And that will be the first step of the method. The attitude will bring that question out of your mouth, or something like that—"What is it you're unhappy about?"—simply because I want to talk about the same thing that you are talking about, so we can talk to each other. And since I want to talk to you about what you're unhappy about, I might say something like "What do you mean? What is there about that that you are unhappy about? Would you be more specific, or would you speak more clearly? Or would you speak more plainly?"

Knowing the Cause of Other's Unhappiness

You may develop, perhaps, a very uncanny ability of being able to discern what people's issues are. It may even resemble ESP—you know as the person walks in the door, you can have him diagnosed instantly, and he hasn't said a word yet. So you are very good at it. That isn't going to help them. Especially if you think it should.

Then you'll be trying to lead them, and you might be absolutely right; but you are not going to help them, because if they get where they go, they went because you led them.

And they may come to very accurate conclusions from your guidance, but they won't be for themselves, it would be out of *your* skills and *your* reality. When you are called upon to remedy practical situations other than in the therapy, then you can call upon some of your perceptive ability to be able to make a recommendation that *may* have a nine-out-of-ten chance of being right, or a ten-out-of-ten chance of being right. There is another saying of mine that "evidence never proved anything to anybody."

It's in the very nature of unhappiness, in the nature of the belief, that just maybe a person is willing to believe you when you tell them why they are unhappy. All the worse. They become happy in order to be good. We can observe something, and in spite of the fact of what we have observed, we can still believe it. It's like being right for the wrong reasons. I was talking to somebody recently who was very reluctant to do something and had very clear reasons, and there were certainly reasons for them not to do it, whatever it was; it would have been very self-defeating. The reasons were clear, but it just so happened that they could never have the freedom to go along with those reasons, because they suspected why they even had the reasons; somehow those reasons were *too* good. They were too pat—they were real, and they were really undeniable, but they kind of meant too much, in the sense of "I am glad I have a reason not to do it," and just that thought can be self-defeating.

Guidance in Questioning

Monday Night Study Group, 1973

QUESTIONER: *What do you do when somebody says "If I really feel good about myself, and I'm really happy, then it will change, and some magic will happen, and I will become unhappy."*

For informational purposes, first I would ask them if they are describing an actual experience of theirs: "Has that happened before?" The next question might be, "If something would ever happen, and you became unhappy, are you unhappy about that *now*? If something happens you believe that you had to be unhappy about, why do you believe that?" If you decide that for some reason you just want to be unhappy, you are only in touch with your freedom, why would you want it to be otherwise? "As long as you don't *want* to be unhappy, would you? As long as you didn't believe you *had* to, would you?"

Then they could get in touch with that they could really have to be unhappy then, if that was the case. But why now? Do they want to be happier now? That's the basic kind of thing you'll always get to: they could be really happy now, and there is nothing *now* to be unhappy about. The feeling is: "Someday there may be something I will have to be unhappy about, and I don't know what it is. And I don't have any reason to believe that this would be so, so I want to cover myself." But the question is, even if that were so, "Would you have to be unhappy now? And if that were so, couldn't you know that if then you had to be unhappy, you could be?" They may start talking about believing that they don't want to be out of touch with themselves, that they don't want to not be unhappy when they should be. They can start to get in touch with their basic freedom, and just explore why they would be unhappy about the other things. And when it is reduced to, "So in your life you would be unhappy about nothing else except some possible unhappiness that you didn't know why," you can address why they believe they would have to be unhappy about that *now*.

Questioner: *I have had the most problems working through this kind of magic: "I can't get too happy, because I'll pay for it."*

I never met anyone who didn't believe in that adage. I wouldn't try to get anyone to accept that it's silly. You see, one thing we know is that they are believing that somehow they think using that frame of mind is going to help them. Ask, "Why do you want to believe that? Why do you believe that, believing this would make you be happier?" And let them answer that.

Sometimes, it's useful to truly work it all the way down, so that they aren't unhappy about anything except the possibility of being unhappy, before addressing that. But in general, I see the belief that if you are happy then you will be unhappy as basically something you just work with like anything else. I mean, I've had people say, "God made me unhappy," or "The devil did," or "Evil spirits."

Questioner: *Someone said, "I'm unhappy, because I'm afraid to be happy. Because if I'm happy, I know that I'm only going to get unhappy."*

Somehow it seems to me that you're talking with your patients somehow about the nature of unhappiness. And once people come up with the reason of "Why do I get unhappy, *in general*," they come up with all kinds of magical answers to explain it. Question, "Why do I have to be happy about a certain particular thing?" You didn't identify what she was unhappy about. Ask, "What do you mean by happy?"

There's so many things you could ask, like, "Why do you believe that you should be unhappy because of some evil spirits? You mean that you didn't want to be unhappy? Somebody made you unhappy? Where was the case where you didn't want to be unhappy but somebody made you? *Who* made you?" When you're into this general kind of hocus-pocus magic kind of thing, they're not talking about anything. They're not talking about being unhappy—there might even be no reason to believe that they *are* unhappy. There's nothing more happening. And then if they say "I'm unhappy being unhappy and I'm unhappy that I could be made more unhappy," you can ask "What could you be made more unhappy about?" Or if they say "I'm not happy just about myself," you can ask "What is it about yourself that you're unhappy about?" "How do you know if you're unhappy?" would be another question. A person says "I'm unhappy because I'm unhappy," and you ask "How do you know you're unhappy? How do you know? How do you know it's not indigestion? Do you want it to be unhappiness?"

Get particular. For example: Question: "Do you want to believe that you're unhappy?" Response: "Yeah, I just do believe it." Question: "What do you mean by that? What do you feel bad about?" Response: "About everything. Well, just everything." Question: "Well, what's one thing, for example?" I've had cases of people who were hallucinating, and believing that they were being made to do bad things—the devil is making them do it, or God is making them do that to be unhappy. But I would ask them things like, "If you were really happy, do you think this would last?" And they did not know. Just like that. "Do you think if you were really happy, God would be talking to you every night?"

Questioner: *What keeps happening is that she keeps getting into storytelling, and then I would keep bringing her back and tell her, "That's fine, but now what are you be unhappy about?" I'm trying to get her out of the storytelling and into working.*

I ask "Why are you telling me that?" There might be a chance for you to reaffirm why you are there—if you are not understanding why a story is being said, just as with anything else, you ask "What do you mean?" If you don't understand the connection, if you don't see the relevance, if you don't see how it's an answer, you might ask them "What does it mean?" You might do the same thing with the story. "Why is it that you're telling me this? What are you trying to say about the story? What is it that you are unhappy about?" And she might try to explain to you what she's unhappy about. And if she goes off into another story, then, "I understand that he makes you unhappy, and I want to try to help you be happier": restate and reaffirm your purpose. And I don't know that you will continue to get stories, because it seems to me if you asked "Why are you telling me?" you have to go somewhere with that; she'd have to tell you and she will tell you why she was telling you that. And if she went to another story, you would say to her, "Well, why are you telling me that? I'm not sure if you're answering my question—why are you telling me that?"

You're not impinging on their freedom. They can go right on with their story; you're not stopping them, but somehow you're making it clear why you're there. If you want, you could say it quite clearly,

"It's *really okay* that you tell me this, but what I'm wondering is *why*? And you can tell me anything you want to tell me, but that's not why I'm interrupting you right now. Why I'm interrupting you is to find out why you want to tell me this." If you think that they are thinking that you're going to try and stop them, you could make it clear that you're not trying to stop them from telling you the story; they can feel perfectly free to tell you, you just want to know why.

Questioner: *Oftentimes when I ask a question, she'll counter with a question like "Would you say it's normal?"*

Ask, "Well, do *you* think it's normal?" You are able find out the reason behind the question, just simply by saying, "Well, do *you* think so?"

They just don't know how you're going to help them. The way you help motivate them to want your help is to just let them know as clearly as you can what you intend to do; then they can make a decision. "I'm here to try to help you, to try and find out what you're unhappy about. When you discover why you are unhappy, you may find that some things that you have believed you have to be unhappy about, you may not, if you look at them more closely. I don't know, but let's find out."

Even though they may come in to you week after week and complain to everybody else about why they are coming to see you, they expect you to really go out and do something about it. And if a person is very repressed and they start getting angry, know that at least they have a way to express their anger. And they go on being angry, and angry, and angry; they stop being angry, and start crying; so now at least they're able to be in touch with where it is really at. All behavior starts to change, and all the behavior that they weren't okay with starts to fall off, and then any behavior can be okay.

Questioner: *Could you know if a person is really happier or not?*

No. What does it mean? I guess the question is "Why would you want to know? Why would you need to know? What difference does it make to you whether they get happy or they don't get happy—or if they get happy, whether you know it or not or whether it shows or not." It might be an indication that someone may really need your patience to get happier, or at least to show their happiness, because they are starting to become happier but they want to do so at their own pace.

Patients estimate their own happiness, and say "I'm getting better," or "I don't think I'm happier," or any such number of things. There was a case in which anybody else would say that a patient had ended up regressed, he was absolutely a sheer mess by any worldly definition. And I just thought I'd say what I felt like saying. I said "I think you're better than you've ever been before," and he screamed, "What do you mean? How could I be? Look at me." I said, "That's why I think so." And then all kinds of things started falling away. I said, "I think you're happy," and that was all that was needed.

Is it within The Option Method attitude? The question is "Well, do you have The Option Method attitude?" I did. I don't know if you consider this actual therapy or not, but that wasn't my rationale—I was not trying to help them feel better or anything, I was just saying where I was and what I felt. And I was perfectly prepared to say that "The reason I think you are better is because I'm happier."

I've taught you technique. I've told you to use the questions, and I said to you that they were models. The models spring from the Option Attitude.

In his way, he was asking, "Do you think I'm better?" and I was communicating, "What you think matters—it all depends on whether *you* think you are happy or not." And so I just thought that I would make what *I* thought totally irrelevant, and I figured the best way to do that would be to be totally honest, and to just say whatever it was I was thinking, and me knowing that it was totally irrelevant might make the difference. It would make the difference as long as I knew that what I was saying was totally irrelevant to where he was at. So I said, "I think that you're happier than ever, and that you're a big actor," and he said he knew that and he smiled; and then he reached over to my wall and knocked on it and said, "Help," and it just became a joke. Somehow he was telling me,"See through me." At least that's what I picked up: "If you can really help me, you should be able to see through me right now," maybe something like that.

As long as my attitude is to do what I consider the best for who it is, whatever is going to follow from there will follow. I did notice that a few sessions later, he thinks of me more as an ally now. We have a little joke that sometimes we use: if somebody says, "If such and such happens, I'm going to really be unhappy," the joke is "You promise?" which then puts it back on ourselves.

Questioner: How do you handle the threat of physical violence? It's so very unthinkable to me, I just don't believe it.

If you've ever been mugged or robbed, perhaps one of the worst things you could say to a person would be, "Could you please not hurt me?" Because in that begging is an accusation that they are rotten, really miserable people, who would be out to hurt you. If you treat people as if they are bad, as if they are robbers, as if they are evil, they will live up to that; they will hate you for the accusation.

If someone threatened me, I'd do whatever I thought was best. I'd be sure to give them some satisfaction. I would let them think they were taking something, rather than giving it to them. "God bless you" is liable to get you punched or killed. You could simply not say anything, and then if you're asked a question, that attitude would come through, whatever you decide to answer.

Using The Option Method with Others

Monday Night Study Group, 1973

It's *not* a pre-condition for The Option Method that you do not believe that your emotions come from somewhere out there. The idea that our emotions don't come from somewhere out there is, if anything, *the message* of Option; but it's for those people who don't believe that that The Option Method would be most meaningful. It's for those people that The Option Method exists, those who always believe their feelings come from somewhere outside. If you asked them why they aren't happy, they have never heard that question before; and every time they've ever answered it before, they've always answered it "Why am I unhappy? Because so and so did this," and they always answer *what* they're unhappy about. They are the very ones you help with The Option Method the most, the ones you'll find the most dramatic change in. "No, I don't mean *what* are you unhappy about, I mean *why* are you unhappy about that, what is there about that that you believe you have to be unhappy about?" You don't teach them that it's a matter of their belief, you just know that it is, and so all your questions are geared toward that.

For those who are mentally retarded, to the degree that they are capable of being unhappy, in that they are capable of making judgments (which is why they are unhappy), they can tell you why they make those judgments. Their reasons might be a little funny, but there they are. I'm not so sure that anyone's reasons that are more conventional are really any different answers. There's different sizes and shapes of delusion, that's all.

Questioner: *Some of my patients just want to be unhappy.*

They don't *just* want to be unhappy. They want to be unhappy for a reason. Ask them "Why you afraid you won't get what you want, if you're not unhappy?"

You can't assure them that they will still want what they want. You don't have to assure them of that. You couldn't. You ask them why they are so sure that they want that. Your role isn't to assure them of anything except to help them find out how to assure themselves. So when you ask them why they believe they just want to be unhappy, and they say "I don't know," you ask them "Well, if you don't know, why do you believe it to be true?" and work from there, until they come up with an answer for themselves.

Questioner: *How can I help if I'm not really that happy?*

You can start off like this, even before anyone walks into your office: Anybody who I'm going to see today, if they want to be unhappy, they can. There's a prevalent belief that you've gotta get your head together before you do good therapy. Are you going to do any less good therapy because of where you're at? You would still be doing the best you could right? And you'd still be doing Option that way. All you're pointing out is that it could be done better. But is ten percent of your potential useful? I suppose even if you were the kind of therapist who, when a patient came in, you started yelling and screaming at him, and said, "You stupid idiot, you know you can be happy inside!" they can use that to be happy if they wanted to, couldn't they? If they wanted to use it, it doesn't have to be the best.

My not doing my best doesn't prevent them, and anything you do doesn't prevent them, from using it if they wanted to use it to help themselves. It's just that if you change your tone of voice, and you feel a little better yourself, it might make it easier to find out what their beliefs are, and would make it easier to use The Option Method.

Questioner: *I work with some people who have such different life histories than mine—they grew up poor, were in jail—and I can't see myself saying, "Why are you unhappy about that?"*

You're afraid they are going to laugh at you when you ask such a question. I think you'll find that they won't, if you really ask sincerely and meaningfully. I've never had anybody who laughed at me. People tell me about these horrible situations they are going through, and I say, "Well, why are you unhappy about that?" or rather, that is the model question. I may say "Well, what is there about that you're most unhappy about, that gets you most unhappy? What is there about that? And why does that get you down?" There are words that you can use rather than "Why are you unhappy?" "What is there about that that bothers you most, and why does that bother you?" If you find the slightest objection, all you say is, "Wait, I'm not saying you *shouldn't* be unhappy. We all have different reasons for being unhappy about that, and I'm asking you what your reasons are, so that I can know better what it's all about."

Maybe they don't have the reason you consider justified. They may have some real crazy reason. So ask and find out. Their reasons are not your reasons, etc. For example, I have never heard anyone tell me that they were unhappy about being hit, or hurt, or beaten, or anything because it hurt. I have got people who were shot, stabbed, and were never unhappy because it hurt.

And that's just my own experience; and possibly somebody would say they *are* unhappy because it hurts, and then you would be on to, "Why are you unhappy about hurt or pain?" But that's rare, I haven't come across it.

Questioner: *What if people are not interested in being happy? They are interested in something else?*

So they are after beauty, truth, productivity. You say, "Okay, why are you unhappy if you don't produce?" That's the relevant part of it. I don't care that everyone says to me, "I'm not here to be happy." I would say something like, "Wouldn't it be nice if you could produce just as much or even more, and did not also have to be unhappy?" They may say, "Yeah, it would but I don't believe it's possible." And I ask, "Why not?"

Questioner: *How about reasons like "I have my parent on one shoulder all the time?"*

They're not saying anything. They accept that they want to change and they have come up with some harebrained reason about why they're not changing. And then, what they have done is they've invented their own therapy and you go along with them. They say, "Because I've got my parent on my shoulder." They could have said, "Because my libido itches," or "My underdog is bothering my top dog."

That's their theory and their reason for believing, "I can't change because my parents are on my shoulder." The obvious question is, "What is there about not being able to change that bothers you? What do you mean by change?" You're not there to help them change. Maybe they want to change in order to do something else, but ultimately they want be happier. In some therapeutic systems, you have a nice contract with your therapist and you say "I want you to help me change this way," and then everybody agrees that that's a very good thing to change into, and the therapist helps you to become that. But that's got nothing to do with therapy; that sounds like a strategy planner and some kind of behavioral engineer.

"What is there about not changing that bothers you? What is there that you are unhappy about yourself that you want to change?" What you are really asking is, "What are you unhappy about and why?" If they say "I can't change because there is a parent on my shoulder and a monkey on my back," you may ask, "What is there about yourself that you're unhappy about, that you want to change?" You may have forgotten that you were trying to help him to be happy, and you thought you were going to try to help him make a change. You were going to try to help them get their parent off their shoulder. I doubt if you could do that because they probably wanted it there, as a way to explain why they can't change. Did you find out that in their dialog with their imaginary parent, they wanted the parent to be exactly how they saw them, and they really were using them in order not to change? If they are willing to negotiate a mutually agreeable contract, what they are saying is that they are willing to change their beliefs, and therefore they go ahead and do change them; because for them to be able to make the contract, they would have had to have worked through their beliefs to some extent.

Why shouldn't they believe whatever they believe? How do you know that they shouldn't believe that? How do you know that what *you're* believing is right? What they're believing is not the problem; it's their unhappiness about it that's the problem. If they believed for sure and absolutely that the world was going to end tomorrow or ended yesterday, what's that going to do with anything? I wouldn't need to change that belief for them at all. You are not concerned with beliefs, or facts, or experience, or about anything other than beliefs about why they have to be unhappy.

For example, I worked with a woman who wanted to save her husband before the world ended, and but so what. The point is, "Why would she be unhappy if he wasn't saved?" We're concerned with happiness, not sanity. I wouldn't consider it like a good Freudian, who would have considered it an obligation to society to talk people out of their superstitions. We are not concerned with what people believe. Insofar as those beliefs come from unhappiness they'll change, so I don't have to judge whether they're good beliefs or bad beliefs, or sane beliefs or insane beliefs, or happy or unhappy beliefs. Otherwise you have to become the world's greatest authority on everything, and it's totally irrelevant to happiness.

Beliefs about having to be unhappy about something are the only beliefs we're concerned with. The other things that you're calling "beliefs" are deductions based on facts and reasoning processes and ways of ascertaining information. They feel that given a certain amount of data, they can go ahead believing certain things. That in itself does not have anything to do with happiness or not. I could really believe that the world is flat, and if I was a happy person I'd also be open to seeing whether it wasn't flat or not. So certain rigidity in beliefs might not allow for openness. But you don't try to get the openness in order to produce the happiness; you help with the happiness, which will then allow for the openness.

Applying The Option Method Personally

November 11, 1995 Lecture

You people want to be happy insofar as you can stand it, and you're willing to be unhappy insofar as you can afford it. And don't tell me that anything else is true or you're all liars.

You're willing to be happy as if it was some kind of . . . "Okay, I'll have a little bit of schnapps, just a wee drop, but I will only float in churches and I'll never dance down the street." You'll only have as much unhappiness as you can stand, and you're willing to have as much unhappiness as you think you can afford; and ah, there's the rub.

Because what happens is once you get unhappy, you get stupid. Well, you do. And before you know it, you start trying to make unhappiness the best thing in the world. You want to say how it was needed and how it was necessary and how it in fact helped you get your feet down the street. It kept them on the ground so you didn't float, because you don't want to be unrealistic.

"Come on! Face it! This is real life. This is something to be unhappy about. Oh well, wouldn't you (*be unhappy about it*)." So it's always a lot of fun when we realize "Oh," when we're not unhappy about a thing, it's like, "Yeah, so what? I don't want to hear about that. I'm done with that. When I'm not unhappy about it I don't want to understand why I was unhappy about it. What's that got to do with anything?"

We quickly are willing to drop our past when we know it doesn't serve us at all. But when you believe you're living down to an image, like, "This is the kind of thing I got unhappy about or I get unhappy about," you get unhappy about it. So to make a long definition even a shorter one, you feel what you think you ought to feel.

That's all that says up there. [Pointing to blackboard.] You feel what you think you ought to feel. Whatever that "ought to" means, there's lots of ways of saying what you ought to be feeling. Like what you think is natural for you to feel, what you think is necessary to feel. Even what you think is unfortunately necessary for you to feel, you'll feel.

You'll even feel what you're afraid you're going to feel, right? You can't be afraid you're going to get unhappy. Gotcha already, gotcha, all right.

So now The Option Method is a method to question beliefs that are in the middle between events and feelings, since they cause results that people don't like. Insofar as someone says, "Gee, I'm sick and tired of being unhappy," I'll be glad to help them look at then how they got unhappy and why they get unhappy.

Once they look at how and why they get unhappy, they're free to decide whether they really believe at that point that that is for them, that it is what they want, that it really does suit them. If they don't believe it does, then they won't be unhappy.

If they no longer believe that they have to be unhappy about a certain thing, they won't be unhappy about it. Now, don't try to jump to a generalization. I said *a certain thing*. What I mean is rotten fish, flat tires, bad checks, losing your jobs. I mean specific certain things. I don't mean, "Oh wow, the universe is good and great and nothing in it to be unhappy about," because that's not what I mean.

The Option Method is not a method for people who are trying to get themselves to believe in happiness; but if you truly see that there's no evil and you truly see that there is nothing to be unhappy about and you mean all things generally and all things in particular, well then, fine. Then you are an instant mystic and can be instantly happy because there really is no reason why you can't be.

It would seem to me the only reason why we're not all immediately happy is because of some beliefs or some belief—one belief, "Too good to be true." How about that? Another belief, "Takes time, I'm slow. I'm merely human." Things like that.

But I would suppose there'd be no reason why, if all of us—individually, personally, for ourselves and ourselves alone—didn't think anything could ever make us unhappy that we would ever be unhappy again. I haven't had the joy much of seeing that, but I've seen a lot of misery on people demanding that of themselves.

One of the things about The Option Method (which I keep not saying what The Option Method is) is that people who experience their first joys of it and are no longer unhappy about something quickly expect that to generalize and to come everywhere. I find that indeed they are unhappier about things than they were before, sometimes because they didn't learn. But that only shows us something that we'll find out in The Option Method—that there are people who get unhappy about making mistakes and learning.

There are people who are impatient when it's time to learn. They're probably people who curse when they make a mistake on the keyboard, and hit themselves on the head when they make a mistake on the piano, and God knows what they do when they make a mistake sexually. You may never see them again the rest of your life.

Okay. We only know that people hate making mistakes; it is one of the things that they hate. One of the things that I caution my students and my clients about The Option Method is that hating falsehood and hating mistakes is no substitute for loving truth. Hating error is no substitute for loving accuracy. Being afraid to fail is no substitute for wanting to succeed and for loving success.

So anyway, people quickly fall back into unhappiness because they're ashamed or embarrassed that they got unhappy again, but they don't call it that. I've rarely met a person who was embarrassed by something admit to the embarrassment, even to themselves. They just avoid it.

There are people who will never talk about it; but there are men who will never go to a lady physician and there are women who will never go to a male physician because of embarrassment. There are people who will die of rectal cancer because of embarrassment. Embarrassment kills, but it also is the biggest secret.

So people don't often tell themselves that what they are is embarrassed. They just act on it; but that doesn't mean that they're not unhappy and they're not greatly unhappy and very unhappy because now they're failing at the thing that they now learned they're in control of. Well no, they didn't learn they're in control of their happiness.

You haven't learned, unless you've learned through The Option Method; you haven't learned in what way you're in control of your emotions. You're not in any more control of your emotions than you've ever been. You're controlling them the exact same way you've always controlled them; but there have always been people who claimed from childhood that they're not in control of their emotions. There are always people who complain that they are over-controlled, etc.

Well, there are people who are always worried about what they're doing to themselves. But you're not in control of your emotions any more than you've ever been or any less than you've ever been. You're in control of them in the same way, by what you believe.

The only reason it might work, see—once you've learned that you don't have to be unhappy with this and you're not unhappy about that and you've learned that there are lots of things that you just don't have to be unhappy about—one of the things that might work if you found yourself getting unhappy is to say, "Oh, I don't believe in that anymore." See, "I don't believe in it" is the important part. Or "that's not me" or some version of that, which is the way of telling yourself that you don't believe it's necessary for you to feel this way. But it has to be you personally, not "It is taught or it is believed by others that I don't have to be unhappy about this."

Using The Option Method with Yourself

WHEN you are unhappy it is because you believe you should be. You feel it is necessary.

Whenever you are unhappy (or angry, sad, frightened; use your own words), you can become less unhappy by asking yourself: "If it were possible, would I like to be less unhappy and suffer less?" If you answer *yes*, then ask yourself these questions.

First, "About what am I unhappy?"

Second, "What about that am I most afraid?" and/or "What am I most afraid will happen?" (Try to be more precise.)

Third, "If that were to happen, why would I be unhappy about it?"

Continue clarifying by repeating the above question.

If you answer, "I always have been," or "Wouldn't anyone?" rephrase the question to mean "What is MY reason now for being unhappy about this?"

When you repeatedly answer, "I don't know," ask this . . .

Fourth, "What am I afraid it would mean if I was not unhappy about this?"

If you answer something like, "It would mean I didn't care," or "It would mean I was crazy," that shows how you are preferring and choosing to be unhappy because you are afraid that happiness would mean you don't care about what you see yourself as caring about.

Ask yourself . . .

Fifth, "Why would it have to mean that?"

Could you not still know that even if you were happy, you are still for whatever you are for, and against whatever you are against; and that being happy is not contradictory to your values unless you fear it is?

COMMENTARIES

by Aryeh Nielsen on

"The Practice of The Option Method"

The Attitude Behind the Questions

This commentary represents the editor's synthesis of ideas Bruce Di Marsico expressed only in fragments.

BEFORE: *Allow.* Feel into the Option Attitude. Know that the clients' unhappiness is not real, and they are welcome to keep it if they wish. You are here to help them *help themselves* be a little less unhappy about something that *they* want to be a little less unhappy about. Note: the whole process may take more than one session.

Anytime: *Clarify.* At anytime, clarify what they mean.

Question 1: *Orient/Initiate.* Orient yourself to how you can help them today. Find out what they are interested in examining (allow the rest), and feel into the pacing (patience).

Question 2: *Identify.* Identify specifically the feeling they don't like, and what event is the presumed cause.

Question 3: *Reason.* Exhaust the reasons they believe that the *event* is causing them to have an emotional feeling they don't like.

Question 4: *Cause.* Explore their belief that having an emotional feeling they don't like is *necessary* (e.g., the emotional feeling is necessary to do what they want to do).

Question 5: *Release.* Inquire if they need to choose a feeling they don't like in order to motivate themselves towards their wants.

Test. Inquire how they would feel, now, in response to the original event. If they still confess unhappiness, go back to questions 1–3.

Support. What do you want? What about that is attractive to you? Why do you want that? This leads to either a confession of happy or unhappy wanting. If the latter, then go back to questions 1–3.

After: *Patience.* Now that the client has the realization that they are *at cause* (though not at fault) for feeling a way they don't like, *they* have the option to feel differently, or not. It is *their* choice, not yours.

Necessity Is the Only Belief that Matters

This commentary is a synopsis of ideas that Bruce Di Marsico expressed in many writings or talks, but did not express summarily in a single writing or talk.

PEOPLE are always doing what they want. But some things are wanted on the basis of being in touch with our perfect freedom, and some things are wanted because we (incorrectly) believe they are *necessary* for our happiness.

So, when someone says, "I don't want to be angry," they mean (a) they *do* want to be angry, *but only because they believe it is necessary for their ultimate happiness to be angry*, and (b) being imperfectly in touch with, but not completely out of touch with, their inherent perfect freedom, they are aware that if they didn't believe it was *necessary* to be angry, they wouldn't be.

The point of The Option Method as Bruce Di Marsico taught it, strictly speaking, is not to question beliefs broadly, but to specifically question beliefs in necessity ("should," "must," "have to," "obliged to," etc.). When someone has the insight that what they believed to be necessary isn't, they may appear to have the identical belief as before, but it is from their freedom. "I have to" can become either "I still want to, but happily," "I want to do something else," or "It's no longer relevant to me."

As Bruce Di Marsico said, you can always pretend to be unhappy. So, using one of his examples, instead of being angry at a bureaucrat who was obstructing you, after using The Option Method you might still choose to pretend to be angry, or otherwise be extremely forceful, but from your happiness. Or you might not, but either way, you'd be in touch with your freedom.

The linchpin of unhappiness is the belief that anything is *necessary* for happiness. Ultimately, all unhappy beliefs rest on a specific case of this belief, and any other detail about a belief, except the "necessary for happiness" part, is ultimately irrelevant.

Option Restores the Awareness of Choice

This commentary represents the editor's synthesis of ideas Bruce Di Marsico expressed only in fragments.

OPTION is from the Greek word for choice.

Unhappiness is never chosen. In fact, the cause of unhappiness is believing that there is no choice but to feel a way that is not wanted.

There are four elements of unhappiness in the above definition:

Belief: the whole-body presumption of what is true, forming the basis of action.

Choice: the awareness of inherent freedom, that if something is (physically) possible to do, it can be done—that God, Existence, Nature, Society, or Existence put no inherent restraint on our doing of actions (here, *doing* of actions is differentiated from the successful *accomplishment* of what we aimed to achieve with our actions).

Feeling: the experience of one's own whole-body emotional orientation. Note that feeling can properly be applied to all organisms, for even single-celled organisms organize and orient themselves to their environment (for example, by changing the permeability of the cell membrane).

Wanting: the awareness of being oriented to move toward or away from some situation, event, or state.

So, unhappiness is the whole-body presumption that what is true is that God, Existence, Nature, Society, or Existence have put an inherent restraint on what our emotional disposition is, as if forces outside of us mandated that our emotional disposition be what we would move away from having (if God, Existence, Nature, Society, or Existence did not mandate it).

Each alternative description of unhappiness summarizes an aspect of this. For example, "Unhappiness is being against yourself" emphasizes that we want to move away from our feelings to other feelings, but believe we cannot. "Happiness is Freedom to the *n*th degree" emphasizes that unhappiness depends upon believing that God, Existence, Nature, Society, or Existence places an inherent restraint on our actions. "Unhappiness is *believing* in unhappiness" emphasizes that unhappiness depends on the whole-body presumption that our emotions are inherently restrained.

Beliefs are a mechanism that are inherently neither happy or unhappy. Everything we do and know comes from our beliefs, and insofar as our beliefs are not about the necessity of feeling a way we do not want to feel, beliefs are not unhappy.

Feelings are a mechanism that are inherently neither happy or unhappy. Insofar as feelings are wanted, they are not unhappy. As for unwanted feelings, the question arises as to why they persist. Note that when there is a *situation* we do not like, we *do* want to feel that we do not like the situation. For example, in general we *want* to feel aversion when our finger is burnt—the alternative is to let the finger get more burnt, instead of pulling away!

Wanting is a mechanism that is inherently neither happy nor unhappy. Some things we want to move toward. Some things we want to move away from. Some things we are indifferent to. Insofar as we are not experiencing wanting to move toward a different feeling but believe that we cannot, there is no unhappiness in wanting.

At the root of unhappiness is choice. Choice, in Option, does not refer to a higher-order cognitive ability, such as deciding between chocolate and vanilla ice cream. Choice refers to the inherent state of perfect freedom every organism has. Trees enjoy (employ) their freedom by doing what they do as trees. Snails enjoy (employ) their freedom by doing what they do as snails. It actually requires higher-order cognitive ability to even imagine not enjoying one's inherent freedom. So choice is more properly thought of as what happens naturally in the absence of the higher-order cognitive ability to impede freedom of emotion. Choice is always present inherently, if it is not actively disavowed.

So, although the context of Option Therapy is beliefs about feelings, Option Therapy is not *fundamentally* purposed to change beliefs or feelings (although it often does). It serves to bring to greater awareness that:

1. Some feelings being experienced are unwanted.

2. There are no inherent restrictions by God, Existence, Nature, Society, or Existence on one's own feelings.

When someone becomes conscious of these two circumstances, then unwanted feelings naturally shift, because the person is aware that they don't have to feel a way they don't want to.

As Bruce Di Marsico said, "The whole point of The Option Method is to help people see that their emotions don't just happen to them. That's the only thing that it's meant to show. It can be used to help people be happy, but that isn't its goal."

The Option Method does not aim to change feelings, and is only concerned, ultimately, with beliefs about the *necessity* of feeling certain ways. Since, additionally, only a given person can know that the way they feel is not wanted, Option only serves to help those who want help. Option may be called the most respectful attitude, in that it truly honors each person's (and organism's) way of being. Option is the least intrusive form of therapy possible, not seeking to change a person's actions, feelings, likes, or dislikes, but only being concerned with restoring the awareness of the inherent freedom of feeling that is the birthright of every organism, from bacteria to trees to snails to humans.

PART VIII
Stories and Meditations

SECTION I

Stories

Going Off to College

WHAT causes unhappiness? Why are we unhappy? Well, The Option Method helps us to see that all behavior comes from our feelings, our emotions, which are themselves judgments. Our emotions do not happen to us. Now, we have in our vocabulary that our emotions happen to us: "That really hurt me." "It made me feel bad." "You made me feel this way." "You made me feel that way." We speak about all of our feelings as very passive things that we happen to receive and they just happen to us. Our unhappiness just happens to us. That's always our experience whenever we're unhappy—that it happened to us; we didn't choose it. But it didn't happen to us. It was a judgment that we made, and perhaps I could demonstrate that.

There's a family of a mother, a father, a brother, a sister, and I'll throw in one other person who's not part of that family, a stranger who is walking down the street. Outside the family home, the older sister is going off to college. That's the simple event. She's leaving for school, and she's saying goodbye. To that event, there are many emotional reactions, and each of those four people who are left all have a different emotional response. Now, to show that the emotions just don't happen to them, let me show you that their emotions are based on their judgment of what they see happening.

The mother of the daughter is crying. She's really feeling bad. Why? Because all she's able to see is that she's losing her daughter. She doesn't believe she needs to go off to college. She's going to miss her, and she sees the whole situation as one of loss, so she feels bad. The father, he has sort of mixed feelings. He feels good about it, and he feels bad about it. He has both feelings. Why? Because he sees it's really a good thing, and it's good for her. She's going to meet the kind of people she wants to be with. She's going to get an education. It's going to help her, and he feels good about that. That's why. And he feels bad because he is going to miss his little girl. They've loved each other very much, and he sees that there's going to be sort of a gap, and he sees some loss, and he feels bad about that, but he also feels good.

Her younger brother, who's about ten years old, is just absolutely overjoyed. The big pest is going away to school. Now he can use the telephone whenever he wants, and he's really just very happy about it. The stranger walks down the street, and he sees this whole thing going on, and he feels absolutely nothing about it. Why? He has no opinion. He has no judgment about what's going on, and he just continues on his way.

Each of the emotional responses is seen very clearly in this example. I picked it and made it simple and set it up that way, and I loaded it to show that each emotional response came from the judgment that was made. When we judge the event as bad, we feel bad about it. When we judge it as good, we feel good about it. When we judge it as both good and bad, we feel both things about it. When we don't judge it at all, we feel nothing about it. That's really where it's at. And so we try to take this view consistently and see that kind of phenomena in all of our behavior. That whenever we're feeling bad, it's because somehow we have judged something as bad. That we cannot feel bad without having first made the judgment, the decision, that it was bad, and that all of our unhappiness comes indeed from that phenomenon, from that dynamic of seeing events and calling them bad.

That's why both you and I could witness something, and something identical could happen to both of us, and I might feel bad about it, and you might feel fine about it. It might not bother you at all. In fact, you might even feel good about it. We could both go to the same play. You might think it was great, and I might think it was horrible. You really had a good time and you feel good about it, and I really feel bad about it. We might be married; we might have two different feelings about our child. It goes on that way. If it's true that we, then, are the ones who make our emotions by our judgments, then it simply cannot be true that things make us feel that way. It simply is not true, for instance, that that daughter, that daughter who was going off to school, made her mother feel bad. Which very frequently, in many situations, would be very much what she'd be prone to thinking, and some would say to her, "Boy, you really made your mother feel bad," and it was somehow her fault.

If that were true, then how come her father didn't feel bad and her brother didn't feel bad and the stranger didn't feel bad, if she's the one who "made" the emotion? Was it the daughter who made the mother feel bad? Or the mother's view, her own personal judgment and belief about what happened?

So what we find is that it's our beliefs about things that cause our emotions.

Holding Your Breath

UNHAPPINESS, to me, is a not doing, and it's very similar to holding one's breath, and it takes effort. One has to find a reason to hold one's breath or else you wouldn't hold your breath, just like being unhappy. One has to find a reason to be unhappy or one would never be unhappy. And that in giving up holding one's breath, there is no pain, there's release. The pain is in actually holding the breath. All you do is stop holding your breath. You don't actually do anything. You stop deciding to hold your breath, you see, and you just start breathing, and there's no pain. In fact, there's relief. In making that choice and that decision, there's no pain, because it is a choice for true happiness, something that's really good for you. It was a very clear thing. The unhappiness was the holding of breath, and that's what takes the effort, and that's what the painful thing is. You can't be unhappy unless you think there's a reason to be, any more than you wouldn't hold your breath unless you felt there was a reason to hold it.

Genesis

ANYBODY remember the Genesis myth of happiness and unhappiness and of good and evil? It starts in the Torah, in the book of Genesis, second chapter, fourth verse.

God created all these things and he said that they were good. They were very good. And it lists a whole bunch of things that were good. They were all good. There was no question, it was just simply stated, these things were good. And man was given control over all these good things, and he had all these good things.

Then, for whatever reason or another, we come to the part where someone tells man, "You can know the difference between what's good and what's not good. Here is the tree of knowledge of good and evil, and if you eat of this, you'll be like gods." All man had known was good. So he ate of the tree because he was lied to. But what was the lie? The lie wasn't that he would know the difference between good and evil. The lie was that there was a difference.

And so then he ran around and started saying, "That's evil, that's evil, that's evil, that's bad," and he covered himself, and in the next part of the story, God comes walking through the garden and he says, "Adam and Eve, where are you? I can tell that you're hiding. Come on out," and he finds certain parts of their body are covered. He says, "Who ever told you that that was bad? That you had to cover yourself?" "We were ashamed. We decided that it was bad." And if you remember, he said, " That's what you're going to do? Now you're going to decide what's bad and what's good? Okay. That's what you're gonna do then, and you're gonna do that for the rest of your life and so will your children." And from now on, we're all cursed to deciding what's good and bad.

All right, it's a wisdom that an ancient culture was able to see that perhaps really still has an application. There was a point where man did not have to believe that things were bad, and decide that they were. He didn't have to say he was unhappy being naked.

It could only be a lie because then they started referring to the person that lied to man as the father of lies, because all lies come from believing that evil exists, don't they? From believing there's a reason to be unhappy, that there is such a thing as evil, and there is something to be unhappy about.

The Troubadour

THERE was a troubadour who traveled in Spain. Every year, he made the cycle. He was in the north during the summer and in the south during the winter, and he went around during the Middle Ages, and he tried to coincide his stops with places of pilgrimages and the various events that were going on, and he made his living as a troubadour. Frequently along the way, he would join up with bands of gypsies and travel part of the way with them. At other times, he would travel with sheep herders. At times, he would travel with the troubadours, sometimes with circuses.

He wasn't a very happy man; in fact, he was a very unhappy man. He was well aware of his poverty and how he had to sleep with fleas and lice, how he had to sleep on the cold roadside, and how people threw things at him. All in all, he was a good troubadour. He sang beautiful songs and sang them beautifully. They had a lot of meaning to everybody but him. He no longer really heard the words and never really listened to what he sang, but other people did.

One day, he was in Seville. The Moors had left the city not too long before, so this was the early 16th century, and there was a whole lot of new wealth for the Spanish. He was very much aware of that, and how poor he was, especially when he got to the city. It used to be a Moorish town, and now it was a Spanish town, and it was filled with castles and alcazars. He was singing in the courtyard—it was a really plaintive song, very plaintive, very sad, very melancholy, about the dreams of wealth and paradise—and it touched one old man very much, who was a new Dom, and gave him such joy that he said, "Come here." And the troubadour went over to the Dom's balcony, and the Dom threw him down a gold coin, which was a fantastic amount of money for this troubadour. Fantastic. I imagine it's equivalent to a year's wages. And he said to him, "You just sing so beautifully. You just sing so tremendously. You're the best troubadour that I've ever heard, and I want you to have this. And when you come back next year, I'll even give you more than this."

Well, from that moment, the troubadour's life changed, and he went on his next cycle, constantly looking forward to getting back to Seville. He heard his own songs, and he changed them to even better ones. He heard what they meant, and he made them even more beautiful. He was the best troubadour that he ever was. He was so happy that the fleas didn't bother him, the lice didn't bother him. His whole life had changed, and he was just living for getting back to Seville. It was fantastic. As he got closer and closer, and halfway around, he was at Santiago de Compostela, and it was a whole new thing for him. He had a fantastic religious experience at the shrine. He just couldn't wait to get back.

Happier and happier, he got back to Seville, and he ran to the house, and said, "Is Dom Pedro here? I'm finally back," and the daughter answered and said, "I'm sorry, señor, but he died about this time last year." And the Spaniard said, "But he had given me a gold coin, and it made me so happy, and I was living all year just to come back here because he said he would give me more." And she said to him, "But he has. He already has." Of course, the troubadour had two options at that point, and that's where the story ends.

He never spent that gold coin, by the way. He kept it. He lived on all the money he made by being such a better troubadour and such a happier person. And what is happiness, then? Was it a gold coin? Somehow he didn't feel that he had anything to be unhappy about. Anything that he was ever going to be unhappy about just wasn't going to be a problem. And all the things that he felt he needed the money for, he didn't even really need the money for.

Why was he not unhappy about the fleas anymore? Or those stupid pilgrims at the shrine where he became one of them? What is happiness? It wasn't a gold coin for him. Yet it was the hope for more gold somehow because the gold meant that he would be happy. And so before he even had what he thought would make him happy, he was happy. And before you even have what you think you have to have in order to be happy, you can be happy thinking you're going to get it before you even have it. It gives you what you want from it, and you don't even have it.

How different would you be if you thought that next year at this time, you would have a million dollars? How different would you be this year? And you wouldn't have had the million dollars yet. How happy would you be before you even had what you said you had to have in order to be happy? So, what is it that you have to have in order to be happy?

Apparently nothing. But there are some things you can't have and be happy, and that's fear and unhappiness.

If you knew that starting tomorrow you'd be a happier person, and if by some miracle, each day, you would be happier and happier, and all your troubles would fall away and you would worry less and less and fear less and less and have less to fear, and that each day from now on for the rest of your life, you'd be happier and happier, how would you feel now? Look at how you're feeling now already.

The Man Who Found Diamonds

Original story written by Wendy Dolber

ONCE upon a time there lived a man who knew no great happiness. It was true that he was content enough, but he, like all his neighbors, had the feeling that something more was needed to be truly happy. One called it a good marriage, another called it a healthy body, still another called it a good crop. Some had no name for it or even an awareness that they wanted anything different from what they had. But if any of them were asked "What would it take for you to have everything in life?" there would always be something that was not yet achieved. Everyone was waiting for something. It was part of their way of life.

Each neighbor had his own way of dealing with this phenomenon. Some traveled far from home in search of answers, some studied the old books, some lived as though they already knew the answer, and some lived as though there was no answer. Even though all day long the neighbors busied themselves with their living from dawn to dusk, one apart from them could clearly see that they looked for the answer in everything they did. Viewed from a distance, what looked at close range like a diverse collection of people, each involved in completing his own isolated task, could be seen as one great animal with its many parts all working together toward one goal—to find this answer. "Is it in the bread I'm baking, the dress I'm making, the earth I'm turning? Is it in this shoe I'm sewing, this house I build? Do I see it in the sky or in the trees? Is it in my lover's eyes?"

How could it be that in all this dedication to a greater happiness, no one could really say in truth that they had indeed found the answer? This is how it was.

The one man who I have spoken of lived in his house and worked his little patch of land to feed himself. He was not the kind to speak to others of what was to be in his life, but he lived each day and did what he did with a steady hand, hoping secretly to himself that behind it all was the recipe to great happiness, but never really affirming or denying the truth of his way. He would daydream, as he worked, of scenes where his neighbors looked at him with a special respect and he loved them all in a most generous manner. It was his habit to wander through the fields of the village in his free time, silently translating his secret longings into episodes of satisfaction as he would have it. It was just such a day when he went wandering and musing that a most extraordinary event occurred.

As he walked he came upon a turn that he had not noticed before, which led to a field of grass. The sun was high in the sky and lent rich new color to its earth. The cries of birds in the air mingled with the distant rush of water, and as he stopped to listen breathlessly, poised with senses alert, his eyes fixed upon an object close at hand, which now caught the sun and shot it back in a twinkling flash of light. Instantly he was captivated. With a stampeding heart he advanced with both hands open, fingers wide apart, held breath in a body of quietly controlled expression about to be born but not yet certain if its time had come. "Oh my God! Oh my God," he whispered softly, tentatively. "Could it be, could it be? Not yet, not till I'm sure." And then approaching, still, as if the thing might sprout legs and run away, he saw indeed that it was just what he knew it to be all along but needed the confirmation of his eyes to believe. Sinking down upon his knees, for his legs could hold him up no longer, he touched what he knew belonged to him. His diamond. His heart lit up with its brilliance and shone with joy that gave his body new life, and for many, many moments he knelt there in total recognition and gladness for what had come to him. He had never before imagined even wanting such a thing, but now that he saw it, his every movement said, "Yes, Yes, this is what I want." He thought of the new freedom possessing such a treasure would bring, and of his new life, as in an act of total gladness he scooped up the earth with both hands, kissing it and rubbing it lovingly into his face; and finally, as if reluctant to part with it, let it run gently through his fingers, even as his tears brimmed over his eyes and ran, streaking his cheeks where the earth still clung.

"But wait. What is this in my hands?" Where one diamond had been, now there were two, as if the earth, in passing, had secretly slipped him another diamond for good measure. To find one diamond was more than he had ever dreamed possible. But two? Somehow, this one seemed alien to him, irrelevant. Possessing one diamond, he had felt full and hopeful and glad, but this second produced an empty place palpable in his breast—an empty, vacant nothing. "I must want this, I must," he protested; but instead of burying his face in the earth, he stood up and, with an air of one who had been "caught in the act," cleaned his face with his kerchief, brushed his clothes, wiped his eyes. He must have looked so foolish acting like that. Acting like what? It was certainly not unjustified to act so after finding such a treasure. Why, then, was he so embarrassed? Oh, it must just be that he, usually being an inhibited sort of person, naturally would be embarrassed to have had anyone watch him display such emotion. That must be it. He was very inhibited. In fact, he would have liked to show the same gratitude for the second diamond, but he just couldn't. He was not the kind of person to show great emotion. When he found the first diamond, it was just that he was so overwhelmed that he was not quite himself. He had gotten carried away.

Feeling thus justified, he squared his shoulders, lifting his eyes to meet the multitude of jeering faces he imagined watched him. Instead, a field of tiny lights seemed to thrust themselves forward as if they had all the time been waiting to be noticed. A field of diamonds. Not *one*, to be hid away and brought out on special occasions to be admired. Not a *second*, to ease the pain if the first got stolen. But hundreds of diamonds everywhere. Diamonds by the armload. Diamonds for the taking. No rare treasure anymore, but as common as the grass between them, as the earth to which he had just been so devoted. A treasure that could be gotten simply by bending down and picking it up. The truth was so much more obvious now. He had been duped, seduced, made to look the fool. No longer the lucky one, but the victim of some cruel joke. Yet if a crowd of his neighbors were to come upon this field now, would he not rush out to gather up as many diamonds as he could? But where were they? Surely if these were truly diamonds, others would be here to reap the harvest, *if* these were truly diamonds.

What he had known and recognized at first glance, he now questioned; and his very questioning was in itself an answer.

He said, "If I found all these things, they couldn't possibly be diamonds." He emptied his pockets and threw the diamonds back onto the field. He said to himself, "If these are diamonds, why isn't everyone else taking them? If these are diamonds, how come there's so many? If these are diamonds, how come I'm the one who is finding them? If I'm the one who found them, they can't really be diamonds. If they were really diamonds, there wouldn't be so many of them." He argued himself out of the fact that they were diamonds. Because he was the one who found them. Because they were in this barren field. Because he had always believed that they were extremely rare.

By the time he turned for home, the sun was low in the sky, the grass lost in shadows, the moon a pale ghost. Now and then as he walked, he felt the hardness of many chips of "glass" under his feet and a great sadness bent down his head and numbed his mind and body as two glistening crystals dropped unnoticed from his hand.

Just because you found a lot of them doesn't mean they aren't diamonds. Just because you find them everywhere doesn't mean they're not diamonds. A diamond is a diamond because it's a diamond. Happiness: because it's plentiful, it doesn't mean it's not there, and because you find it everywhere and you can see it, and it was something you never thought you could see, it doesn't mean it's not true.

SECTION II

Meditations

Choice

PEOPLE choose their beliefs, every belief.

People choose what they have hope in. People choose what they have no hope in.

People decide what they want, and they decide what they don't want.

People choose to believe that they can't do something, or can do something.

People choose to lie or tell the truth.

People choose to make believe and say they know what they do not know, OR they choose to admit that they do not know. People choose to make believe and say they don't know what they do know, OR they choose to admit that they do know.

People choose what they feel about anything.

People are free everywhere, and yet choose to believe that they are constrained in their opinions, beliefs, attitudes, decisions, and *options*.

Why do people believe thus?

They choose to believe that they do not choose. In some way they must believe that they would be responsible for something bad if they had to realize that they freely choose. People fear being free because if they were free they would be "too" free and would do evil or something bad.

People make choices.

This is not wrong, nothing is. There just are consequences.

These consequences of choices are not good or bad.

Good and bad are also choices of judgment.

It is also not wrong to judge. There are just consequences for that.

The consequences of judging are not good or bad.

The consequences are happiness or unhappiness.

People choose what to do, and choose what not to do.

This is not wrong. People choose what to feel emotionally, and choose what not to feel emotionally.

This is not wrong. People choose what to forget, and what to remember. People choose their postures. People choose their mannerisms.

People choose their speech, language, inflections. People choose what they learn.

People choose their tastes, opinions, attitudes. People choose their superstitions and religions. People choose what they believe is proof of anything. People choose what they believe is relevant and pertinent.

People choose what they think about their lives, their dreams, their memories, their thoughts, affections. People choose whatever they think about anything.

The Absolute Truth Is Simple

September 7, 1975

THERE is no such thing as unhappiness. People have believed there was. You have been one of those people.

There is nothing, absolutely nothing to cause unhappiness.

Since there is no unhappiness and never can be, no one has to be afraid of anything.

There is nothing to be afraid of, or angry about. Nothing that happens can bring about unhappiness.

There have been many symptoms of people who have believed in unhappiness.

No symptoms of unhappiness exist, but symptoms of *belief* in it have.

Once you know the truth that all is happiness, you will have reminders.

All that is can be the cause of your awareness of the truth.

If you believe that unhappiness could happen, in any of the many ways you can do that, your body, your mind, your heart, your very self will remind you of what you were believing.

You will not like what you are thinking, doing, feeling.

In order to make the reality of happiness real in your lives, there is only one thing to do:

have the perfect awareness that unhappiness does not exist,

have the perfect awareness that you have changed,

have the perfect awareness that you do not believe what you used to believe,

have the perfect awareness that happiness is the cause and destiny of all you are and do and all that is.

Every feeling is a reminder.

All feelings and thoughts are awareness.

Each feeling and thought makes you aware of what you believe about your future.

Happiness permeates all that is real and that happiness will naturally manifest itself to you, and in your life.

Give it room. Make room.

Remind yourself always of the truth: "You are never going to be unhappy."

Cor Super Ratio

July 1982

To enter into a new life, which is in our sense spiritual and miraculous, it is possible to do so by choice.

One can choose a way of life and state of mind that makes it possible to receive the gifts and graces which are fruits of being in union with happiness and the cause of all knowledge and action, especially quiet action.

The essence of God is Happiness. The fruit of union is knowing. The love of knowing is Quiet Doing.

Deus Super Omnes Beatus
Super Omnes Sanctitude,
Scientia est Vita,
Facientia est.

To be the channel and expression of knowing and doing, to enter into miraculous union, to live in habitual joy, confess that no one has to be unhappy, and do whatever you want.

Listen to your heart, for that is where knowledge acts.

Do only what attracts you.

Do what you feel like.

Cor super ratio. The heart above logic.

If you are lost, it is because you ignore your source. Turn around and you will be instantly miracled. There is no delay, no punishment, no more old life. Look inward to see what you want to do and be glad to do it. Being obedient to your heart is not obedience; it is your life and joy. Your whole reason for existence.

PART IX

A Comprehensive Overview

A Brief Compendium of The Option Method for The Option Method Professional

How to Use This Compendium

This compendium of the principle, axioms and fundamental ideas of The Option Method is intended primarily as a quick reference for the advanced student of The Option Method who already has had substantial experience with his or her personal analysis as well as seminar training. I realize that it may also have value for the layman and welcome your interest.

Because the basic idea of Option is simple, the insights of The Method can be expressed in many cases as aphorisms. The goal in this exposition is to be succinct. In most sections the ideas expressed are merely restatements of another idea, or the same central truth in other words. I realize that there is really only one truth of happiness, and that truth can be expressed in various ways. My hope is to try to be relevant to the concerns of the different kinds of reader; whether a curious person, a novice, an advanced student or an Option analyst practitioner.

Since I intend this compendium to be easy to use for a more effective practice of The Option Method (by providing insights and a reliable reference), it has a decidedly axiomatic tone, with Laws, Corollaries, and the like. That is intentional. It in no way is meant or is able to supplant the personal experience of using The Option Method. It is a practical handbook for the application of what you may already know. When a reminder or maxim is not pertinent or useful, nothing can substitute for The Option Method itself.

Although there is much to know because of The Option Method, and many applicable concepts that can be taught as a result, there is nothing didactic about The Option Method as method. It is first, foremost, and solely an analytic technique; a maieutic and heuristic method of questioning. Its heuristic quality is what makes it The Option Method. I never intended to create it as a preaching procedure; a way to tell people that they need not be unhappy. Option Method is a maieutic method also, and as a helping tool is meant to aid people to discover for themselves what their role is in their happiness and unhappiness.

It is simply a question of effective competence that the underlying rationale be axiomatic and accepted as indisputable by those who wish to practice: i.e., *the individual is the sole determiner of his or her emotional states*. The proper application of the method requires this knowledge. The Option Method practitioner (when actually using the method itself) never teaches, advises, or challenges the client. Self-analysis and discovery is the value of The Option Method.

Notwithstanding that I affirm that The Option Method is not a teaching tool, it still has been desirable to teach interested persons about it. Those who hope to help others can especially benefit from the knowledge that there is, indeed, a canon of truisms about happiness, unhappiness, and the many names unhappiness goes by.

If what, at first, seems too dogmatic and simplistic in my style puts you off, please be patient. I only mean to make a cogent whole out of many years of experience, and various attempts to teach The Option Method in the most effective way. The Laws and Principles expounded herein are meant as a teaching guide. Although I hope it can be used to answer most questions, I know that there are areas I have not even touched on, let alone exhausted, in this brief reference aid.

In any case, when the various sections are studied and explored (in no particular order), I think that an understanding of the simplicity will emerge. The ideal aim of using this little guide to further your own explorations and expertise in the employment of The Option Method is the best use it could have. Your life as a happy person is the only life you truly want. This Compendium is dedicated to the fact that happiness is really your option. I hope Option will be your way to know that.

Let the motto of The Option Method Institute be yours: *Beata Vita Omnia Est*: Happiness Is Everything.

Have fun with the ideas in here.

Bruce M. Di Marsico
January 28, 1992

SECTION I

The Option

Option is from the Latin word for choice and the Greek word for servant. Both roots are quite appropriate for the name of a method whose goal is to serve by helping people realize the role that personal choice plays in their emotional states. This section is an exposition of the basic insights of The Option Method regarding the nature of unhappiness and other emotions.

The Natural Laws of Happiness

First Axiom: All people seek happiness.

Second Axiom: When happiness seems impossible, then all people seek to avoid the greater unhappiness.

Third Axiom: All other things are sought as a means to the greatest happiness, or to avoid the greatest unhappiness.

The Option to Be Happy

The value of knowing how emotions are derived is in order to use that knowledge to serve ourselves in our quest for greater happiness. Since people choose their emotions, they can be happy.

This Is How We Work!

By Our Choice of Beliefs: The Primary Operating Principle of Emotions

We choose our emotions by means of our beliefs alone. Once the belief is held, the equivalent emotion necessarily follows. They are the same. The belief is operative as the emotion.

First Law

I. The First Law of the Option

We feel happiness or unhappiness according to what we believe we will feel.

The Prime Examples of The Option Method's First Law.

Beliefs about happiness and unhappiness, psychological attitudes, moods, moral judgments, and emotions are the same experience.

Emotions are beliefs about the causes of happiness and unhappiness.

Attitudes are long-held beliefs about the causes of happiness and unhappiness.

Attitudes are emotional states which are applied and experienced instantaneously, according to perceptions. The perceptions can be subtle or gross. The attitude comes into play whenever it seems to the believer as relevant.

Emotions are judgments as to the relevance to happiness or not: "good for" or "bad for" happiness.

I.1 First Corollary of the First Law

We would always be happy if we did not believe we had to be unhappy.

Happiness is believing you are going to be happy or happier.

Examples:
a) You are happy whenever you believe there is something to be happy about.
b) You are happy when you believe something makes you happy.

I.2 Second Corollary of the First Law

Whatever we believe is bad for happiness (i.e., causes unhappiness) is feared. If it happens, we get unhappy. Fear or worry is believing you are going to be unhappy or more unhappy. Unhappiness is believing you have something to be unhappy about.

Examples:
a) You are unhappy whenever, and only whenever, you believe that there is something to be unhappy about.
b) You are unhappy only about whatever you believe is something to be unhappy about.
c) You have fear only whenever you believe something will make you unhappy.

Second Law

II. The Second Law of the Option

We can never get unhappy about something we don't believe is something to get unhappy about.

We can never get happy about something we don't believe is something to be happy about.

II.1 Second Law Corollary

Whatever emotions of happiness or unhappiness you believe you are being caused to feel, you feel now. Whatever emotions you believe you are going to feel (in the present or in the future), you begin to feel now.

Third Law

III. The Third Law of the Option

The belief that our beliefs are irrelevant makes us fearful and feeling like we need help.

We don't understand and realize that the first two laws of emotions can be used to be happy. We feel like victims to our emotions because we don't realize that our emotions are determined through our beliefs about the causes of unhappiness. We can question those beliefs and then either affirm or change them. We no longer need to feel like victims. We can understand our choices.

III.1 Third Law Corollary

Nothing makes you unhappy. Your belief that something does is what causes unhappiness.

What you are unhappy about does not make you unhappy, your belief that it can does.

Conclusion:

Therefore, you can use The Option Method to not be unhappy, and be happier. The Three Laws of The Option are demonstrable and can be experienced through use of the questions of The Option Method.

Fourth Law

IV. The Fourth Law of the Option

Believing "Happiness is Bad" is Unhappy: We are afraid of unhappiness as what we mistakenly believe is happiness. We think we fear happiness, but what we really fear is unhappiness under the name of happiness. We believe that, in some cases, being happy would be "self" destructive. We believe that happiness is not true, but a denial of the "reality" of unhappiness.

IV.1 First Corollary of the Fourth Law

Because we believe we are bad, we believe "happiness" will make us disregard or forsake our truly held values.

IV.2 Second Corollary of the Fourth Law

We believe that if we are "happy" we will not take care of ourselves or what we love.

IV.3 Third Corollary of the Fourth Law

We believe it is bad, crazy, unreal, wrong, immoral, sick, inappropriate, unloving, contradictory, etc. NOT to be unhappy about certain things or losses.

IV.4 Fourth Corollary of the Fourth Law

These concepts (beliefs) of "happiness" are merely ways of believing that if you do not get unhappy (just because you don't want to) when you should, then you will have to be unhappy eventually, anyway, because you must be lying, bad, crazy, etc. and against your true self.

Conclusion:

The "happiness" we fear is not happiness, but a misunderstanding of unhappiness under the name of happiness.

Fifth Law

V. The Fifth Law of the Option

Believing "Unhappiness is Good" is Unhappy: Unhappiness is experienced because we believe that unhappiness is good, healthy, sincere, sane, moral, loving, appropriate and self-affirming when properly experienced.

V.1 First Corollary of the Fifth Law

You believe that if you are not unhappy about something, it "means" that you are not really or sincerely against it, even though you know you are. You wouldn't be concerned with this seeming paradox otherwise.

Conclusion:

You know which things you have decided are against your values. Being happy is being free to still know that, without needing to be unhappy to "prove" it.

V.2 Second Corollary of the Fifth Law

You assume that if you are believing that something is bad for a value of yours, it means that you must be unhappy. In order to be on "your side," you get unhappy about your predicament.

Conclusion:

You have no predicament. Holding values is a freedom. Not all events cooperate with your values. You are actually merely unhappy about not getting what you want.

Sixth Law

VI. Sixth Law of Option

Wanting is happy. Needing is unhappy. Wanting, or believing in needing, are the human motivations. We are motivated as we experience our beliefs about happiness and unhappiness. We either want as a free, self-motivated or self-affirmed choice, or we believe we have needs in order to have happiness or to avoid unhappiness.

VI.1 First Corollary of the Sixth Law

Happy Motivation: Desire, Wanting

We believe we will be happy if we get what we want, or avoid what we don't want.

VI.2 Second Corollary of the Sixth Law

Unhappy Motivation: Needing, Fearing

We believe we will be unhappy if we don't get what we want (need), or don't avoid what we don't want.

Seventh Law

VII. Seventh Law of Option

Free Will: All choices are free, and none are not free.

VII.1 Seventh Law Corollary

All desires are freely chosen since no particular desire, or lack of any one is necessary to happiness.

SECTION II

Further Axioms of Option

This section contains further examples of the fundamental laws of human emotions in topic form. These can also serve as a quick reference for summaries and answers to essential questions about The Option Method.

Feelings

If you believe something is the type of thing that makes you unhappy, you will believe it is currently making you unhappy. That is what you will seem to feel.

As long as you believe something will make you unhappy, you will keep experiencing the fear that it will make you unhappy.

Regarding Unhappiness

a) If you believe that something makes you unhappy, you will feel that it makes you unhappy.

or, in other words:

b) If you believe that something makes you unhappy, you will feel unhappy just as if it actually made you unhappy.

or, in other words:

c) If you believe that something makes you unhappy, you will believe that you feel unhappy just as if it actually made you unhappy.

or, in other words:

d) If you believe that something makes you unhappy, you will "feel" your believing just as if it actually made you unhappy.

Regarding Happiness

a) If you believe that something makes you happy, you will feel that it makes you happy.

b) If you believe that something makes you happy, you will feel happy just as if it actually made you happy.

All Human Emotions

Past feelings were caused that same way, as described in the First Law.

Future feelings will be caused that same way, as described in the First Law.

If you believe you are going to get unhappy in the future, you become unhappy now.

If you believe you are going to get happy in the future, you become happy now.

Beliefs

* A belief is accepting something as true, as a fact.
* A belief is assumed to be true.
* A belief is not caused; it is created by choice.

Another's belief when affirmed by you is re-created as your own. The other's belief does not cause yours. Likewise, unhappiness is not caused, it is created as a feeling by a belief.

Choosing Best

* All people choose what they believe is best for them, and can do no other.
* Given the choice between seemingly good things, we will always choose the better (best) or the believed highest good of our choices as the best choice.
* Given the choice between a believed good or bad, we can only choose the good, which we judge as the best.
* Given a choice between only bad things, we can only choose what we believe is the less worse or least bad of choices, which we believe is best.
* When we cannot (do not) decide which is the best choice, we then choose the method we think is best for deciding, or we choose what we believe is best for us when not deciding. If we choose to make no choice, then that is because we believe that that choice is best.

Axiomatic Corollaries of Option

Pertinent and Relevant Corollaries

There are numerous corollary insights, which are as varied as the forms of unhappiness. They will be discovered in your life as they become relevant and pertinent to your awareness of your desire for happiness. They range from mild annoyance to livid rage, from slight disappointment to bleak depression. From a nagging feeling of something undone or forgotten, to dread of doom, demons, and suicidal fears. From feeling guilty for another's bad feelings, to feeling hated by God. From phobias (things or behaviors you "must" avoid) and manias (things or behaviors you "must" do) of all sorts, to feeling stupid and worthless. These are just a few examples of almost countless forms of unhappiness that we believe are caused by something or another; by phenomena, events, others, or ourselves.

Why There Seems To Be Many Forms of Unhappiness

The various names and forms of unhappiness and happiness are related to what is believed to be the "cause" of those emotions; not the real cause, of course, which is revealed in the above axioms.

Examples of Fears, Truths, and Other Analyses:

Phobia Something you "must" avoid. (Also, something you must do in order to avoid what you must avoid.)

Mania Something you "must" do. (Also, something you must avoid in order to do what you must do.)

Worry If you believe there is something you must do to avoid unhappiness, and you're not sure you will, that is worry and anxiety.

Boredom If you believe there is something you must do to be happy or happier now, and you're not sure you know what it is, or that you will do it, that is boredom.

Fear and Hate If you believe that something can cause your unhappiness, that is fear, and loathing of it.

Terror If you believe that something will happen, and it will cause your unhappiness, that is terror.

Owing No one owes anything to anybody, or even to themselves. If we want to give, we may give. No one should do anything, or must do anything. We do as we choose.

Owning We only own what we can effectively control, and only for as long as we control it. We may lose ownership. We may try to regain ownership.

Rights We always have the right to be happy. Unhappiness is believing we do not have that right.

We have the right to do anything we have the power to do, or the ability to do. We have no right to anything we do not have. We have the right to try to get anything, or keep it.

Prudence We exercise our rights or use our power and abilities accordingly, as we think best.

Blame Your belief that you can or will get unhappy is the cause of unhappiness, not what you blame or believe is the cause.

Enemies Neither anyone nor anything ever caused your unhappiness. Your belief that they had that power was the cause. You feared what they did or what happened.

Innocence You do only what you believe is best for your happiness. This includes believing you must be unhappy when you have believed that was true.

Freedom to Be Different People don't make you unhappy by not doing what they "should," or by doing what they "shouldn't." Your unhappiness is caused by your belief that there is a way people should be. There may be ways you want people to be, but that does not, in itself, determine what motivates them, or what they believe is best for them. Of course, the same goes for you. You don't have to be what others expect.

"What" Doesn't Matter It doesn't matter what you believe can cause your unhappiness; what matters is only (the part) that you believe you will be unhappy. That is the cause of unhappiness.

"As If," the Illusion of Unhappiness Nothing causes unhappiness, it merely seems that it can be caused. Merely believing that something can cause unhappiness makes you fear *as if* something can. Merely believing that something will cause unhappiness makes you feel *as if* something will. Merely believing something is making you unhappy makes you feel *as if* something is making you unhappy. Still, it is only that you are feeling as you believe you will.

For example: the feeling that one is being cheated does not mean that the actuality of being cheated causes that feeling. The feeling, in itself, certainly does not mean that one is truly being cheated.

You don't need to be cheated to feel cheated; you only need to believe you are. The feeling that something makes you unhappy doesn't mean that it actually does, or even can. All you feel is that you "feel" (believe) it can and does. You don't need to be ever actually "made unhappy" to feel that you are. You only need to believe you are being made to be unhappy.

Unhappy against Your Will You cannot be made unhappy by anything that you do not believe is something to be unhappy about.

Evil There is no evil. Since by the word "evil" is meant that which can make someone unhappy against their will or choice, it does not exist. All unhappiness is "caused" by the believer's belief that he or she must be unhappy, not by a being or an event other than that belief.

Bad Nothing or no one is bad in itself. Things are bad "for" or "to" something we want or value.

Bad in Essence Nothing is bad for our happiness, except unhappiness; and that's for only as long as it lasts. It lasts only as long as we believe we deserve it.

Eternal Happiness We would always be happy if we did not believe we had to be unhappy.

Bad Vibes, Evil Spirits, Manifestations, Apparitions, Etc. The belief in evil makes it seem that evil exists.

Things That Seem against You Because things are destructive to what we love or want does not mean that they are evil, or that they should not be. It means that they are destructive, and we do not love them, and do not want them.

Freedom to Be against While Happy We do not have to believe that something is evil, bad, or causes unhappiness in order to be free to be against it, or not want it. We don't want it because it seems to be against what we do want.

Freedom of Taste We cannot be happy if we believe that we are not allowed our own tastes and preferences in life. You are free to not like whomever or whatever you choose for any reason or no clear reason. You are free to like anyone or anything for any or no reason. You are also free to change your mind.

Freedom of Choice You do not have to justify or explain your preferences or choices, ever. You may wish to privately explore your motive or rationale. You may choose to explain to gain another's agreement, but you do not have to in order to be satisfied that you have the right to your choice.

All That Is, Is The belief that there are things or phenomena anywhere in the universe that should not exist is the belief in evil.

Fear of Being Evil Feeling you are evil is believing you are not unhappy when you should be, or happy when you shouldn't be. The modern version is feeling crazy, self-defeating, sick, etc.

Hatred of Evil People Believing another is evil is the fear (believing) that they cause unhappiness and are happy or indifferent about their "evil" or another's unhappiness when they shouldn't be. It is the belief that they shouldn't cause unhappiness. The fear of evil people or beings is the belief that they may desire our unhappiness, and that they can achieve that.

Guilt Guilt is feeling bad for not feeling bad when I should. It is believing that I will feel bad for not having felt bad, or for not having believed something would make me unhappy. It is feeling bad for "making" someone else feel bad instead of me. It is feeling bad for making or allowing myself to feel good when I should not have felt good. It is believing that being happy makes me evil. It is believing that being evil will make me unhappy (see the Fourth Corollary of the Fourth Law).

Fear All fear is the fear of unhappiness. Does anyone fear poverty in itself, or is it the unhappiness that poverty is believed to bring? In other words: do we fear being poor, or poor and then unhappy? Does anyone fear being sick, or sick and then unhappy? Loss? Or loss and the "resulting" unhappiness? Alone? Or unhappy loneliness?

Fear of Desires Since all fear is the fear of unhappiness, this fear is likewise also. The feared desire is believed to be a "wrongful" desire because the object is believed to cause unhappiness. If I got what I wanted it would be "bad" because it would or should "cause" unhappiness to me or another. (see "Guilt" and "Fear of the Motivating Cause of Desires")

Fear of the Motivating Cause of Desires

The Fear of Being Crazy We fear that what is behind some desires is bad for us. We fear that the cause of a desire is not what it should be. This is the fear of self-defeating desires. It is also the fear of being crazy.

The Fear of Selfishness Fearing our motivation is fundamentally the fear of selfishness. We can only have this fear because we have believed that it is wrong to be selfish. The only sense that being selfish could be believably wrong is because it would somehow ultimately make us unhappy. The fear of mysterious punishment (guilt) would follow from this. Secret terror is the fruit of this fear.

Selfishness is believed to be wrong because it may lead to behaviors that are harmful (cause unhappiness) to others or to our greater good (mysteriously defined). This greater good is understood or inferred to be our greater happiness. This is simply the belief (fear) that we are somehow against our greater happiness.

Fear That "Something Is Wrong with Me" This is expressed by the feeling that: "There is something wrong with me. Deep down inside I have something wrong with me. I'm crazy." The fact that we would, of course, fear this, shows how evidently untrue it has to be. Why would I fear my deep self-destructive urge toward unhappiness if that was in me? How could it disguise itself as a desire? Simply, the concept is full of internal contradictions. I only could fear self-defeatingness out of a desire to avoid self-defeatingness; just as I feared unhappiness because of my desire to avoid unhappiness. Is not that desire from my selfishness, which I should not trust? What shall I then trust? My fearful distrust and my suspicions of my selfish desires would still have to be a manifestation of that inherently selfish desire to protect myself from the punishment of greater unhappiness.

Fear of Making Mistakes This is the fear of selfish, self-defeating, desires that is the same as all fear. (See above entry.) It feels like you can't trust yourself. It goes by the names of hysteria, paranoia, schizophrenia, anxiety.

Fear Called Hysteria Belief in the absence of self-actualizing desires:

You fear that you might not do what you can do to cause being loved, and fear you don't need or want love. That is worry and the fear of regret (guilt), which is believing you will be unhappy about the powerlessness of yourself. It feels like you can never say enough, do enough, or give people enough love to satisfy them. You believe you are lacking passion. People seem demanding, selfish. It feels like people don't understand how innocent and loving the real you is. You actually feel that the skills and abilities that you use and show are almost beyond your true abilities. You struggle to keep up.

You are quietly angry and resent criticism, especially the nagging urging of others. You don't question yourself to justify yourself when you are embarrassed by criticism. You simply blame them for insensitivity and fussiness.

Fear Called Paranoia Belief in the presence of self-defeating desires:

You fear that you might do what you should not, and will cause your not being loved, which you fear you need for your happiness. That is anxiety and the fear of regret (guilt). You feel like you should not love or want people as much as you do. It seems like you do, say, or want more than they want you to. You believe you have too much passion. People seem to avoid you, disdain you or hate you. You believe they can't or won't love the real you. It feels like people dislike you because they suspect your selfish motives. You start to feel like you have more powers than you use or show. You struggle to play it cool. You miss the lack of encouragement from others. You secretly question yourself in order to justify yourself when embarrassed by the criticism of others. You blame them for over-sensitivity and ill will.

Fear Called Borderline Personality Belief in self-neglect, accident proneness:

If you believe that you might not do what will cause your happiness, that is feeling like a loser or worthless, or a martyr. Hysteria competes with paranoia in many areas. You can be "diagnosed" as a hysterical paranoid or a paranoiac hysteric. You are judgmentally fussy and monumentally neglectful. You strain out gnats and swallow camels. Image is extremely important, and you confess tremendous faults. You fear being hysterical because you are convinced you are. You have many physical/psychosomatic symptoms and mental/ emotional symptoms as well. You find fault with most people and yet are envious of their normal successes, happiness, and luck.

You fear being paranoiac because you believe you are. You confess to having delusions of grandeur and egomania and yet hate yourself. You think you're too unworthy of love, and yet more worthy of admiration than you are credited for. You are too small and too big. You believe you are impotent, lazy and a fake. You believe you are brilliant, driven and cheated. Like most people, you believe you are a contradiction; only more so.

Need

Nothing is necessary for happiness.

Nothing, other than belief in unhappiness, causes unhappiness.

Believing something is necessary for happiness is unhappiness.

Believing something else is necessary for happiness, other than stopping fearing being unhappy, is unhappiness.

Nothing is necessary for you to be or do or want in order to be happy. Be as you will. There is nothing that must be done for you to be happy.

Perfect

Everything is what it must be.

There is nothing wrong. Everything is precisely and exactly how it should be. Everything that is now has come necessarily from what caused it.

Freedom to Change the Perfect

You may change or wish to change anything that is. There is nothing wrong in that either. That is perfect.

SECTION III

What Is Option About?

Option Ontology and Epistemology

THE whole subject of happiness and unhappiness is what The Option Method is about.

Life is knowing happiness or believing in unhappiness.

Unhappiness is a matter of belief and opinion.

A belief about a thing's existence is not the same as its existence.

A belief is what a person assumes or holds to be true.

What is, is. What is not, is not.

Beliefs about what is, or is not, are merely beliefs; and as such they only have a kind of experiential, functional existence; but merely as self-affirmed beliefs—not as the reality of proof of the truth of what is or is not, but simply as the feeling of the proof and experiential truth of what seems to be or not.

Illusions of truth or reality are not the experience of truth or reality, but instead the experience of the beliefs about it.

What Is the Purpose or Meaning of Life?

EACH person will answer this for himself or herself. How you answer determines how you live.

This life means *your* life. It does not have to be other than what it is. But since all want true happiness by whatever name, one could suppose that unless the decided purpose of your life is happiness, it would not seem to be a happy life unless you had what you wanted.

What is the purpose or meaning of your life? Is your life for you to be happy, or would you prefer your life to be for something else, or nothing? Would that make you happy? Whatsoever you seek, you still seek the cessation of unhappiness and the satisfaction of happiness.

Justice? After you have Justice, what would you feel? Happy?

After Truth? After Health? After Riches? After Charity? After Peace on Earth? Then will your happiness be allowed? Happiness for the good and punishment for the evil? After you have your wishes, what would you be? Happy? Any goal or ideal is the means through which you are ultimately seeking happiness. You believe these things are necessary first. If you don't believe true happiness is possible or desirable without them, why?

Using an extreme example: Are there people who would be willing to die, even, to save another? Then that idea of seeing themselves as loving the other so much, even to self-sacrifice, makes them happy.

You do all that you do for happiness. You may not have realized that.

SECTION IV

Summary

The Option Message

EACH person and all mankind can always be happy and never unhappy again. Since we choose our emotions, we have the option to be happy.

The Option Invitation

If you want to be happy, do not be unhappy now and be happy.

If you don't believe you can be happy now or can stop being unhappy now, use The Option Method to feel better.

The Decision to Be Happy

Because of Knowledge of the First Law:

I can expect to be happier and happier since I want to be, and absolutely nothing has the power to prevent it.

I am never going to be unhappy, because absolutely nothing causes it except a belief that it could be caused, which I don't have anymore.

That's how we work.

The Hope of the Option

Whenever I discover or realize that I may be feeling in a way I think may be unhappiness, and since I don't want to be unhappy and want to be happy, I will decide that I do not believe that what I may have been unhappy about is something that, in itself, can cause my unhappiness. I don't need to be unhappy about it. I may happily continue to have my values and desires, and not value what I believe is against them.

The Right to Be Happy

All people are allowed to be happy at all times, forever. This is happiness: to know you are always allowed to be happy no matter who you are, what you do, and no matter what happens to you.

All people have the right to be happy. It is never wrong to be happy. Those who know it are happy forever.

You have the right to be happy no matter how rotten others think you are; no matter how sinful, or stupid, or selfish, or sick, or horrible, or thieving, or lying, or arrogant, or shy, or failing, or murderous, or monstrous. You absolutely have the absolute right to be happy always; no matter how others may hate you, or hurt you, or try to punish you.

Those who disagree will be unhappy.

Blessed are those who know they are happy. Happy are those who know they are blessed.

To be blessed is to have the right to be happy. To be born is to be allowed to be happy.

To know you are allowed to be happy is to be blessed.

Happiness is being allowed to be happy. Happiness is not believing it is wrong to be happy. Happiness is not believing it will become wrong to be happy. Happiness is not fearing you will have no right to be happy. Happiness is not believing you should be unhappy. Happiness is not believing you have to be unhappy. Happiness is not believing it is right to be unhappy.

It is evident. God permits you to be happy no matter what or when. Nature permits you to be happy no matter what or when. The only permission you need is yours to be happy all the time.

You don't have to deny your happiness, ever. It is not wrong to be happy always.

COMMENTARIES

by Aryeh Nielsen on

"A Comprehensive Overview"

A Summary of Option Teachings

The Option Method Demonstrates How Emotions Happen

The Option Method is about discovering, for yourself, how you become happy, unhappy, or indifferent about things, events, circumstances, people, ideas, or anything at all.

When you discover this, you will find out it is never necessary to be unhappy about anything.

Although The Option Method can be used to become happier, it has no point of view that people should be happy. When you learn that it is no longer necessary to be unhappy about something specific, you will know that, if you want to, you are free to no longer be unhappy about that specific thing. You are free—that means you are free to remain unhappy, if that is what you decide is best for you.

The Option Method demonstrates how emotions happen *in specific cases.* Sometimes, this learning generalizes: the reason someone is unhappy about slow service in a restaurant may generalize to slow service in a shoe store. Sometimes, not.

You Do Not Have to Be Unhappy

The Option Method demonstrates that you, alone, do not have to be unhappy *in a specific situation.* Some who learn The Option Method believe that the abstract knowledge that they do not need to be unhappy should release them from all unhappiness, and wonder why it doesn't.

You have *your* reasons to be unhappy about any situation which you are unhappy about. Although The Option Method can demonstrate that every reason you have to be unhappy does not *force* you to be unhappy against your will, until you know that each particular reason cannot make you unhappy, the reason holds sway over you.

If you thought that Paris was in England, and you found out that you were mistaken, this discovery will not correct any other mistaken ideas you have about cities.

Your reasons are *your* reasons. If two people are unhappy about something, they each have their own reasons. If two people are unhappy about their incomes, one might feel not valued at work, while another might feel they can't afford what they wanted to buy.

The Option Method Does Not Say You Should Be Happy

If you believe you *should* be happy, you have added another reason to be unhappy to all the reasons you already have. If you desire greater happiness in your life, there are simpler ways, more complex ways, and impossible ways.

The simplest way to be happy is: just be happy.

The next simpler way is: stop being unhappy about not being happy. Paradoxically, those who are not unhappy about not being happy find themselves not unhappy at all.

The next simpler way is The Option Method.

You have your reasons to be unhappy. When you realize your reasons are mistaken, you will no longer be unhappy. To try to be happy without inspecting the reasons you have to be unhappy is like stressfully trying to relax: counterproductive and fruitless.

You can never be happier by becoming more unhappy about being unhappy.

Cause vs. Fault

If you mistakenly thought a friend of yours liked candy and you gave your friend candy as a gift, and your friend hated candy, you were the cause of your friend receiving a gift she hated.

You were not at fault for giving an unwelcome gift; you had no intention to do so.

Similarly, you are the cause of your unhappiness by virtue of mistaken beliefs you have that it is necessary for you to be unhappy in certain situations. While you are the cause, you are not at fault; you would never cause yourself to be unhappy if you did not believe that it was necessary.

As you use The Option Method, you will discover that *you* are the cause of your unhappiness, not events or things or whatever you thought was the cause. This is good news; when you find out that you have been mistaken, you can gladly rejoice in no longer being mistaken. That you *were* the cause of your unhappiness is no more of a reason to be unhappy than anything else.

There Is No Way You Should Be

The Option Method does not propose an ideal way of being.

The Option Method supports you in becoming the way *you* most want to be.

If there was a "best" way to be, and it was the way you wanted to be anyway, why do you need a "should"? Why do you *need* to be obligated (by God, the universe, nature, duty, or whatever force would obligate you) to do what you *want* to do anyway?

If there was a "best" way to be, and it is not the way you *want* to be, why do believe it is the best way to be? If you truly, with your whole body, believe that the "best" way to be truly *is* the best way to be, then it will be the way you want to be. Until then, you are demonstrating that you really don't believe that it is the "best" way to be.

Only you can judge the best way to be *for you*. There is no greater authority on what is best for you than *you*.

Happiness Is the Taste in Your Own Mouth

There is a reason that stores carry a variety of foods; as you know from experience, some people find some of the foods that you greatly enjoy to be distasteful, and vice versa. There are no foods that taste good, period. There are only foods that taste good *to you*.

Happiness is the taste in your own mouth. To believe that what brings you joy would bring *everyone else* joy also, is similar to believing that everyone would have the same favorite food as you do.

Indeed, even if many, many people have the same taste as you, that tells you nothing about the taste of anybody in particular. They may be one of the many, many people who have the same taste as you, or not.

You are the perfect and sole authority on your happiness. No one else is, and you are not an authority on anyone else's happiness. Even if your predictions about other's taste seem to be perfectly accurate for years on end, you still do not know *with certainty* what they want *now*.

Happiness Is Personal

Happiness is a word that has many meanings.

Some define happiness as pleasure, experienced in the moment.

Some define happiness as satisfaction, contemplating their past.

Some define happiness as having meaning in their lives, looking forward to the future.

All of these may indeed be part of your happiness, but that is for you to find out.

The Option Method defines happiness as your ultimate desiring, whatever that may be. You may be most moved toward pleasure, satisfaction, or meaning. You may not be.

However you define happiness, it is something *you* want. If you are defining happiness as something you don't want, that is unhappiness under another name. Any true definition of happiness cannot be defined as causing unhappiness.

Happiness Is Not a Particular Mood

Many moods are often described as "happy" moods: being calm, being excited, being cheerful, and many more.

If you do not want to be in a particular mood, it is not a happy mood for you at that moment. If you are at a party, and you are feeling very calm, and all around you people are asking you "why you aren't more excited, why aren't you *happy*?" you know that being excited is not what you want. It is not your happiness. You want to be calm. Those who presume you to be unhappy are mistaken. If you do not feel that you should be excited, you will just know that you are calm, and will be happy to be as you wish to be.

The only happy mood is the one you want right now.

You Are Already Happy

Happiness is your ultimate desiring, whatever that may be. Your desiring is not dependent on getting what you want. You cannot do anything but desire what you desire.

What you desire changes in every moment. If you desire something, and don't get it, you may find that you no longer desire it. Or, you may find that your desire increases.

If you desire something, and get it, your desire also may change. Before dinner, you wanted to eat. After dinner, you no longer want to eat.

Since you are always desiring what you desire, you are always perfectly happy. Except . . . you can mistakenly believe that what you desire could be against your happiness.

The Option Method demonstrates that you could never be against your happiness; you can only mistakenly believe you are. Since you *are* perfectly *for* your happiness, you are already perfectly happy, but you can mistakenly believe that you are not.

Happiness as Freedom

Happiness is knowing your perfect freedom. Happiness is knowing that you are perfectly free to desire whatever you desire, and that you will always act from your greatest desire.

You can do what you can do. In other words, you are allowed (by God, nature, the universe, etc.) to do whatever you are capable of doing. The question of unhappiness is, "If I am free to do anything, might I act against my best interests, against my happiness?"

A perfectly free person would never act against their best interests, insofar as they are aware of them. Imagine: if you had a choice between acting on behalf of what you understood to be your best interest (including all expected consequences), and making a choice not in your best interest, would you ever choose the less attractive option?

Those who know they are perfectly free can only do what is most for their happiness. This is not a restriction on freedom, but the revelation that perfect happiness and perfect freedom are the same.

Happiness as Your Ultimate Desire

If you define happiness, and it is not what you want most, then you have not truly defined happiness. Happiness includes the absence of what doesn't belong there.

If you are believing that you don't want to be happy, then you are being aware of something that you want *more* than happiness *as you define it*. Whatever that is, is a better definition of happiness, for you.

For example, if you don't want to be happy because you believe it would be unsafe, then *your* happiness includes safety. If you don't want to be happy because you believe it would be boring, then *your* happiness includes being engaged.

What you don't want can only be *someone else's* happiness, which has no relevance to you because you cannot enjoy someone else's happiness; you can only enjoy your own. The happiness of your past self is someone else's happiness. The happiness of your ideal self is someone else's happiness.

Your happiness is *your* ultimate desiring, *now*.

Believing There's Something Wrong with You

For many, the most accessible description of unhappiness is the belief that "there's something wrong with you."

There's something wrong with you if you don't get what you want.

There's something wrong with you if others don't behave the way you want them to.

There's something wrong with you for not being as you "should" be (more cheerful, less angry, kinder, more assertive, etc., etc.).

There's something wrong with you for believing there's something wrong with you.

"There's something wrong with you" is also felt as being against oneself, being self-defeating, not looking out for your own interests, somehow not knowing what is best for you, needing help, feeling you *should* be different, feeling that there is something wrong with you if you *want* to be different.

What You Don't Want vs. Unhappiness

You may believe that if you don't get what you want, or if you get what you don't want, or if you fail to avoid what you want to avoid, you will become unhappy.

The Option Method demonstrates that if you become unhappy when you don't get what you want, it is because you believe unhappiness is best for your ultimate happiness. When you question your unhappiness using The Option Method, you can find out if, in each particular case, this is true.

Perhaps unhappiness is a bad-tasting medicine you take to best help yourself when you don't get what you want. Perhaps unhappiness is an *ineffective and useless* bad-tasting medicine.

You already know what is best for your ultimate happiness; you don't need unhappiness to remind you. But there is no ultimate harm in using unhappiness—when you realize it is ineffective and bad tasting, though, you may no longer be inclined to use it.

Believing We Are against Ourselves

The question is: could we ever act against our own best interests, as we understand them at the time? Hindsight may reveal to us that if we had acted differently, we would likely have more of what we want now. But we could never act against our best interests in every moment we act.

If we suspect that we may not be able to predict the consequences of our actions well, we may choose to search for more information to better predict the consequences of our actions. We may decide that to delay acting has its own consequences. But what if we believed that we had discovered that we have bad judgment? If that is so, how can we trust that our judgment that we have bad judgment is correct?

We can be certain that we want to have the best outcome of our actions for ourselves. We can be certain that *right now* we know everything we know *right now*. It is impossible to know *right now* what we only discover in the future, the actual consequences of our actions. To insist to yourself that you know now what you will only know in the future is to give yourself a truly impossible task.

Not Believing Ourselves

Unhappiness is not believing our feelings. If feel the strong desire to run away from a bear, that is the desire to avoid a bear. If we don't believe ourselves, we will feel bad about wanting to avoid the bear, instead of enjoying our body's natural response of fleeing.

If we really care about something, and we find ourselves wanting to be forceful in accomplishing our goals, if we don't believe ourselves we will feel bad about being forceful. The quality of forceful *and* feeling bad is anger. Both we and others feel the difference; there is a core feeling of problem in anger that is not present in mere forcefulness.

If we want to eat a cake, and we doubt ourselves, the doubt is instead of being in touch with whether we *more* do not want to eat the cake, for whatever reasons. If we have prepared a special cake for someone's birthday, and we are in touch with our desire to present them with the cake, we don't have to disbelieve that we want to eat the cake right now. If we do want to eat the cake now, we do. And also, we may *more* want to save the cake for later.

"Should, Must, Have To" Are False

The idea of necessity can be expressed in many ways: should, must, have to, ought to, owe, obliged, etc. All verbs of necessity have an object. The full meaning of "You should do this" is "You *should* do *this* in order to, in my estimation, be the most likely to succeed at achieving *that.*"

Often, "You should do this" means "You should do this in order to succeed at being happy." Since happiness does not depend on anything, this is a lie. It is a statement on the order of "You should do this in order to help you remember to digest your food." You cannot forget to digest your food. Similarly, you cannot do anything to make yourself happy; you can only stop believing that you need to be unhappy in a given circumstance.

To believe you should be wanting other than you do is believing you are wanting the wrong thing for your happiness. You can only want what you believe ultimately leads you to happiness. If you change your mind about what you want, you changed your mind freely, and it wasn't because you *should* have changed your mind.

Believing That the Future Will Be Unhappy

If you knew that at this time tomorrow you would be perfectly happy, how would you feel now? If you knew that at this time tomorrow that you would be perfectly unhappy, how would you feel now?

You can only feel unhappy now by believing that you are going to feel unhappy in the future.

Since the purpose of our unhappiness, ultimately, is to be happy, if we knew that we would be happy in the future as a result of our unhappiness, we would be happy now.

So unhappiness has within itself the tacit acknowledgment that it doesn't work: at the same time that we use unhappiness to try to become happier, we are not believing that it will actually make us happier.

This is why if you are not unhappy about being unhappy, you will no longer be unhappy at all. It is impossible to stay unhappy if you really believe it is really helping you become happy!

Unhappiness Is an Always-New Event

If you drink water every day from your faucet, and one day you heard on the news that the water would be of undrinkable quality that day, you wouldn't drink the water that day. When you know you don't want to do something, even decades of doing the same act daily will have no hold: today, you are not going to do what you did yesterday.

There is no such thing as habitual unhappiness. Each time you are unhappy, you may be believing a belief similar to what you believed yesterday, but it is only a similar belief, not the same belief—just as waves on the beach today may be similar to the waves yesterday, but will never be the *same* waves as yesterday.

If you no longer believe that something is a reason to be unhappy and you find yourself unhappy about it again, it is not that you have "backslid," or are believing again what you no longer believe. You cannot believe again what you no longer believe. The unhappiness of right now is a new situation. You are never "up against" any momentum of history or habit.

Unhappiness Doesn't Actually Exist

Unhappiness is believing something impossible: that you could be against yourself, that there's something wrong with you, that you are not free to feel as you wish to feel.

In this sense, unhappiness is like believing in being demon-possessed. If you believe that you are demon-possessed, you may build your life around this knowledge, and experience what it feels like to be demon-possessed. But despite your believing, we can know that you are not demon-possessed.

The whole-body tacit revelation of the non-existence of unhappiness is gradual until it is sudden. The greatest unhappiness, perhaps, is to believe that you *should* know in every cell of your body that unhappiness doesn't exist. When you actually know this, you will know this. Until then, you can enjoy being happier and happier.

Emotional Feelings vs. Physical Feelings

The feelings that The Option Method is concerned with are emotional feelings, not physical feelings; that is, physical sensations.

If you have very mild pain—for example, a scrape—you may feel neither happy nor unhappy about it. You have no emotional feelings about your physical sensation. On the other hand, there are people who, each for their own personal reasons, feel unhappy about very strong physical sensations of pain. The physical sensation and emotional feeling appear as if they are one event, but the emotional feeling actually *follows* the physical sensation very closely.

Emotional feelings always bring with them physical sensations; without a sensation in the body (tightness in the gut, elevated heart rate), you would not experience an emotional feeling.

Emotional feelings are a bodily orientation and relationship toward what is happening. Physical sensations are knowledge of what is happening, but not an orientation.

Feelings Are an Attitude of the Whole Body

The mind extends from above the scalp to below the toes. Emotional feelings are a whole-body, tacit (non-verbal) attitude. Emotional feelings are the general attitude you take to best orient yourself to what is happening. For example, the emotion of caution is a bodily attitude of care, examining in detail, and surveying for risks. Anxiety is the emotion of caution *and* feeling bad (being unhappy).

Emotional feelings in themselves are never unhappy before they are believed to be reasons for unhappiness. They are simply the whole body, mind, and self expressing the best attitude for itself in response to what is happening and what is wanted to happen.

When emotional feelings are *believed* to be not in your own best interest, then they cannot function as they naturally do, in your best interest. Note that emotional feelings are not what we express to others; that is *public expression* of emotional feelings. They are what we feel as our orientation toward what is happening, independently of how we are moved to express them.

Feelings Are a Form of Knowledge

Feelings are your knowing of what you want to do.

Why, then, do feelings sometimes seem to be leading you in a direction you *don't* want? Because the feelings are mixed with unhappiness.

Having feelings, and being unhappy, is understanding your own feelings through a murky window. At root, your feelings are perfectly reflective of what you want. But when you have feelings and are unhappy, it seems that your feelings could lead you to be against yourself. Without unhappiness, feelings reflect your knowing what you want *most*.

If you feel like doing something that is "bad for you," you are feeling what you are feeling *because* you believe you could be bad for you. When you are no longer looking through the murky window of unhappiness, you will certainly not feel bad. And if, in your estimation, you are doing something that would not be beneficial to you, you won't feel like doing that. How could you, knowing it wouldn't be beneficial to you?

Emotional Beliefs vs. Practical Beliefs

Beliefs are a prediction of the future. A belief is in the form, when *this* happens, *that* happens. There are two significantly different kinds of beliefs: emotional beliefs and practical beliefs.

A practical belief is: "This knife is good for cutting," or "This knife is bad for cutting." An emotional belief is: "This knife is good for my happiness (or the happiness of the universe, or others)," or "This knife is bad for happiness (or the happiness of the universe, or others)."

Emotional beliefs are evaluations of how something may make you, others, or the universe happy or unhappy. Since nothing can *make* you, others, or the universe happy or unhappy, emotional beliefs are all false.

Practical beliefs are informational, and have no implications for happiness or unhappiness.

When you are happy, you can make a belief up, a justification for your happiness, and what harm does it do? Question unhappiness only. Unhappiness is the lie that hurts.

Beliefs Are in the Body

Beliefs are not mere thoughts. Every predictive inclination in your whole body is a belief. The purpose of all these predictions is to best serve your well-being. Your breath is a prediction about how oxygen best serves your well-being.

Everything you do is a manifestation of your beliefs. You can only do as you believe is best for you. If you believe that it is best for you to hold your breath forever, and find out that it isn't, then your actions are a reflection of what you *actually* believe.

Sometimes, what you *think* you believe is only what you *want* to believe, what you aspire to believe, but not what you *actually* believe. If you are insisting to yourself that you really don't care about something, you may want to believe that; but if you *really* didn't care, you wouldn't have any motivation to be insisting to yourself that you don't care!

You cannot believe two things at once, but you can oscillate between two beliefs in close succession.

Testing Your Beliefs

What if your beliefs are wrong? With practical beliefs, you find out. For example, if you thought there was a door in a wall, and it turned out to be only a painting of a door, you find that out when you walk into the wall. Beliefs are always held as perfectly true until they no longer are. A belief that is "held tentatively" is actually a recognition of a possibility: "This knife might be sharp; it might not be."

Regarding emotional beliefs, the belief behind unhappiness is, "This is a necessary reason for me to be unhappy." Like practical beliefs, emotional beliefs are held as perfectly true, until they no longer are. If you realize "This might be a necessary reason for me to be unhappy, this might not be," then you will be free to not be unhappy, if this is what you desire, because unhappiness only occurs when you are *certain* that something is a reason to be unhappy.

The Option Method is concerned with exploring beliefs about the *necessity* of unhappiness. It is not concerned with proving that something is not a reason to be unhappy, but merely with demonstrating that it does not *necessitate* being unhappy.

Attraction: The Question, "How Much Do I Want This?"

Attraction does not mean you want something. It means you are asking yourself the question, "How much do I want this?" Everything is more or less attractive; "unattractive" really is: less attractive than other alternatives. For example, cancer may be attractive compared to death. The idea of death may be attractive compared to the idea of eternal torture in an "afterlife."

When you are absolutely certain how much you want something, that is knowledge that is acted on. The question of "How much do you want this?" then, does not come into awareness. You are often not aware of how attractive food is on your plate. You eat what you want and don't eat what you don't want. If you notice a choice as attractive, you are noticing the process of evaluating something to determine how much you want it.

Attraction, or the question "How much do I want this?" can lead to wanting, or moving toward (for a reason). When there are no more reasons to move toward something, then you just do (move toward without reasons).

Wanting: Moving Toward

Wanting is moving toward. If you want something, you move toward it. If you want two things, and cannot move toward both of them, then you move toward whichever you want more. If you do not move toward either, than you are moving toward deciding which of the two you want more. Once you are certain, for example, that you want to wear a green shirt more than a yellow shirt, you put the green shirt on. If you do not, it is only because you also may want to not wear a shirt at all, and are deciding also if you want to wear a shirt more than you do not.

Wanting has the implication of "for a reason." If you ask yourself why you want something, you will find out that you want everything for something else. Ultimately, you will discover everything you want, you want for happiness, which is defined as "that which you most move towards," which is synonymous with your own understanding of your well-being (as opposed to what outside authority may define your well-being to be.)

Doing: Moving without Reasons

There are no reasons necessary for happiness. You do not *need* to do anything to be happy. So what does a happy person want? Nothing. So what does a happy person do? Whatever they do.

"Just doing" can be observed all around you. Trees just do. They do not conceive of themselves as having reasons for their doing, or having lacks. They have no justification for stretching their roots out to water. That is just what they do, a manifestation of their being.

Only humans (and perhaps a few other species) sometimes require a justification for their doing. You do not require justification for your liver to do what it does, or your intestines to do what they do.

Ultimately, what you do *is you*. Some fear that without reasons, they would not do anything. Amoeba and trees do without reasons, and flourish in their well-being. Whatever you do without reasons can only be the best doing for you.

Stimulus, Organism, Response

In a stimulus-response system, cause creates effect. For example, pushing a pin into a paper with sufficient force will puncture it.

The idea that "things make people happy" is a stimulus-response concept. It neglects the organism. In living beings, stimulus is the stimulus *of an individual organism*, and response is the response *of an individual organism.*

In living beings, a stimulus happens, and that particular being has an individual response. Even though two responses may look similar, they are never the same. Living beings change continuously, and take the context of the whole known world into account when making any response. Additionally, stimuli that occur to living beings have a great variety. No two stimuli are alike outside a perfectly controlled laboratory.

So we could say that the organism chooses the response to the stimulus, but only in the sense that the response is not caused directly by the stimulus; the response does not "happen" to the organism as a result of the stimulus.

Beliefs Produce Feelings

How are emotions created? Emotions are whole-body attitudes, or orientations toward what is happening. Emotions are created based on whether what is *believed* to be the meaning or consequence of what is happening (whether internal or external, real or perceived) is judged as "good for me" or "bad for me." Emotions are the root response to the stimulus of an event.

Good for me/bad for me has two meanings:

1. Good or bad for my wants.
2. Good or bad for my happiness.

Although these often appear as the same, they are not. If you do not get what you want, you can still know that you want what you want (if you still do want it after you don't get it). This knowing that you are "on your own side," that you are indeed, "for what you are for," that "there is nothing wrong with your wanting," is the knowledge of happiness.

If an event happens, and you believe that it means or has the consequence that you will become unhappy, you will be unhappy now. That belief is the only cause of unhappiness.

Degrees of Unhappiness

We feel as unhappy about things as we believe we ought to feel. Often, a principle of comparison is used: if to lose a little money will make us somewhat unhappy, to lose a lot of money is reason to be very unhappy.

You feel as unhappy about everything that you feel unhappy about with the intensity you believe you should.

Many forms of unhappiness are believing that the intensity with which we feel an emotion is to the wrong degree. Someone we love has died, and we do not feel particularly sad. We didn't get awarded first prize at the state fair, and, twenty years later, we still feel devastated. In both cases, there is a belief that there is a "right" intensity of emotion we *should* feel (as "good" people, as "caring" people, as "sane" people), and we are not feeling the "correct" intensity of emotion.

Or we feel that we are not joyful enough about the achievements of our friends, yet too joyful about our own achievements. Again, we are believing that our intensity of emotion is not right.

Self-Motivation through Happiness and Unhappiness

Unhappiness is fundamentally a self-motivator. The purpose for our unhappiness is to better move us toward what we want. In other words, we are only unhappy because we believe that ultimately, it will be happier to be unhappy.

Unhappiness can *seem* an effective motivator. But the hidden driver behind the motivation of unhappiness is the movement toward happiness.

For example, if you are unhappy that you didn't get what you want, that can only be because, indeed, you want what you want. It can seem that unhappiness is helping to motivate you towards what you want, but it is entirely riding on the coattails of your underlying (not unhappy) wanting.

If you are unhappy about not getting what you want, and you truly realized that you didn't want what you are unhappy about not getting, you would instantly no longer be unhappy. You couldn't be unhappy about not getting what you didn't want, or getting what you want (though there may be secondary unhappiness related to each of these).

Using Unhappiness to Motivate Others

Unhappiness is often used to motivate others. For example, anger at others is often used to motivate them to do as the angry person wishes. Sorrow is often used to motivate others to give a sad person what he or she desires. Fear is used to motivate others to not do something, for the reason that it would "cause too much" fear in the fearing person.

Relative to others, the appearance of your unhappiness may indeed be the strongest motivation for them. But it is not necessary to *be* unhappy in order to *appear* unhappy. Actors do this all the time.

There is never a circumstance where appearing to be unhappy would have any different effect than actually being unhappy. So, from a practical point of view, actually being unhappy is a medicine that tastes bad . . . and doesn't work.

The threat of unhappiness can be used as a punishment, and the promise of unhappiness as a reward, to motivate. Regardless of how effective as motivators these are, it is not necessary to *actually* make your happiness dependent on others.

You Are Always Doing What You Want

People are always doing what they want insofar as *they* are doing it. If someone has got strings tied to his or her wrists and is being moved like a marionette, then whoever holds the strings is doing the movement of the body, not the person whose body is being moved.

Sometimes, people are doing what they want based on the mistaken belief that it is necessary to do what they want to do in order to feel the way they want to feel. This could be called "unhappy wanting," because it is wanting in the context of believing that unhappiness exists. It is doing what you want, based on having a fundamental misunderstanding about the nature of reality.

Even when people are acting based on this mistaken belief, people are still aware of what they *really* want ("in touch with their desires"). By "really want" is meant: what desires they are aware they would act on if they did not believe that it was necessary to do anything in order to feel the way they want to feel. All unhappy wanting derives initially from happy wanting, but is distorted by unhappiness.

Wanting vs. Needing

Starting from being unhappy is starting from a negative position, to try to motivate ourselves toward what we want more.

An alternative is to start out from being *not* unhappy, and move toward being happier. This is moving from love, not fear.

Needing is wanting, and fearing being unhappy if you don't get it (or wanting to avoid, and fearing being unhappy if you get what you want to avoid).

The only practical difference between wanting, loving, and becoming happier, and needing, fearing, and becoming less unhappy, is that the former feels far better than the latter—and is more effective.

Love of wealth, health, and intimacy is a far better motivator than fear of poverty, sickness, and being alone.

Doing without Motivation

You are your happiness. Ultimately, the feeling of wanting is the feeling of a gap between where you are and where you are moving towards. In perfect happiness, motivation falls away, because there is no more moving from a state of less happy to more happy.

But there is still movement in perfect happiness. Your intestines function without any motivation. And the rest of the body, mind, and self are no different. Without a trace of unhappiness, you just *do*.

Motivation is a confession that a reason is required in order to move. There are no reasons for happiness. Reasons *can* be made up to move, there is no reason not to.

Your being and your doing are perfectly coincident in perfect happiness. All that is happening is you being *you*, perfectly.

Wanting Something More than Something Else

We often want two things that are not practically compatible: for example, to be honest in a conversation, and to be agreeable. Then we might get unhappy that "we have to act agreeable towards you" in order to ensure that we act agreeable (which is what we wanted *more* than to be honest), and to ensure that we don't fall "victim" to the "temptation" to be honest.

All unhappiness could be called self-distrust; in particular, a distrust that you actually want *more* what you do indeed want more than something else. If you know that you want health more than cancer, then there is no need to be unhappy about cancer; in fact, someone could only be unhappy about having cancer if they wanted to be healthy *more* than they wanted to have cancer, *but* somehow were not acknowledging this to themselves.

In every moment, there is one thing you are doing and an infinite number of things you are not doing; you do not need to know all the things you don't want to do, only that which you do want to do.

Wanting the Whole Package

Some wanting is wanting of intermediate steps. For example, we often don't want a job in itself; we want the benefits that money brings. We use unhappiness in the form of "I have to go to work" in order to stay in touch that we do want to go to work, as an intermediate step towards the benefits we want that money brings.

Oftentimes, what we do unhappily, perhaps even protesting that "We don't want to do it," is what we *want* to do as part of the "whole package" of what we want in itself, and all the intermediate steps we foresee as necessary to achieve what-we-want-in-itself.

Ultimately, everything we want to do is part of the "whole package" of our happiness. When we are no longer unhappy, we are free to see the practical sense of "have to, must need to," which no longer imply "have to" for happiness, but only "have to" as a step towards getting what we want.

Wanting Something Similar

Oftentimes, we know exactly what we want, but there are other things wanted as part of that wanting. For example, "I want to go to that party (and I want to bring a friend, or I want it to start earlier)." In other words, I want something like what you propose but not exactly as proposed. We may choose to negotiate, or we may decide that negotiation has its own consequences that we would prefer to avoid.

We may want to do something, as long as we reasonably predict that any secondary consequences of our actions will be as we want. We may want to wait and see if, with time or information, we are able to predict with more certainty which of two actions is more likely to have the consequences we desire.

The common dilemma, "I want to, *but* . . ." is being aware that you want to do something *only if* further criteria are met, or you want more certainty about practical consequences of the action. If there are apparently two choices which you want exactly equally, and which have unknown outcomes, then you can simply know that your choice cannot make you unhappy.

Wanting You to Want

A happy person might want to dress in the same way their parents want them to dress. They might not.

They might want to dress in the same way their parents want them to dress because they have similar tastes as their parents. They might want to dress in the same way their parents want them to dress because they want to show their parents they care about their parents' taste.

They might not want to dress in the same way their parents want them to dress because they do not have similar tastes as their parents. They might not want to dress in the same way their parents want them to dress because they want to show their parents they are indifferent to their taste.

This is knowing your freedom in relation to others wanting you to want something. Unhappiness is needing to either want what someone else wants you to want, or needing to not want something because someone else wants you to want it.

You Are the Expert on You

You are the perfect authority on what you want. No one knows you as well as you know you, yourself. If you receive guidance and you choose to follow it, you choose to follow it because the actions proposed by the guidance seem attractive to *you*. What makes an action attractive is that you predict it will have consequences you want, and you may base that prediction on your judgment of how accurately an "expert's" prediction is likely to be.

Events do not cause unhappiness.

If you give someone advice, and they follow it, and are happy, you are not the cause of their happiness. If you give someone advice, and they follow it, and are unhappy, you are not the cause of their unhappiness. If they agree with you, they chose to "try on" a similar point of view as yours, freely and by their own choice. If they "follow" your advice, they freely chose to act in a way co-incident with your suggestion, because they, in their own reflection, decided that it was a good path of action to take.

Are Others Allowed to Be as They Are?

Two ideas co-arise: "I should be different," and "others are not allowed to be as they are." If you knew that the universe allows everyone to be as they are, then you would know that the universe allows you to be as you are.

In particular, the universe allows all to be unhappy. Fearing unhappiness is in itself a form of unhappiness, a feeling that you shouldn't be unhappy. The universe doesn't care. If anything, the universe "knows" that you are not really unhappy, just experiencing what it feels like to believe that you are.

If you are unhappy about being unhappy, you will be unhappy. If you are unhappy about others being unhappy, you will be unhappy.

If you know that unhappiness doesn't exist, then you will know that those who are unhappy are mistaken, but you will also know that you don't need them not to be mistaken in order to be happy.

"Negative" Emotions: Guilt, Sadness, Anger

So-called "negative" emotions are feeling bad or wrong to feel as you feel.

Guilt is feeling bad about feeling good. In particular, it is the apparent dilemma between "what I want to do (in itself)," and "how I want to appear to others (or presumed others)," which often becomes, in time "what I *should* do." There is no actual dilemma. You already know if there is a difference between what you want to do and how you want to appear to others; that is already taken into account. Guilt is an unnecessary reminder to balance these two desires.

Similarly, anger is feeling bad about feeling forceful or aggressive. Sadness is feeling bad about feeling withdrawn, inward, or feeling bad about crying.

All "negative" emotions are feeling exactly how you want to feel *and* feeling bad or wrong about how you feel. The only part that feels bad is *feeling bad*. Feeling forceful or crying doesn't feel bad in itself, but feeling bad about feeling forceful or crying does.

Falsely Deducing That You Are Unhappy

There are three common reasons that people deduce they are unhappy: pain, bodily symptoms, and not caring.

Pain is not a form of unhappiness. It is a sign of wanting to avoid. If the sign is informative, then it is useful. If it is believed to convey no more information, then if you do not get unhappy about it you may naturally seek to minimize the pain. If pain is not informative, and has been minimized, then the sensation may simply not be of interest.

Unhappiness can generate bodily symptoms (for example, a racing heart). But these same bodily symptoms may or may not be caused by unhappiness. Running fast, for example, can also cause a racing heart. Often, bodily symptoms are used as evidence of unhappiness. Because they can arise either from unhappiness or other causes, they are not evidence.

Finally, not caring is often used as evidence of unhappiness. Every culture has a point of view about what things a member of the culture cares about (and to what degree) and what they do not. But, if you don't care—you don't care.

"Happiness Isn't Possible"

If someone seeks help, it can only be because they believe that more happiness is possible. For those who know without question that happiness isn't possible, there can be no desire to seek help.

The Option Method does not presume that happiness is possible. If it is not possible, then that will be discovered. If there is a "core" unhappiness that just happens, and about which nothing can be done, and there is unhappiness about this "core" unhappiness which does not just happen, then The Option Method can help people be happier by helping them to be a little less unhappy about their "core" unhappiness.

If all unhappiness is "core" unhappiness, and this is discovered, then The Option Method can help settle the question of "Can I be happier?"

The Option Method can help, insofar as unhappiness does *not* just happen.

"Happiness Isn't Safe"

A common argument against happiness is: "Perfect happiness would make me a willing victim of others, or would cause me to not take care of myself." There is the idea of the fool whom everyone takes advantage of, or who sits grinning on a log, not seeking food and starving to death.

Perfect happiness is the absence of whatever doesn't belong there. And if, for us, what we would want in our happiness is to be assertive, safe, and taking care of ourselves, then to define our happiness as not including these qualities is merely to call unhappiness "happiness," and then argue against unhappiness.

For many, after happiness, safety may be what is most desired. Safety is always *personal* safety. It is our personal calculation of how much we wish to be exposed to seemingly unavoidable risks as we move toward what we want. If we are cautious while walking on the edge of a cliff, it may be because we have a good estimation of our level of coordination, and wish to reduce the likelihood of our slipping and falling.

If I Were Happy, I Wouldn't . . .

There is a class of arguments against happiness that happiness would mean that you wouldn't value what you value.

If you are happy, and find out that you no longer care about something, then you will not care that you don't care. You have changed many beliefs in your lifetime. When a belief was truly changed, then there was no appeal in the old belief. Wanting to care about something *is* the same as caring. You could never find yourself truly not caring about something and yet wanting to care. Wanting to care about something is actually a form of caring about it.

Similar logic applies to the two similar ideas, that if you were happy you wouldn't want what you want, or wouldn't enjoy what you enjoy. Happiness is what you desire most. If you truly desire to enjoy something, then *your* happiness includes such an enjoyment. Any happiness that is not you feeling the way you *most* want to feel about everything is merely unhappiness under the name of "happiness."

Behavior

Insofar as behavior is caused by an unhappy belief, it will change when the belief changes. Insofar as the behavior is not caused by an unhappy belief, it won't. Either way, the concern of The Option Method practitioner is unhappiness, not behavior.

Knowing that you have perfect freedom of behavior includes both knowing that you have the freedom to change your behavior whenever you wish, and that you have the freedom to not change, to repeat any behavior as long as you see fit.

Such roles as "the professional" in a professional relationship are descriptions of prototypical or expected behavior when in a certain configuration of relationship. If you choose to adhere to the behavioral prototype, that is a choice. Oftentimes the prototypical behavioral patterns have great utility. The universe allows you, though, to behave in a way not in accordance with a role if you find it beneficial.

No Reasons or Beliefs Are Necessary

Happiness is you being you. You cannot be other than happy, but you can believe that you are against yourself, or that you are unhappy.

No reasons are needed to be happy, no beliefs are necessary to be happy, only to consent to experience your own happiness.

Since you are your happiness, your happiness does not depend on you understanding yourself or knowing anything.

You will experience unhappiness if you believe you need to understand yourself in order to be happy.

You will experience unhappiness if you believe you need to know something in order to be happy.

Consenting to Happiness and Gladness

Gladness is the acknowledgment that now is a perfect time and circumstance to be happy. Now is the perfect time to feel just the way you do about everything.

You can be glad that you like things. You can be glad that you don't like things. Gladness is what you feel when you consent to your happiness, which is consenting to feeling the way you feel about everything.

Joy is the active bodily attitude of happiness. It is being not done with what you are doing, for now; being engaged in a motion.

Peace is the inactive bodily attitude of happiness. It is being done for now, having completed a motion, resting in the satisfaction of completeness.

Quiet is the knowing that nothing ever needs be done. Quiet can be known in the midst of a riot, or not known sitting in meditation.

Love

To love is to be happy, and want the other to be happy or happier.

Loving can be defined negatively as not believing someone is the cause of your unhappiness. Loving can be defined positively as wanting someone to be happy (not happy because of what I give them or not, but unconditionally). Putting these together, we find the full meaning of loving: wanting someone to be happy, and not fearing their unhappiness.

Since nothing can make us unhappy, we can always not be unhappy with anyone.

The only reason we might not want someone to be happy or happier is if we believed that their happiness could cause our unhappiness.

Happiness is perfect love. Love of an individual is happiness in the context of that relationship.

Wait, Watch, and Enjoy

Wanting is not unhappy, but in perfect happiness doing and wanting become coincident. Beyond "not unhappy, and wanting to be happier" is "happy, and doing." There is no longer a gap between wanting and doing.

What do you do when perfectly happy? Wait, watch, and enjoy what happens in you and around you and *as* you. You have no reasons to do anything, and you don't need a reason to do anything.

Wait, watch, and enjoy what is happening *as* you, which is only your happiness.

Happiness is being glad for who you are:
liking that you want what you want,
liking that you don't like what you don't like,
liking that you change your mind whenever you
think that's best,
liking that you don't change your mind until you
really change your mind,
liking that you don't like not knowing how to have
what you want,
liking that you don't like being mistaken,
liking that you feel just the way you like to feel about
everything you do,
liking that you feel just the way you like to feel about
everything that happens.

Bruce Di Marsico

Acknowledgments

My deepest thanks and gratitude to the many hands that helped birth this book. Aryeh Nielsen had the vision for this project; without his ideas, archival preservation work and enthusiasm, this book would still exist only in our imaginations. Richard Banton caught all of the big mistakes as we began to work with the raw material. Wendy Dolber, Bruce's student and friend, spent months reviewing; her watchful eye, editing skills and comprehensive understanding of Option was essential in making sure we "got it right." Frank Mosca's further review, editing and feedback was invaluable and put me at ease, knowing we had not missed anything important. I'd also like to thank Frank for his Foreword for this book as he so eloquently captured how so many of us feel about Bruce's work. Finally I would like to thank all of The Option Method students the world over who have patiently supported our efforts.

Deborah Mendel

The Editing Process

Bruce Di Marsico primarily taught in a group context. He often wrote short essays as seeds for group discussion, and would read the essay at the start of gatherings, followed by interactive discussion and commentary.

These essays sometimes were descriptive, and sometimes were poetic meditations. Bruce also wrote some essays for personal use, working out how best to convey an idea or to communicate to a particular person about a particular issue.

Bruce primarily worked through the spoken word, not the written. He recorded tapes of group gatherings from the 1970s through the 1990s, and over 500 hours of tapes exist. This represents an overwhelming amount of material, and so this work contains only a selection of materials from these tapes.

Both written and verbal works have sometimes been edited quite a bit for presentation here. While some pieces are exactly as written, others may have been modified by removing secondary themes to create a more focused essay, by weaving together two essays or talks on the same subject, by cutting whole sections of interactive discussions, or by adding a few extra words to clarify what did not need to be clarified in the context of an ongoing discussion. The principle was to only do what could be done with the confidence of maintaining the integrity of his authorial intent, as judged by some of Bruce's closest students.

The commentary sections in these volumes are to bring forth points that are felt to represent Bruce's ideas but for which good source material could not be found for using Bruce's own words. Some commentary is a synopsis of ideas that Bruce Di Marsico expressed in many writings or talks but did not express summarily in a single writing or talk. For example, a wide-ranging discussion about a topic over six hours of tapes might leave a very clear impression of Bruce's teachings on a subject, but present a great difficulty in extracting his word directly into a short, relatively linear essay.

Other commentary represents the editor's synthesis of ideas Bruce Di Marsico expressed only in fragments, such as intriguing short asides. In this case, there is more editorial extrapolation.

Finally, some commentaries are based on the editor's understanding of Bruce Di Marsico's teachings, often created in response to common misunderstandings of Option. These commentaries are not directly traceable to Bruce's words but may be edifying nonetheless.

The relationship of a given commentary to Bruce's work is stated at the opening of the commentary. Additionally, whenever an essay or talk can be traced to a particular date (and the vast majority can be so traced), the date is included so that future researchers of the archives of Bruce's material can easily check the edited version against the original.

The archives contain great quantities of materials that are wonderful and valuable, but were not presented here both for the sake of limiting the size of the volumes and not delaying their release by a period of decades! What is *not* here is the complete history of Bruce's playing out of Option in all the lived situations that actual people brought to him.

On that point, since Bruce often used a questioner's own language, a given talk might use a given term very differently than another talk, because the talk was in response to a different person. The context will make this clear.

As we continue to research the archives, and respond to questions for clarification, subsequent editions will invariably be created. Yet what is collected here is unquestionably more than sufficient for a complete understanding of Option. Enjoy!

About Bruce Di Marsico

Bruce Michael Di Marsico was born in 1942 in Weehawken, New Jersey. He was the first child born to Onofrio (Alfred) Di Marsico and Elizabeth (Bette) Bauer. In their first child they found an exceptionally bright and precocious boy. While Alfred tried disciplinarian methods, Bette turned to Dr. Spock in raising him. As he grew older he became so adept at reasoning with his mother when he wanted something that it became obvious it was she who was learning from him.

Bruce was a restless child in school and was advanced a grade in elementary school after being tested by a psychologist. When it came time to attend high school he requested that he attend a Catholic school. He was drawn to a spiritual quest at a very young age. Upon graduating high school he was still seeking an immersion in theological study and chose to pursue a monastic life. He entered the Trappist order. After spending some time there as a novice he realized it was not the right path for him.

He decided to attend university and explore psychology and philosophy. He was fascinated by mankind's eternal pursuit of happiness. He thoroughly enjoyed the spiritual passions of the heart and soul. He always kept a volume or two of Butler's *The Lives of the Saints* at his bedside, loving the mysteries of the mystics. It was his own quest for happiness—the same desire that drew him to Catholic school, the monastery and the study of the works and teachings of many, from Buddha to Freud—that he came to create the Option teachings and Attitude. However, it was because of the joy he derived from helping others that he naturally came to develop The Option Method.

Bruce drew upon the wisdom of ancient philosophers. It was the Greek philosopher Epictetus who said, "Men are not worried by things, but by their ideas about things. When we meet with difficulties, become anxious or troubled, let us not blame others, but rather ourselves, that is, our ideas about things." Bruce realized it was not what was happening that made people unhappy, but their beliefs about what was happening that created their emotional responses. He developed his Option Method Questions based on the Socratic Method of teaching using non-judgmental questions. The theory of recollection, according to Socrates, means that before we are born we possess all knowledge. We are never taught anything new, but instead are reminded of things we already know. Bruce felt this was true about our happiness. He believed that every one of us already possesses everything we need to be happy.

Bruce became a psychotherapist, and around 1970 introduced Option at a paraprofessional school called Group Relations Ongoing Workshops (GROW) in New York City. Bruce's classes became "standing room only" as he taught laymen and practitioners from a variety of backgrounds his Option Method. Over the years Bruce offered various workshops and groups in and around New York City, Long Island and New Jersey. When GROW closed, a group of students asked him to continue teaching them. He created what came to be known as the "Monday night group" at his home in Montclair, New Jersey. A closeness and camaraderie developed among them and oftentimes discussions would carry on into dawn, with breaks for Fettuccini Alfredo family-style in the large eat-in kitchen. You will find transcripts of recordings of these groups throughout this book.

In the 1980s and 1990s Bruce continued to conduct workshops and groups from his home in Montclair as well as seeing private clients in his office in Greenwich Village, New York City. You will also find material from these workshops within these pages. It was during this time that Bruce was diagnosed with heart disease and later diabetes. Through years of physical pain and suffering he continued to teach as he did in his last recorded lecture on November 11, 1995, transcribed in these volumes. Bruce was a testament to his own Option realization that pain itself cannot cause us to be unhappy. Bruce passed away on December 4th, 1995, with several of his last students at his side.

Deborah Mendel

Index

A

Allow 402
Anger 402
Attraction 394

B

Bad 367
Behavior 405
  changing 3
  repetitive 4
Belief, defined 311
Beliefs
  as cause of feelings 396
  as embodied 393
  as unnecessary 83, 102, 405
  emotional vs. practical 393
  in necessity 270
  testing 394
Blame 366
Body 34
Boredom 365

C

Choice 321, 345
Choice, defined 311
Contemplation 228

D

Death 60, 62
  fear of 63
Doing 395, 399
  what you want 398

E

Emotions
  as happiness 205
  as problematic 149
  cause of 383
Enemies 366
Evil 201, 367

F

Fear 366, 369
  of desires 369
Feeling, defined 311
Feelings
  as attitudes 392
  as knowledge 392
Freedom 366
  experienced in the body 153
  of choice 368
  of taste 368
  to be against 368
  to change the perfect 372
  to not change 183
Future 167

G

Gladness 193, 405
God 209, 226

Good
all things as **135**
as state of everything **133, 135**
Gratitude **194**
Guilt **369, 402**

H

Habits **14**
Happiness
after perfect happiness **406**
and miracles **130**
and moods **386**
and the future **6**
and values **404**
and way of being **385**
as "Yes!" **162**
as freedom **127, 387**
as impossible **403**
as knowing there is nothing wrong with you **160**
as motivation **397**
as personal **385**
as present state **386**
as right **380**
as ultimate desire **387**
as uncaused **101**
as unsafe **404**
as you **27, 154**
as your present state **115**
awareness of **347**
being lived by **223**
consenting to **405**
emotions as **205**
enjoying **123**
known as God **223**
no obstacles to **89**
now **125**
perfect **116, 156, 168, 176**
requirements for **117**
summary wisdom of **349**
without reason **107**
Hate **366**
Healing **63**
Health **59**

I

Importance **17**
Innocence **366**

J

Joy **191, 228**

L

Learning **152**
Love **406**

M

Mania **365**
Meaning of life **67, 376**
Mind **29**
Mistakes **16, 370**
Motivation **397**
Mysticism **231**. *See* Option Mysticism
Myths **13, 14**

N

Necessity **270, 320**
Need **372**
Needing **399**
Now
Experiential vs. Intentional **44**

O

Option
described axiomatically **355**

ontology and epistemology **373**
Option Method
and those not interested **283**
as free of statements **272**
attitude of **275**, **292**
general guidance on applying **300**
helping with **276**, **278**
how to do **241**
introduction to **246**
learning **239**
non-necessity of **285**
using with others **306**
using with yourself **311**, **315**
Option Method Questions
attitude of **319**
dialogue model **264**
guiding **268**
in response to **270**
introduction to **259**
variants of **266**
Option Mysticism **216**, **221**, **223**
Option Theology **216**
Owing **366**

P
Past
and feelings **46**
Peace **191**
Phobia **365**
Play **203**
Pragmatism **216**, **223**, **231**
Privacy **151**
Prudence **366**

Q
Questions **241**
Quiet **187**

R
Religion **220**
Rights **19**, **366**

S
Self **27**, **34**, **36**, **74**
as location **36**
hidden **31**
Self-trust **401**
Sex **53**
Should **389**
Society
participating in **144**
Sorrow **402**
Stimulus-Organism-Response **396**
Stories
college **329**
diamonds **338**
Genesis myth **333**
holding your breath **332**
troubadour **335**
Summary of Option **353**, **383**

T
Terror **366**
Time **43**

U
Understanding yourself
as unnecessary **91**
Unhappiness
and fault **384**
and the future **390**
and the present **390**
as believing something is wrong with you **388**
as believing we are against ourselves **388**

as meaningless 107
as motivation 397
as non-existent 391
as not believing ourselves 72, 389
believing in necessity of 44
causing others 139
degrees of 397
falsely presuming 403
non-necessity of 383
no reasons for 90
to motivate others 398
vs. physical symptoms 391
vs. what you don't want 388
Unhappy
acting as if 203

W

Wanting 395
in a practical context 400
more 399
not justifying 110
others to want 401
to do nothing 184
vs. needing 399
with provisions 400
Wanting, defined 311
Will 27, 68, 367
free 28
Work 9
World 39, 76
as you 41
Worry 365

Y

You 70

Lightning Source UK Ltd.
Milton Keynes UK
UKHW010019180221
378934UK00001B/23